MW00777136

THE · FILMS · OF · SAMUEL · FULLER

A series from Wesleyan University Press
Edited by Jeanine Basinger

The new **Wesleyan Film** series takes a back-to-basics approach to the art of cinema. Books in the series will deal with the formal, the historical, and the cultural—putting a premium on visual analysis, close readings, and an understanding of the history of Hollywood and international cinema, both artistically and industrially. The volumes will be rigorous, critical, and accessible both to academics and to lay readers with a serious interest in film.

Series editor Jeanine Basinger, Corwin-Fuller Professor of Film Studies at Wesleyan University and Founder/Curator of the Wesleyan Cinema Archives, is the author of such landmark books as *The World War II Combat Film: Anatomy of a Genre*, *A Woman's View: How Hollywood Spoke to Women, 1930–1960*, *Silent Stars*, and *The Star Machine*.

*Anthony Mann*
by Jeanine Basinger

*The Films of Samuel Fuller*
*If You Die, I'll Kill You!*
by Lisa Dombrowski

*Physical Evidence*
*Selected Film Criticism*
by Kent Jones

*Action Speaks Louder*
*Violence, Spectacle, and the American Action Movie*
Revised and Expanded Edition
by Eric Lichtenfeld

*Hollywood Ambitions*
*Celebrity in the Movie Age*
by Marsha Orgeron

# The Films of

# SAMUEL
# FULLER

## If You Die, I'll Kill You!

### Lisa Dombrowski

WESLEYAN UNIVERSITY PRESS
MIDDLETOWN, CONNECTICUT

Published by Wesleyan University Press, Middletown, CT 06459
www.wesleyan.edu/wespress
© 2008 by Lisa Dombrowski
Printed in the United States of America

5   4   3   2   1


Library of Congress Cataloging-in-Publication Data
Dombrowski, Lisa.
The films of Samuel Fuller : if you die, I'll kill you! / Lisa Dombrowski.
p.   cm.
Includes bibliographical references and index.
ISBN-13: 978-0-8195-6866-3 (cloth : alk. paper)
ISBN-10: 0-8195-6866-X (cloth : alk. paper)
1. Fuller, Samuel, 1912–1997—Criticism and interpretation. I. Title.
PN1998.3.F85D66 2008
791.4302'33092—dc22    2007037126

*For the kids in the screening room*

# Contents

# Illustrations

# Acknowledgments

My passion for Samuel Fuller originated during my undergraduate years at Wesleyan University in Middletown, Connecticut, where Jeanine Basinger has been teaching his work for over forty years. The depth of her knowledge and her love of cinema have inspired me throughout my career. I would not have thought to undertake this work—nor been able to complete it—without her.

I produced a fledgling version of this book under the patient tutelage of Lea Jacobs and David Bordwell at the University of Wisconsin–Madison. I am indebted to them for their comments on drafts, as well as to Vance Kepley, Tino Balio, and Noël Carroll. Much thanks also to my Madison cohort—Jim Kreul, Jane Greene, Jonathan Whalley, Chris Becker, Chris Sieving, Jennifer Fay, and Jim Udden—who provided me with encouragement, beer, and pie when I needed them the most.

At Wesleyan, Richard Slotkin offered invaluable advice on the project, while my colleagues Leo Lensing, Scott Higgins, Jacob Bricca, Lea Carlson, Marc Longenecker, Leith Johnson, and Joan Miller have all supported my scholarship in countless ways. Thanks also to Sam Wasson, Lucas Dietrich, Shahruk Chowdhury, and Dan Butrymowicz for their research help. My editor at Wesleyan University Press, Eric Levy, has been a gem, as I tell him all the time. Much thanks to Eric Lichtenfeld for heartily recommending him.

I am tremendously grateful for the early assistance provided by Mike Pogorzelski and Joe Lindner at the Academy of Motion Picture Arts and Sciences and the access they offered to Fuller's personal film collection. I'd also like to thank Lauren Buisson at the University of California–Los Angeles Young Research Library Arts Special Collections, Maxine Fleckner Ducey at the Wisconsin Center for Film and Theatre Research, Barbara Hall and Faye Thompson at the Academy of Motion Picture Arts and Sciences Margaret Herrick Library, as well as Haden Guest, a true gentleman, who opened the doors for me at the Warner Bros. Archive and shared his own work on Fuller. Jon Davison and Kelly Ward discussed their memories of Fuller with great honesty and enthusiasm; they made the man come alive, which I truly appreciate.

My family—Chuck, Carol, Eleanor, Mike, Helen, and Henry—have experienced the highs and the lows of this project along with me. Their unfailing love convinced me I could do what I never conceived to be possible. Brett, my partner in crime, receives the biggest bear hug of all.

His commitment, confidence, and cheers carried me through. We plan a sitcom.

Finally, I offer my heartfelt thanks to Christa Lang Fuller, her daughter Samantha, and her granddaughter Samira. The generosity of these bright, strong, funny women knows no bounds. No wonder Sam loved them so! I look forward to seeing their stories of him in print one day.

THE · FILMS · OF · SAMUEL · FULLER

# Introduction

man eyes a woman on the subway. She returns his gaze. Two other men watch. A pocketbook is picked.

An outlaw shoots his best friend in the back, then proposes to his girlfriend.

A woman furiously beats the camera with her bag to the sound of wailing saxophones. Her wig falls off. She is bald.

An African-American pulls a white pillowcase over his head and cries, "America for Americans!"

A woman's face cracks like a broken mirror, shattered by a gunshot.

A young solider pumps round after round into a Nazi hiding in a concentration camp oven.

A newspaper editor pummels a man against the base of a Benjamin Franklin statue.

A sergeant shoots a prisoner of war, then yells at him, "If you die, I'll kill you!"

With their startling subject matter and emphasis on conflict, contradiction, and kineticism, Samuel Fuller's films are designed to hit you—hard. His stated goal was to "grab audiences by the balls!" By upending expectations, disregarding conventional norms, and combining realism with sensationalism, violence with humor, and intricate long takes with rapid-fire editing, Fuller created films that produce a direct emotional impact on the viewer. He wanted to unsettle the assumptions of audiences, to surprise them, to instruct as well as to entertain, always striving to reveal the truth of a given situation. His are daring and stimulating films, and they have inspired fascination in generations of fans.

As the recurring narrative and stylistic tendencies in Fuller's films are so readily apparent, his work has repeatedly been the subject of auteur study. In the late 1950s in France, the young lions at *Cahiers du Cinéma* discovered in Fuller a prime example of the delightfully aggressive nose-thumbing they celebrated in Hollywood's genre pictures and began to describe his aesthetic as primitive. When structuralism inflected auteur criticism in Britain and the United States a decade later, a collection of essays edited by David Will and Peter Wollen for the 1969 Edinburgh Film Festival, as well as monographs by Phil Hardy in 1970 and Nicholas Garnham in 1971, refocused attention on the motifs, themes, and dichotomies in Fuller's narratives, elevating his stature as one of the preeminent cinematic critics of American society.[1]

This book aims to rethink earlier portraits of Fuller by examining his films in the context of the practices and pressures of the industry in which he primarily worked: Hollywood. In doing so, I am following in the footsteps of scholars such as Paul Kerr, Justin Wyatt, Lutz Bacher, and others who have demonstrated the necessity of considering auteurship in relation to economic, industrial, and institutional determinants.[2] I draw on in-depth formal analysis as well as previously untapped primary sources, including script, production, payroll, legal, and regulatory files; trade and popular publications; and interviews. This book focuses on Fuller's directorial work in film, and as such necessarily neglects much of his vast written output for page and screen, as well as his television efforts. A particular emphasis is placed on understanding the narrative structure and visual style of Fuller's films, as these topics have previously received little systematic analysis.

As a writer, director, and frequently, producer, Fuller had multiple means of creative influence over his films, a situation that was highly unusual for directors of his era, particularly those operating—as he often did—in the low-budget arena. Though he labored in a wide range of production circumstances for more than forty years, Fuller's many-layered involvement in his films contributes to the distinctiveness of vision exhibited by the totality of his work. Within the history of American cinema, Fuller is the model of the idiosyncratic director, one whose films frequently push the boundaries of classicism, genre, and taste. His work contains the potential to reveal the contemporary limits of what is considered socially and aesthetically acceptable to present onscreen.

Fuller did not direct in a vacuum, however, and his filmmaking was molded by competing influences whose nature and weight varied over time. Fuller began his directorial career in the late 1940s during a transitional period in the American film industry marked by the decline of the studio system and the rise of independent production. The changes in Fuller's working conditions and degree of production control allow for an examination of how economic, industrial, and institutional forces impact a director's aesthetic tendencies. The recognition that multiple causal determinants shape the nature of Fuller's work is crucial to explaining its variation in form and relation to classical conventions and production trends. Such an approach acknowledges the director as a conscious craftsperson engaged in formal decision making while constrained by rival concerns, providing an alternative to conceiving of authorship strictly according to the director's biography, psychology, or choice of recurring motifs.

The length of Fuller's career also enables an assessment of the opportunities and challenges facing directors in the decades following the 1948 Paramount antitrust decision, which prompted the major studios to cut payrolls and move toward financing and distributing independent productions. Rather than drawing all of their cast and crew, equipment, and other resources from a single studio, producers now assembled the means of production on a film-by-film basis, each time creating a distinct "package."[3] Fuller provides a case study of the impact of the shift to the package-unit system on a director's films and career, revealing that operating as an independent producer or freelance talent—rather than as a director under contract to a studio—could both aid and frustrate creative expression and professional development. In particular, Fuller's case complicates the promise of artistic freedom associated with incorporation as an independent producer while offering a corrective to popular conceptions of studio-director relations as obstructive to individuality and innovation. While the details of Fuller's case are specific to him, the choices he faced when navigating the changing industrial landscape in Hollywood were shared by fellow directors emanating from the world of low-budget B movies. Industrial determinants can partially account for the fates of Anthony Mann, Budd Boetticher, Joseph H. Lewis, Phil Karlson, Andre de Toth, and Jacques Tourneur— gifted filmmakers who, like Fuller, struggled to maintain their careers by the 1960s.

Like cultists everywhere, Fuller followers tend to seize on those elements in his films and his biography that most excite and use them to proselytize the cause. So Fuller becomes a filmmaker ahead of his time; one who makes movies that reek of headline-blaring tabloids; who transforms every picture into a war picture; who is a primitive, an outsider, a maverick. There is some truth in these characterizations, but as a newspaperman would say, they don't tell you the whole story. A close examination of Fuller's body of work reveals greater variety and complexity than is generally acknowledged. My goal in this book is to account for the total Fuller: those films and portions of his career that match his legendary persona, as well as those that do not. While Fuller's primary artistic impulses remained consistent throughout his professional life, the manner and means through which he expressed them differed over time. The following discussion of Fuller's biographical legend, his aesthetic interests, and his working methods lays the foundation for a long-overdue analysis of his rich and influential legacy.

## The Fuller Biographical Legend

Over the years, publicists, critics, and Fuller himself have shaped the details of his life and his career into a biographical legend, a persona that has influenced how his films are generally understood.[4] At the heart of the Fuller biographical legend is Fuller's own colorful personal history. Fuller began directing films only after successive stints as a journalist, solider, and screenwriter, and his real-life adventures clearly shaped his worldview and his work. As publicists and critics wrote about Fuller's action-packed life and films, his legend took on a wistful, nostalgic quality; to many of today's writers he is an icon of lost authenticity, a reminder of an era when American moviemakers learned about storytelling on the streets rather than in film school. Fuller's biographical legend is further defined by his reputation as a "primitive" filmmaker and a maverick who worked outside of Hollywood studios, characterizations that gained popularity during the 1950s and 1960s and have been widely repeated ever since. The Fuller biographical legend foregrounds important aspects of his story but is only the beginning of our journey toward understanding his films.

Fuller's first career was as a crime reporter in New York City, where he haunted the streets for the *New York Evening Graphic,* the town's most sensational tabloid. In the midst of the Depression, he quit the paper and headed west, writing his way across the country until he landed a job covering the waterfront for the *San Diego Sun.* Fuller's journalism provided the foundation for three pulp novels he wrote during the late 1930s and enabled him to begin collaborating on film scripts and submitting story ideas to Hollywood studios. From his years as a newspaperman Fuller learned the value of a punchy lead and the importance of speaking the truth. He frequently cited this period as providing significant fodder for his screenplays, and from the late 1950s to the present, critics have highlighted the tabloid flavor of his films.[5]

In December 1941, while writing a new novel, *The Dark Page,* Fuller enlisted in the army. At age thirty, he left behind journalism and Hollywood for World War II. Fuller served with the Twenty-sixth and Sixteenth Intrantry Regiments, First Infantry Division in North Africa and Europe, landing on Omaha Beach on D-day and participating in the liberation of the Falkenau concentration camp in Czechoslovakia. Fuller kept a diary during the war and incorporated many of his infantry experiences into the screenplays of his combat films, culminating in his autobiographical triumph *The Big Red One* (1980). Fuller's years as a soldier fueled his subsequent reputation as an action-oriented director who made authentic, real-life movies. Fuller suggested the impact of his war

Corporal Samuel Fuller in Sicily during World War II, flanked by a pack mule and a young boy. Mules and children pop up in almost every Fuller combat film. *Chrisam Films, Inc.*

years on his cinematic worldview during his cameo appearance in Jean-Luc Godard's *Pierrot le fou* (1965): "Film is like a battleground: Love. Hate. Action. Violence. In a word, emotion."

The years Fuller spent in Hollywood immediately after the war taught him the importance of acquiring production control over his own stories. The screen rights to *The Dark Page* had been purchased by Howard

Hawks; Hawks later sold the rights to the newspaper murder mystery, which Phil Karlson eventually directed as *Scandal Sheet* (1952). Three different studios then hired Fuller to write original scripts, all of which exhibited the hard-boiled sensationalism characteristic of his later films and none of which were produced. Despite concerns regarding the controversial nature of his stories, Fuller remained in demand as a screenwriter, even resisting a contract offer from MGM in the hope that he might be able to direct his scripts the way he wanted. Finally, in 1948, Fuller received a phone call from Robert Lippert, a West Coast exhibitor and independent producer, who offered him the opportunity to helm his own feature.

Over the next sixteen years, Samuel Fuller made seventeen films, operating both as a contract director and as an independent producer, much like fellow action experts Robert Aldrich and Anthony Mann. He wrote and directed three low-budget films for Lippert Productions, eventually receiving producer status and significant production autonomy: *I Shot Jesse James* (1949), a psychological western; *The Baron of Arizona* (1950), based on the true story of a nineteenth-century forger; and *The Steel Helmet* (1951), the first Korean War picture released in the United States. The astounding critical and commercial success of *The Steel Helmet* catapulted Fuller to the attention of the major studios as a hot new director of action genres.

The creative energy of production head Darryl Zanuck drew Fuller to Twentieth Century–Fox, where he signed an option contract as a director and screenwriter. Fuller wrote the original script for *Fixed Bayonets* (1951), his second Korean War picture, but shared screenwriting credit on his subsequent directorial efforts at the studio: *Pickup on South Street* (1953), a gritty espionage and crime thriller; *Hell and High Water* (1954), a submarine adventure; and *House of Bamboo* (1955), a cops-and-robbers picture set in Tokyo. While on leave from Fox, Fuller produced, wrote, directed, and completely self-financed *Park Row* (1952), a sentimental yet raucous view of the newspaper business in late-nineteenth-century New York City. Though he mounted an extensive promotional campaign, the picture flopped.

In 1956, after Fuller parted ways with Fox, he established Globe Enterprises, an independent production company, and initiated a series of financing and distribution deals with RKO, Fox, and Columbia. In addition to two failed television pilots, Fuller wrote, directed, and produced six films under the Globe banner: *Run of the Arrow* (1957), *China Gate* (1957), *Forty Guns* (1957), *Verboten!* (1959), *The Crimson Kimono* (1959), and *Underworld, U.S.A.* (1961). Following the collapse of Globe, Fuller worked as a freelance director on the World War II combat picture *Merrill's Marauders* (1962); he subsequently wrote and directed two adult exploitation films for Allied Artists, *Shock Corridor* (1963) and *The Naked Kiss* (1964), neither of which produced sizable domestic returns. In 1965, Fuller left Hollywood for Paris to write and direct a science-fiction adaptation of Aristophanes's *Lysistrata*, but the film never got off the ground. Unable to acquire financing for independent production in the United States and finding freelance directing work only on television, Fuller increasingly immersed himself in his writing.

Although he wrote countless scripts and treatments over the next twenty years, Fuller directed only six subsequent films and disowned one of them: *Shark!* (1969, from which he removed his name after losing control of the editing), *Dead Pigeon on Beethoven Street* (1972), *The Big Red One, White Dog* (1982), *Thieves After Dark* (1984), and *Street of No Return* (1989). Ironically, his production decline was accompanied by his critical ascension, and young directors such as Wim Wenders and the Kaurismäki brothers kept him busy throughout the 1970s and 1980s with acting jobs in their movies. Even as Fuller struggled to find financing and distribution for his films, his difficulties only further clinched his reputation as a rebel, one too challenging to be embraced by Hollywood studios. After a debilitating stroke, Fuller died in 1997 at age eighty-five.

While Fuller's biography has played a dominant role in critical assessments of his work, early characterizations of him as an artistic primitive and a Hollywood outsider have also proven a resilient part of his biographical legend. Critics in the 1950s and 1960s associated the seemingly untutored visual quality and emotional authenticity apparent in several of Fuller's films with a primitive approach to filmmaking, a notion that in one form or another dominates discussions of his work to this day. In addition, beginning in the 1960s, newspaper profiles highlighted Fuller's struggles as a low-budget independent producer and developed his reputation as a maverick. Through repetition over time, the labels of "primitive" and "indie maverick" have become the primary touchstones for critical discussions of Fuller.

Critics who draw on the concept of the primitive to describe Fuller's style typically aim to valorize his often nonclassical aesthetic. According to one definition, a "primitive" artwork that appears instinctive and immediate rather than carefully constructed according to classical rules acquires an aura of primal emotion, sincerity, and originality.[6] It is precisely this notion of simplicity and spontaneity as more emotionally compelling than the normative style of classical cinema that many critics respond to in Fuller's work. In a 1959 *Cahiers du Cinéma* article, Luc Moullet initiated the critical association of Fuller with the term by describing him as an "intelligent primitive." Fuller's ignorance of film school conventions and reliance on his own instincts, Moullet argued, enable him to produce a vision of life more spontaneous and real than rule-bound classical cinema.[7] In later years, film critics following in Moullet's footsteps—such as Andrew Sarris, Manny Farber, and Jean-Pierre Coursodon—continued to use "primitive" and the concepts associated with it to describe Fuller's movies.[8] For these critics, Fuller's stylistic unpredictability is a characteristic worth celebrating and is what links him to primitives in other art forms.

In a related argument, J. Hoberman more recently considered Fuller as a pioneer "abstract sensationalist," one of several twentieth-century American artists versed in the trashy aesthetic of the tabloids. Hoberman describes the abstract sensationalist as a typically untrained artist who produces sensational work for a mass audience. In particular, he focuses on how abstract sensationalists embrace the tabloid aesthetic of "shock, raw sensation and immediate impact, a prole expression of violent contrasts and blunt, 'vulgar' stylization."[9] In championing Fuller as a rough-edged producer of urban, low art, Hoberman highlights the same aesthetic traits seized on by those who have labeled the director a primitive.

However they appropriate or alter the meaning of the term, critics who evoke the primitive to describe Fuller and his work participate in a critical tradition that values an artist's rejection of classical norms. The longstanding association of the primitive with the instinctual, however, can unfairly characterize artists who produce primitive work as acting without conscious thought or training. As Paul Klee noted, "If my works sometimes produce a primitive impression, this 'primitiveness' is explained by my discipline, which consists of reducing everything to a few steps. It is no more than economy; that is the ultimate professional awareness, which is to say the opposite of real primitiveness."[10] In distinguishing between the *impression* that is created by the final work and the *thought* that goes into an artist's working process, Klee rightly cautions against confusing the appearance of simplicity in an artwork with a lack of intention. This caution is particularly appropriate when considering a medium such as film, which requires the coordination of masses of people, equipment, and money. Simply because an artist creates a stripped-down, anticlassical, emotionally raw work does not imply that he or she is working from instinct alone. As subsequent sections of this introduction illustrate, Fuller's impulses often challenged classical conventions and produced an appearance of spontaneity, yet his working methods and artistic strategies were quite deliberate. Casting Fuller as a primitive simply does not do justice to the complexity and contradictions evident within his work.

In addition to the "primitive" nature of his films, Fuller's reputation as an independent filmmaker who thrived in the fast-and-loose world of

B movies is central to his legendary persona. Fuller's maverick image arose in the press right as his career stalled in the mid-1960s and has been perpetuated widely ever since. The first in-depth profile of Fuller, a 1965 *New York Times Magazine* piece titled "Low Budget Movies with POW!" describes his typical film as being shot in ten days on $200,000. Fuller himself is portrayed as a "filmic fireball," "dedicated to depicting, at rather small cost and in vivid visual terms, the abnormalities of the world around him."[11] This article cemented Fuller's reputation in the American press as an outsider filmmaker who voluntarily embraced the world of B movies in order to work in opposition to mainstream Hollywood. By the time British and American auteur critics discovered Fuller in the 1960s—as French critics had a decade before—the terms by which his career would be discussed were already in place: he was the primary author of his films, his movies had low budgets, and he worked independent of the grip of Hollywood's commercial talons.[12] These characteristics positioned Fuller as "a role model for maverick filmmakers," a romantic example of what personal vision and self-sacrifice could achieve.[13] The difficulties Fuller faced in getting projects off the ground in his later years only further solidified his outsider persona.

As with the description of Fuller's work as primitive, his status as a B-movie maverick contains some elements of truth: he often shot on a low budget, and he did have primary creative control over many of his films. Nevertheless, in order to romanticize Fuller's outsider status, this portrait overlooks the varied production conditions under which he worked and downplays his frequent reliance on Hollywood studios even when he was an independent producer. Throughout his career, Fuller championed the distinctiveness of the auteur voice and struggled to direct his own scripts his own way. In this sense, he was a maverick. But he also recognized that some of the best production circumstances he enjoyed in his five-decade-long career occurred not when he was an independent but while he was working in the studio system.

The dominant aspects of Fuller's biographical legend have only brought us so far. His years as a journalist, a footsoldier, and a struggling director provide us with a lens through which to view his work, but it is hardly an exhaustive lens. Biography limits us to considering how his life impacted his movies while neglecting other forces that influenced his aesthetic, such as classical norms, industrial trends, and market conditions. The focus on Fuller's willingness to break classical realist conventions in the criticism of those who describe him as a primitive offers a useful contribution to the study of his films; however, the short articles that dominate this critical strain never explore in a systematic fashion how Fuller's aesthetic manifests itself through narrative and stylistic choices in individual pictures. Finally, when critics describe Fuller as an independent maverick, their tendency is to portray the studios and their executives as villainous watchdogs who inhibit his creative freedom. This simplistic approach to industry relations fails to consider the variety of needs that bind directors to studios and distributors, as well as the ways these relationships can enable as much as constrain the creativity of directors.

Considering Fuller's work as a reflection of competing influences enables us to understand more fully the complexities of his films and his evolving strategies as a director. As his career progresses, classical and genre norms, production circumstances, censorship, and industrial conditions shape Fuller's films to varying degrees, resulting in a body of work that utilizes a range of techniques to express defined artistic interests. Exploring Fuller's aesthetic vision in the context of his contemporary industrial conditions highlights the most significant aspects of his biographical legend while qualifying and contextualizing longstanding assumptions about his career. A survey of the relationship between Fuller's narrative and stylistic goals and his working methods further clarifies how he attempted to translate his particular worldview onto the screen.

### Fuller as Storyteller

Fuller passionately believed "the story is God,"[14] and he fought to film his yarns with minimum interference his entire career. His status as a screenwriter enabled him not only to shoot his own scripts but also to rewrite the work of others, offering him a higher degree of control during preproduction than that enjoyed by many directors of his midlevel stature. Fuller's screenplays reveal a unique authorial sensibility, one that combines an interest in history and realism with a desire to entertain in an often sensational fashion. In a 1992 self-penned article, "Film Fiction: More Factual Than Facts," Fuller offers an analysis of the Mervyn LeRoy film *I Am a Fugitive From a Chain Gang* (1932) to illustrate how the fictional presentation of an event can appear more "true" than reality: "The more we are Muni [Paul Muni, the actor playing the protagonist], the more the fiction of brutality in the movie becomes factual. Why? Because we are hit with hammer-blows of emotion."[15] These "hammer-blows of emotion" are what Fuller sought to create in his films, crafting his scripts to convey a hard-hitting form of truth through scenes that shock and startle the viewer. This storytelling strategy took hold in Fuller during his career in journalism, was manifested in his films through their narrative content and structure, and was shaped by his screenwriting process.

Fuller himself has confirmed—as several critics suggest—that the tabloid aesthetic and "illustrated lectures" featured in his films are

Samuel Fuller in his office while working on *Park Row,* flanked by statues of Charles Gut-tenberg (left) and Benjamin Franklin (right) that appear in the film. Ever the newspaper-man, Fuller wears a reporter's visor. *Chrisam Films, Inc.*

rooted in his years spent in the newspaper business.[16] Although Fuller began hawking newspapers on sidewalks in junior high and worked in journalism through the 1930s, his stint as a young crime reporter at the *New York Evening Graphic* arguably had the greatest impact on his brand of storytelling. A cross between the *New York Post* and the *National Enquirer,* the *Graphic* mixed an impassioned defense of the common man with tawdry stories of sex and violence. There, Fuller learned the art of "creative exaggeration" and the power of a compelling lead, two storytelling techniques that characterize his self-written films.[17] As a journalist on the crime beat, Fuller witnessed and then wrote about murderers' confessions, suicides, executions, and race riots. "Every newspaperman has such a Hellbox to draw from," he later wrote. "Every newspaperman is a potential filmmaker. All he or she has to do is transfer real emotion to reel emotion and sprinkle with imagination."[18] Fuller's journalistic career thus provided him not only with strong copy that he could transform into screenplays, but also with an approach to storytelling that de-emphasized exposition and analysis in favor of blunt "truth" and bold-faced, revelatory thrills.

The desire to stretch beyond fact-based reporting led Fuller to begin writing novels and screenplays, yet he retained a tabloid approach to truth-telling throughout his career. His first books published in the 1930s—*Burn, Baby, Burn!*, the story of a pregnant woman on death row; *Test Tube Baby*, on artificial insemination; and *Make Up and Kiss*, an exposé of the cosmetics industry—reveal the topicality and dark humor that infuse the more outrageous of Fuller's later films. When he began writing screenplays, his goal was "to use the screen as a newspaper."[19] His interest lay in "truthful revelation," in dramatizing "anything that's informative and always entertaining."[20] Most significantly, he believed film to be an unrivaled medium in its ability to educate as well as entertain:

One day the greatest educational medium will be the film. Millions of children will watch a moment in history told through drama so gripping that dates of events will become dates of exciting moments, instead of numbers to crowd their reluctant minds. . . . There is no art medium that can accomplish this and reach as many people as the art of film.[21]

Such quotes have led some critics to suggest that Fuller's scripts reveal a definite ideological agenda.[22] To be sure, Fuller does not balk at revealing the failings of American society, and his films repeatedly engage race and gender in a frank and uncompromising manner rare for their times. Yet Fuller's contradictory narratives defy coherent political analysis, leading him to be described in the press as everything from a liberal to a fascist to an anarchist. While he may intend to educate, the "creative exaggeration" Fuller employs in the storytelling process results in films that agitate the viewer, physically, intellectually, and emotionally, rather than offering a clear political position.

Fuller's storytelling goal is to arouse emotion, and his screenplays combine hard-boiled characters, ironic contradictions, excessive conflict, and a selective embrace of classical and generic conventions in order to shake the viewer up. Fuller called his characters "gutter people," outcasts who lived by their own code in a shadowy world he found more inherently dramatic than that occupied by clean-cut, well-behaved Americans.[23] In their own lingo, they are "retreads," "doggies," "cannons," "grifters," "wetnoses," "ichibons," and "bon bons." Typically criminals (*I Shot Jesse James, The Baron of Arizona, Pickup on South Street, Underworld, U.S.A., The Naked Kiss, Shark!, Thieves After Dark*), misfits (*The Steel Helmet, Fixed Bayonets, Hell and High Water*,

*Run of the Arrow, The Big Red One, Street of No Return*), or obsessives (*Park Row, Forty Guns, Shock Corridor, White Dog*), Fuller's protagonists lie, cheat, steal, betray, or kill in order to achieve their desires. For them, the ultimate triumph is merely survival. While Fuller draws from stock "underworld" types—thieves, prostitutes, cops, and reporters—he uses them to reveal the bitter ironies of life. He shows us an American footsoldier shooting a POW, a pickpocket laughing at patriotism, politicians in bed with criminals, children learning to become terrorists—the veneer of polite society and civilization stripped away to expose the shocking truth.

Fuller's narratives place his protagonists in extreme situations fraught with conflict and contradiction in order to produce "emotional violence." Fuller's favorite example of an emotionally violent film was David Lean's *Brief Encounter* (1945), a bittersweet romance about two people who fall in love but are married to others:

Now when you have a married man and a married woman, they're gonna cheat. They're all scared, scared, scared. But these two won't even touch hands on a bed; they've never kissed. The guilt! They're guilty, and they haven't done a damn thing—but in a way they have. And the violence is against themselves. That's better than any barroom stuff.[24]

At first, this may seem a strange example for Fuller to embrace, given the vast tonal and stylistic differences between his pictures and the comparatively restrained *Brief Encounter.* Yet what Fuller responds to in this film is the inner conflict of the two protagonists: they want to respect their marriages, but they also want each other. Fuller equates emotional violence with the severe psychological turmoil that results from an individual having two opposing desires that cannot both be satisfactorily fulfilled. This is the sort of narrative situation that most frequently confronts his protagonists, from *I Shot Jesse James*'s John Ford, who believes he has to kill his friend in order to marry his girl, to *The Naked Kiss*'s Kathy, who desperately wants to marry the town millionaire and lead a clean life but discovers that the millionaire is a sexual predator and clean living is dirtier than she thought. Fuller's embrace of paradox often results in irony, a bitter recognition of truth's complexity.

Fuller's interest in creating intensified narrative situations in his screenplays often overrides the powerful influence of classical conventions. Classical Hollywood narratives tend to feature tightly woven chains of cause and effect; each scene leads directly into the next, with no additional scenes that are extraneous to the dominant narrative action.[25] These norms help to ensure consistency, coherence, and verisimilitude within screenplays—qualities Fuller was often willing to sacrifice in order to achieve heightened conflict. Fuller's original scripts sport looser, more episodic structures designed to contrast the rhythms and tones of scenes and to unsettle audience assumptions. Action may arise quickly—and with little apparent motivation—and be followed by another unexpected event. The narratives of some of his movies, such as *Park Row, Forty Guns, Shock Corridor, Dead Pigeon on Beethoven Street, The Big Red One,* and *Street of No Return,* even appear overstuffed, as if Fuller thought of too many great plot points and simply decided to keep them all. Sharply contrasting action, sudden shifts in tone, surprising plot developments, and multiple lines of conflict all contribute to creating intensified narrative situations in Fuller's films, even as they often undercut viewer expectations of clear causal links, consistent character psychology, and careful plot motivation. It is telling that film trade publications described the vast majority of Fuller's pre-1970s pictures as melodramas, applying a longstanding definition that associated the term with thrilling, action-packed stories.[26] This trend is a potent reminder that Fuller's work is a variant of a cinematic tradition that extends back to the serials of the silent era, in which coincidental, implausible, and often confusing narratives function to create heightened emotion and sensationalism.[27]

While reference to genre conventions helps to motivate many of Fuller's narratives, his films just as often challenge our generic expectations. With a few exceptions, Fuller's movies participate in the war, crime, and western genres—standard territory for low-budget action films.[28] Genre films contain highly conventionalized protagonists, settings, situations, themes, and iconography; while variations on each element occur, their repetition over the course of a genre's development shapes viewer expectations regarding what is "appropriate" for the genre. Although Fuller's genre films often employ conventional character types and situations, they tend to twist some genre elements and completely ignore others, even while relying on genre to motivate unexplained action. Rather than using genre to explore a defined cultural conflict—in the western, for example, the way of the gun vs. the rule of law—Fuller selectively invokes generic elements in his films as a foundation for his own narrative interests. Fuller's preferences for brutish characters and heightened conflict lend themselves easily to some genres, such as crime and war; his westerns and social problem pictures, however, are less conventional and often contain narrative structures and plot elements not usually found within the given genre. After Fuller started his own production company in the late 1950s, his use of excessive sex and violence further warped his genre narratives, and several of his subsequent films are primarily structured around sensational set

"SHORT ROUND"
WEARING PRAYER ON BACK ASKING BUDDHA TO MAKE SGT. ZACK LIKE HIM——

Fuller's preproduction drawing of the character Short Round from *The Steel Helmet*. *Chrisam Films, Inc.*

pieces (*Shock Corridor, The Naked Kiss, White Dog,* and *Street of No Return*). Genre conventions thus provide a convenient structure on which Fuller can build his own ideas; some structures are strengthened by his fresh approach, while others buckle under the weight of his distinct worldview.

Fuller's writing process enabled him to visualize the development of his screenplays and to orchestrate narrative elements for maximum emotional impact. His scriptwriting involved copious research and detailed planning. An early profile of Fuller written at the beginning of his tenure at Twentieth Century–Fox describes how he initially developed a story by drawing pictures of characters, locations, and key action before sitting down at a typewriter.[29] Later interviews suggest this process could also be contemporaneous with the actual writing of the screenplay but confirm Fuller's tendency to cast actors according to his character sketches. He also produced drawings of sets that functioned as blueprints for the art department and drafted upwards of seventy-five drawings detailing how scenes should be shot.[30] Fuller's penchant for visualizing his stories as he was writing them harkens back to his years in journalism, when he often picked up extra cash from drawing cartoons; more significant, however, is how this process underscores his tendency to think in pictures, to imagine how a story can be told through visually arresting images.

When working on several scripts at a time, Fuller also used a system that enabled him to keep track of the narrative structure of each project on a blackboard. The blackboard for each script contained a chart of the film's plot, with white chalk indicating exposition, yellow chalk for the introduction of a character, blue chalk for romantic scenes, and red chalk for action and violence.[31]

If I can end the first act with one or two red lines, the second act with two or three red lines, and the third act with four or five red lines, I am going uphill. So I can get a pretty good idea of the balance of the violence and of the romance or anything I want on that board.[32]

While Fuller admits he did not use the blackboard to map out every script, profiles and interviews suggest he continued to strive for a high degree of preparation and careful plotting of scripts in order to develop contrasting emotion and accelerating action. As Fuller's screenwriting process favored heightening dramatic conflict and varying the tones of scenes over producing a tight, three-act, causal narrative, it is little wonder that the norms of verisimilitude, clarity, and coherence embraced by classical Hollywood filmmaking are not always apparent in his movies.

Samuel Fuller considered himself first and foremost a storyteller, and the way he told stories on film reflected how his narrative preferences were filtered through cinematic conventions and industrial pressures. While his early scripts produced by Lippert and Twentieth Century–Fox reveal closer adherence to classical and generic norms, Fuller's move into independent moviemaking in the late 1950s enabled him to film scripts that had previously been rejected as too unconventional. In the process of establishing his identity as an independent and targeting an adult audience, Fuller's stories became increasingly sensational, topical, and sometimes less than tasteful. Throughout his career, his narratives put to work the lessons he learned from his years in journalism and demonstrate a willingness to flaunt custom and propriety in order to create challenging, startling viewing experiences. At their best, his narratives are exercises in arousal, a surprising blend of brutality, humor, and pathos. The shocking thrills contained in Fuller's scripts are amplified onscreen by his production methods. A review of his visual style provides a helpful introduction to the strategies he used to bring his punchy yarns to two-fisted life.

### Movement and Conflict

During the studio era, Hollywood operated according to a mode of production that encouraged speed, efficiency, and original approaches to classical conventions. Fuller's early track record of shooting fast, spending little, and delivering genre hits made him an attractive find for Darryl Zanuck and the other studio executives who courted him in the early 1950s, but Fuller never fully embraced the "invisible" style of directors like George Cukor and Howard Hawks that dominated Hollywood in the studio era. According to the Fuller legend, the characteristics that constitute classicism—balance, order, and unity—should not even be included in a sentence bearing the name of Samuel Fuller. While Fuller's films do frequently appear unbalanced, incongruous, and disunified, they are not so all of the time. In fact, Fuller was entirely capable of adhering to classical norms, and many of his films, particularly those produced by Twentieth Century–Fox, contain scenes that are models of conventional staging and editing. Any argument concerning Fuller's visual style must acknowledge the complete range of its expression, taking into account both the traditional and the weird, what worked within the studio system and what changed without.

Although Fuller's films may often appear haphazard or unstructured, their visual style is less the result of negligence, instinct, or limited production resources than of a number of conscious strategies designed to maximize the visceral impact of the viewing experience. Fuller's work is shaped by his tendency to shoot long takes as the primary foundation of scenes; to juxtapose long-take scenes with those reliant on montage; and to develop kineticism, sharp contrasts in tone and style, rhythmic and graphic editing patterns, and stylistic "weirdness." Fuller's dominant stylistic strategies complement and support each other, distinguishing his films from those made by directors who worked with similar resources in like genres. While not all of these characteristics are contained within every Fuller film, and they are manifested through different techniques in different films, even the most classically constructed of Fuller's pictures contain at least two of these general strategies. In conjunction with the narrative, these tactics are designed to startle the audience and produce the "hammer-blows of emotion" that Fuller so desired.

Few production and postproduction records survive for Fuller's films, yet interviews with him and his crew members, as well as the films themselves, provide some indication of how Fuller's working methods contributed to the creation of visceral effects. While his production periods were often quite short, Fuller made time for rehearsal before shooting even on his low-budget pictures, suggesting that the intense planning he put into preproduction carried over onto the set.[33] What most distinguished Fuller's approach to filmmaking were his ideas concerning how a scene should be shot. Classical Hollywood filmmaking typically strives to maintain continuity in space, time, and action in an effort to communicate the narrative clearly and efficiently. A conventional scene might begin with a wide master shot to establish the space, then cut in to a medium shot or two-shot that isolates significant action, then subsequently cut into close-ups or shot–reverse shot patterns that highlight character reactions and emotions, and finally cut back out to a medium or wide shot to re-establish the space as a new line of narrative action is initiated. This type of editing pattern, often described as analytical editing, presents the totality of the space and then breaks it into parts, firmly directing the viewer's gaze to ensure clear and efficient exposition of the narrative.[34] In order to provide coverage for a scene—or enough camera angles and compositions for editors to choose from—a director customarily films the complete scene once in the establishing master shot, then shoots sections of the scene again from closer angles and shot scales. While Fuller embraced the concept of a master shot, the general lack of analytical editing and coverage in most of his films, particularly those made outside of Twentieth Century–Fox, suggests that for him, the master shot functions less as an opportunity to establish the space than as the very foundation of the scene. Rather than acting as a jumping-off point for shot–reverse shot or point-of-view shot patterns, the master often becomes the dominant shot for scenes in Fuller's films, intercut with only a few quick close-ups or cutaways.

Fuller's tendency to favor the master shot was rooted less in a desire for economy than in a desire to exploit the tension produced by the technical requirements of a long take. "I don't like to shoot a scene from a close angle, medium, long shot, and then take it into the editor and see if we can do anything with it," he said. "I want to see the excitement on

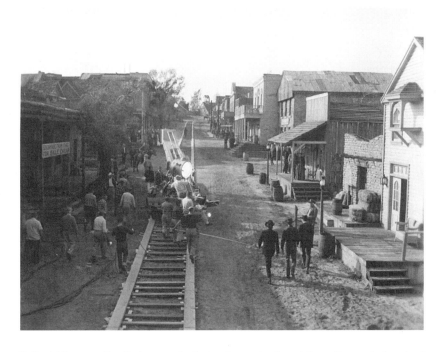

Fuller laid extraordinarily long tracks during the production of *Forty Guns*—the length of Twentieth Century–Fox's back lot—in order to film the characters of Griff, Wes, and Chico walking down Main Street in one continuous shot. Extended tracking during master-shot long takes is part of Fuller's stylistic signature. *Chrisam Films, Inc.*

the set, while we're shooting."[35] Joseph Biroc, Fuller's director of photography on *Run of the Arrow, China Gate, Forty Guns,* and *Verboten!* also pointed out that by forcing the actors to perform a scene in one extended take, Fuller was able to capitalize on their nervous energy, as well as on unexpected reactions or bits of business. "Sam felt—and he was right—that the longer you make the shot, the better the people can act it out, the more real it all seems, instead of making it in small pieces—cut, cut, cut, the way it is usually done."[36] As the master-shot long take requires cast and crew to focus their attention and be "in" the scene for a longer period of time, it increases the potential for unexpected interactions between actors that might speak to the narrative within the scene.

When combined with his tendency to shoot only one or two takes for each shot, Fuller's preference for the master-shot long take often resulted in a lack of coverage for scenes that troubled his editors and challenged their ability to "fix" continuity breaks. Yet these "mistakes" appear to

have concerned Fuller little, as they often contribute to his preferred stylistic strategies. Gene Fowler, Jr., Fuller's editor on *Run of the Arrow,*
*China Gate,* and *Forty Guns,* explained:

Sam is a guy who shoots very long scenes, no cuts, and usually shoots just
one take. So if anything turned out to be wrong with the take you were
screwed. . . . If an actor would flub a line in the middle of a take it presented
quite a problem for me because you had nothing to cut away to.[37]

An advantage to shooting a scene from multiple angles and shot scales is
that adequate coverage enables the editor to use a different shot of the
same action if there is a problem with dialogue, acting, lighting, sound,
cinematography, etc. However, if no other shot of the action exists, the
editor must either leave the error in the shot or create an unconventional
way to mask the error. Fowler and Fuller's other editors thus frequently
resorted to cutaways to contiguous but irrelevant spaces or alternate
takes of the same master shot to cover technical problems. While these
solutions might effectively mask the mistake, they can glaringly violate
the continuity of the diegetic world—the world of the film's story.

Fuller's editors also used close-ups and optical process shots to create
visual variety in scenes recorded primarily in one long take with little or
no camera movement. Static long takes could significantly slow the pace
of a scene and offer fewer means of directing the viewer's attention to important narrative information. One strategy seen over and over again in
Fuller's films is the use of the close-up and optically processed blow-up
or zoom to vary the scale of the image and emphasize significant emotional moments. Gene Fowler, Jr., explained in an interview how he
worked with Twentieth Century–Fox's optical department to produce a
zoom that looked like a dolly in postproduction in order that he might
have the freedom to move into a close-up and back out to a long shot
during extended single takes in *China Gate.*[38] Optical process shots are
also used in *I Shot Jesse James, Park Row, Run of the Arrow, The Crimson Kimono, Underworld, U.S.A.,* and *Verboten!* While optically processed close-ups and zooms draw attention to themselves due to a slight
increase in the grain of the image, they enabled Fuller and his editors to
stretch the expressive boundaries of the master-shot long take in the absence of character blocking and camera movement.

Fuller's preference for shooting master-shot long takes rather than
complete coverage was not unique in postwar Hollywood filmmaking.
The films of directors such as Vincente Minnelli and Otto Preminger typically display much greater average shot lengths than those of Fuller, as
they contain more scenes shot in one long take and a generally more uni-
form use of the long take throughout. Fuller, on the other hand, only

produced two pictures with average shot lengths in excess of the era's norm: *Park Row* and *House of Bamboo*.[39] While Fuller often uses the master shot as the foundation of a scene, the editing strategies discussed above, as well as the juxtaposition of long takes with heavily edited scenes, tend to reduce the average shot length of his films. What makes Fuller's interest in shooting with little coverage and few takes notable is how it contributes to his dominant stylistic strategies. Long takes with rapid camera movement heighten the kineticism of scenes; when juxtaposed with a montage sequence, long takes can produce startling shifts in tone; and master shots intercut with close-ups, optical process shots, or extraneous footage can disorient the viewer.

In addition to staging scenes around long-take master shots, Fuller also builds more heavily edited sequences around quick takes of medium shots and close-ups. Fuller's montage-based scenes typically employ constructive editing. Instead of cutting into a detail from a wide master shot as is common in analytical editing, constructive editing eliminates establishing shots and suggests space through the juxtaposition of images. Movement and screen direction connect action from one shot to the next. The viewer then constructs the entire action mentally by uniting the parts of the action seen in separate shots. Fuller frequently draws on constructive editing to suggest spatial relations through eyeline matches— when the shot of a character's glance is juxtaposed with a shot of the object that is being seen—as in the openings of *I Shot Jesse James* and *Pickup on South Street*. He also utilizes constructive editing for more explosive purposes, repeating a series of compositions multiple times to create a percussive rhythm.

One memorable example of constructive editing in *Underworld, U.S.A.* illustrates how this technique contributes to Fuller's desired emotional effects. Gus, an assassin, has been ordered to kill the daughter of a crime witness, so he runs the girl over with his car while she is out riding her bike. The scene is organized through ellipses, as medium shots of the girl's head and shoulders on the bike, Gus's head and shoulders in the car, the girl's legs and bike wheel, and Gus's car wheel are intercut ever more rapidly to suggest her pursuit. Increasingly tighter shots of the girl's mother in the window watching her daughter's race for life occasionally interrupt the chase, until the mother screams and closes her eyes. The last shot shows the girl sprawled on the concrete with her mangled bike beside her, the victim of a moment of impact the viewer is led to imagine but never actually sees. The rhythm and pacing of the editing in the scene, as well as the need for viewers to link the shots together mentally, heighten our visceral response and multiply our horror.

One of the most distinctive aspects of Fuller's aesthetic signature is his propensity for "weirdness." This was actually a technical term for him.

Frame enlargements of the final shots from a murder sequence in *Underworld, U.S.A.* joined together via constructive editing. Constructive editing relies on the viewer to piece together the spatial relationships between each shot. This technique was often used by Fuller to involve the viewer in acts of extreme violence.

As he tells Jim Jarmusch in the documentary *Tigrero: A Film That Was Never Made* (1994), any time his cameraman or assistant director came across a "W" in the margin of the script, he knew to ask Fuller what to do. The "W" stood for weirdness: an aggressive disregard for classical conventions governing the presentation of space, time, and movement. Weirdness creeps into Fuller's pictures beginning in the Globe era and escalates from there, appearing most frequently—but not exclusively— during subjective sequences. Even relatively stylistically tame sequences can be defined as weird if narrative and stylistic logic fly out the window. Explosions of weirdness are one of the defining aspects of what makes a film a Fuller.

Because the visceral effects Fuller sought could be realized in a swift and inexpensive manner—as they relied on a minimum of camera setups and necessitated only the most basic production design—his stylistic preferences were not entirely out of step with the efficiency championed by the classical system. By adapting his interest in conflict and kineticism to the available resources and production circumstances of each film, Fuller could produce original storytelling in an expedient manner, thereby helping to make his stylistically unusual films more acceptable to the studios and major distributors. Nevertheless, his willingness to draw attention to stylistic choices in a manner not widely embraced in Hollywood made Fuller's visual style somewhat problematic, especially when exercised in less action-oriented genres that do not inherently strive to shake up the viewer. The varied expression of Fuller's stylistic preferences reflects his journey into and out of big-budget studio productions in the mid-1950s, his heightened creative control after becoming an independent producer, his progression toward increasing sensationalism, and the eclectic experimentation of his final films.

All too often critics highlight the rough, occasionally crude construction of Fuller's work and its various excesses without fully considering the range of his aesthetic choices and their intended effect on the viewer. Luc Moullet's attitude toward Fuller typifies that of many who consider him a "primitive" genius: "Perhaps no other director has ever gone so far in the art of throwing a film together. Whatever the extent of his negligence, one cannot but be fascinated by the spontaneity it brings with it."[40] Yet as we have seen, Fuller was hardly one to "throw a film together." His working process was detailed and deliberate, and he was consistently disposed toward narrative and stylistic strategies that aroused and provoked the viewer. The following chapters describe how production conditions, studio and regulatory oversight, and market trends shape the articulation of Fuller's artistic impulses, beginning with his early years at the low-budget studio Lippert Productions. While his first two pictures flirt with unconventional narrative and stylistic choices, in-depth analysis of *The Steel Helmet* reveals the blossoming of Fuller's personal aesthetic and its roots in movement and conflict.

# CHAPTER ONE

# The Lippert Years, 1948–1951

uller began directing films at the end of the 1940s, when the structure of the studio system underwent a seismic shift. After 1946, decreasing theater attendance and skyrocketing production costs eroded profits for the studios, while the 1948 Paramount antitrust decision altered distribution practices and divorced the exhibition arms of the major studios from their production and distribution wings. In an effort to cut costs, the major and minor studios made fewer films, shedding their low-budget B units and funneling available money into high-profile blockbusters, a trend already underway from the early 1940s. The reduction in the number of released films threatened to starve exhibitors, especially those who maintained double-bill screenings and frequently changed their schedules. In response, small, low-budget studios rushed to fill the empty screens vacated by the major and minor studios with genre-oriented action fare.

The low-budget studios were just as hungry for talent as the majors, and the success of Fuller's novel *The Dark Page* soon attracted the notice of Robert Lippert, a West Coast exhibitor and independent producer. Lippert owned Lippert Productions, Inc., a low-budget production unit, and was the president of Lippert Pictures, Inc., a distribution outfit that grew out of Screen Guild Productions in 1949. Lippert released mainly sixty- to sixty-five-minute B westerns and genre pictures destined for the second half of a double bill. The company's motto was: "You get *action* from Lippert Pictures!" During its early years, Lippert films were generally produced for $75,000 to $100,000 and financed through cash advances from Lippert franchise-holders.[1] In addition to abbreviated running times and limited budgets, Lippert films contained other qualities of B pictures made by lesser studios: no stars and shooting schedules of three or fewer weeks.

With an eye toward investing in higher-budget production, Lippert was on the lookout for writers and directors who could put over a spectacular story with speed and efficiency, and he found such talent in Fuller. Eager to direct his own work after over a decade of writing scenarios and scripts for others, Fuller agreed to both write and direct his first Lippert film, *I Shot Jesse James*, for minimum pay.[2] Lippert gained a screenwriter experienced in action genres and insured himself against Fuller's directorial inexperience by pairing him with producer Carl K. Hittleman, a veteran of budget westerns and adventure stories; for his part, Fuller finally had a shot at directing his own scripts. All three of his Lippert films were among the company's most expensive to produce and were designed to be distributed as either headliners or supporting features. Their limited budgets insured a profit if any of them were a hit, and on his third try, *The Steel Helmet*, Fuller hit it big.

Working for Lippert offered Fuller an opportunity to experiment with visual storytelling in a relatively low-risk environment while retaining maximum production control. *I Shot Jesse James* and *The Baron of Arizona* find him developing the obsessive characters, contradictory desires, and themes of deception and betrayal that are central to so many of his pictures, while adopting a range of stylistic strategies that combine production efficiency with emotional impact. The strengths and weaknesses of these two pictures prepare Fuller for *The Steel Helmet*, his first film to express a distinct aesthetic in a unified and coherent fashion. Multiple lines of conflict, sudden shifts in tone, and use of irony emerge as primary narrative characteristics, tools that upend viewer expectations in the service of entertainment and revelation. On the stylistic level, Fuller experiments with both extended master shots and montage editing, seeking a variety of strategies to heighten the physical and emotional impact of his images. While Fuller's limited resources at Lippert certainly affected what he was able to achieve visually, the artistic freedom he enjoyed allowed him to develop the aesthetic instincts he would favor throughout the rest of his career.

## The Marketplace for Low-Budget Films

The low-budget B picture was the bread and butter of Hollywood during the height of the studio system, produced both by major studios to maximize the use of their equipment and personnel and by smaller Poverty Row studios as their sole product. B pictures featured lower budgets, shorter shooting schedules, less established actors, and briefer running times than A pictures and typically played the bottom half of a double bill.[3] The status of a B picture was determined not only by production factors, but also by distribution and exhibition, and sometimes a film could move between the A and B designation. Unlike A pictures, Bs were distributed for a flat fee, allowing studios to calculate their return precisely and to budget their production costs to insure profitability.

Because Bs had limited selling potential, their distribution was not as co-ordinated as that of As, nor was it supported by national advertising campaigns or widespread press coverage. Instead, distributors tapped Bs when and where they needed them to fill out a double bill, resulting in a more random release pattern often to smaller theaters over the course of several months to several years.[4] Box office and critical response could shift a film's designation, however, as successful Bs might be promoted to the top of the bills at better houses, while failing As might be relegated to diffused distribution as supporting features.

As B pictures were made by studios with a wide range of available re-sources, their characteristics varied dramatically. The most prestigious low-budget films were programmers, also known as "in-betweeners" due to their status in between the high-gloss A and the quick-and-dirty B. Programmers shared aspects of both As and Bs, featuring higher-paid actors, larger budgets and shooting schedules, and longer running times than the average B, but still lacked the prestige and high-gloss produc-tion values of the full-blown A. The major studios dominated the in-betweener category during the 1930s, but by the 1950s lesser studios increasingly initiated programmer production. Programmers had the flexibility to play either half of a double feature depending on the the-ater and program and could be supported by national publicity cam-paigns or receive general press coverage. Brian Taves notes that market conditions often made the programmer a risky venture, however. While a hit programmer stood to make a tidy profit due to its lower budget than most As, a less successful programmer could fail to make back its costs if it quickly disappeared from the A market or was exhibited pri-marily as a B.[5] Successful programmers thus had to sell themselves like As—using stars, brand names, genre appeal, or gimmicks—while still featuring budgets closer to Bs.

While exhibitors' embrace of the double bill during the 1930s spurred the growth of B pictures and programmers, the studios' movement away from mass production during the 1940s and 1950s threatened the sur-vival of low-budget films and left exhibitors wanting. The divorcement from studio theaters relieved the majors of the need to produce large numbers of films to fill yearly programs and maintain efficiency. As the major and minor producers cut back on lower-budgeted production in the 1940s and early 1950s, smaller outfits such as Republic and Allied Artists, which previously cranked out Bs, followed their lead and also turned to more expensive productions.[6] Exhibitors found themselves with both fewer people coming in the door and less product to put up on the screen.

The double-bill policy that remained standard in 70 percent of U.S. theaters even through the 1950s made the film shortage particularly acute.[7] The loss of B pictures especially hurt smaller independent and neighborhood theaters that changed lineups more frequently and relied on programmers and B pictures to fill in the schedule between major releases. Smaller houses were loath to abandon double bills due to their popularity with the segment of the audience that exhibitors most wanted to attract: young people. Smaller, indoor exhibitors' need for product was also shared by the drive-ins. According to the *Journal of Property Management,* many drive-ins changed their schedules three times a week in 1953—like the neighborhood theaters—and incorporated both first-class pictures and action films.[8] In addition, drive-ins were "the temple of the double feature," and outdoor owners supported the continuation of double bills into the 1960s, even as other exhibitors called for their elimination.[9] Small, independent movie houses, drive-ins, and first-run theaters that maintained a double-bill policy thus formed the primary market for low-budget films when Fuller began his directorial career with Lippert. Fuller's deal with Lippert aligned him with an established, low-budget studio at a time when demand for its action-oriented B pictures and programmers remained strong. The rest was up to him.

Although hampered by limited budgets and speedy shooting schedules, as well as by genre expectations that he did not always fully embrace, Fuller found at Lippert an opportunity to develop as a director and to gain increasing control over his screenplays. The success of *I Shot Jesse James,* described by the *Motion Picture Herald* as "the sleeper of the year," prompted Lippert to sign Fuller to a three-picture contract, granting him script approval and cash plus participation in profits.[10] While disappointed by the response to *The Baron of Arizona,* his second, more ambitious feature for Lippert, Fuller negotiated producer status for his third, *The Steel Helmet,* as well as a third of the profits and final say on the film's screenplay, direction, and editing.[11] With *The Steel Helmet,* Fuller was particularly proud of his tight control over production, boasting before the film's release, "Lippert never even read the script or saw the picture until it was previewed."[12]

With just three films, Fuller managed to become a writer-director-producer and to receive profit participation, a sort of deal usually reserved for much more experienced directors like Hitchcock and Hawks who worked for major studios and top independent producers. To Fuller's advantage, he was in the right place at the right time: Lippert was looking to expand slowly into higher-budget programmers, and once Fuller had proven himself, Lippert's offer of greater control and financial compensation temporarily kept Fuller from defecting to a larger studio.[13] The Lippert years turned out to be a golden era for Fuller, a time when he could pursue his interests and try new ideas while facing limited risks and exposure. As was true throughout his career, he made the most of the opportunity he was given.

*Early Experiments:* I Shot Jesse James *and* The Baron of Arizona

*I Shot Jesse James* emerged out of Fuller's interest in assassins and in what motivates a man to kill someone he loves. Although he first pitched Lippert the story of Cassius, the Roman senator who plotted to murder Julius Caesar, Lippert warmed more quickly to the tale of Robert Ford, the James gang member who killed Jesse with a shot to the back.[14] Ford's story placed Fuller's first Lippert picture squarely in the genre most associated with the studio, promised enough gunplay to please action fans, and enabled exploitation of the outlaw's legendary name. Budgeted around $110,000 and filmed in approximately ten days, *I Shot Jesse James* starred character actors John Ireland, Preston Foster, and Barbara Britton. Part of Lippert's bid to expand into programmer production, it cost more and ran twenty minutes longer than most Lippert westerns.[15] With its name-brand title, recognizable actors, higher production values, and longer running time, *I Shot Jesse James* contained the potential to play in first-run houses on the top of a double bill. More significantly for Fuller, the film's emotionally charged narrative provided suitable opportunities to experiment with visual storytelling.

*I Shot Jesse James* centers on the motivation for—and effects of—Bob Ford's betrayal of Jesse James. It opens with Fuller's calling card, a beautifully choreographed James Gang bank robbery, after which Bob (Ireland) loses all the loot and Jesse (Reed Hadley) saves his life. While the gang is in hiding, Bob learns of an amnesty that is offered by the governor to anyone who turns Jesse in, dead or alive, and visits the actress he loves, Cynthy (Britton). Cynthy declares that she wants them to marry and settle down on a farm, but Bob knows that if he turns himself in, he faces lengthy jail time. He concludes that the only way to marry his sweetheart is to kill Jesse, his closest friend, thus gaining amnesty for his crimes, but his obsession with Cynthy prevents him from anticipating the consequences of his actions. Cynthy's love turns to hate once she learns of Bob's betrayal, and Bob is haunted in his mind and in public by the cowardly murder. When an honorable marshal (Foster) emerges as a rival for Cynthy's affections, Bob blames him for Cynthy's change of heart, forcing him into a standoff that leads to Bob's death. With his dying breath, Bob tells Cynthy that he's sorry for what he did and that he loved Jesse.

While Lippert sold *I Shot Jesse James* as a western, the film does not engage with generic conventions so much as use them to explore Fuller's own narrative and stylistic interests. The characters, settings, iconography, and situations typical of westerns are all here: dance-hall girls, marshals, and outlaws; saloons and clapboard Main Streets; guns, horses, and cowboy hats; and bank robberies, fistfights, and shootouts. Yet these generic indicators function primarily as narrative devices, efficiently sketching the relationships between characters and their world and conveniently providing motivation for plot points. Fuller demonstrates no interest in exploring the conflict between the "untamed" world and the "civilized" world that is at the heart of the western genre, nor in grappling with the mythic status of Jesse James in particular or of the outlaw-hero in general. Jesse James could just as easily have been Julius Caesar. What excites Fuller is the psychology of his assassin and how Bob Ford's love of Cynthy drives him to betray and murder Jesse, whom he also loves. The film's narrative structure highlights the irony of Bob's situation: Jesse's death can help Bob marry Cynthy, but murdering Jesse kills Cynthy's love for Bob. *I Shot Jesse James* thus introduces themes that will become hallmarks of the Fuller film: as with a love that leads to violence, truth is often contradictory and absurd.

The irrationality of Bob's emotions and his obsessive fixation on marrying Cynthy propel the story forward, even as digressive subplots threaten to diffuse the film's narrative focus. Fuller fully immerses the viewer in Bob's subjectivity, using dialogue to externalize his thoughts and feelings; Bob's self-interest is so total that even his conversations come across as monologues. Ireland plays Bob as a love-struck dreamer, childishly blind to all but his own desire, making him appear more pathetic than villainous. The actor adopts languid, feline poses, and his line readings, expressions, and movement physicalize his character's slow-witted single-mindedness. The effect is entrancing, and while viewers are unlikely to identify with Robert Ford—he has few redeeming qualities—Fuller's script and Ireland's performance enable us to understand him and to pity him.

Narrative and style work together in *I Shot Jesse James* both to provide viewers with subjective access to Bob's thoughts and feelings and to distance us from his pain, producing competing kinds of emotional engagement with the protagonist. One memorable example occurs during the first act after Bob makes the decision to kill Jesse, when sudden tonal shifts emphasize both Bob's hesitation to strike and the comedic irony of his situation. Following Bob's declaration that "nothing's gonna stop me from marrying Cynthy," the sequence cuts to Jesse bathing in a tub, accompanied by upbeat music on the score. Jesse yells out a cheery, "Hey Bob!" as Ford enters the bathhouse laden with pails of hot water. Although the setup is lighthearted and playfully homoerotic, after Bob pours the water in to freshen Jesse's bath, the score shifts to a threatening crescendo, punctuating a cut to a medium-close-up of Jesse's back from Bob's optical point of view. We remember Bob's promise and recognize that he spies an opportunity, and as the significance of the moment sinks in—surely Jesse will never be this naively exposed and vulnerable again—Fuller ups the ante, cutting out to a long shot of Bob picking up a Colt 45—a gift from Jesse, and a convenient murder weapon. As the scene cuts between Bob's point of view of Jesse's back and a low angle of him fondling the gun and looking nervously at Jesse, the audience is placed in Bob's subjectivity, recognizing his anxious indecision and how it is heightened by his mentor's generosity and good spirits. At the same time, however, the clichéd sexual symbolism can't help but shine through: a naked man has just given another man a gun—in a bathhouse! The dramatic suspense and campy comedy are held in tension as Fuller exerts even more narrative pressure, overlaying a shot of Jesse's back with his exhortation to Ford: "Well go ahead, Bob. What are you waiting for? There's my back . . . scrub it." And then, given motive, opportunity, and means to shoot, Bob chooses to . . . scrub.

This scene provides an important moment of narrative suspense—will Bob kill Jesse or not?—while also underlining Jesse's unquestioning trust in Bob and Bob's hesitation in murdering Jesse. More significant, however, is how Fuller achieves these narrative goals, placing the viewer in Bob's subjectivity while simultaneously highlighting tonal counterpoints. Although the bathhouse scene stands alone in *I Shot Jesse James* as an example of unexpected tonal play, this narrative strategy becomes much more widely used in Fuller's later work.

As with the narrative, the visual style in *I Shot Jesse James* reflects Fuller's search for techniques that will effectively heighten the viewer's emotional involvement while maintaining production efficiency. The quality of the overall staging is uneven, however, and lays bare both Fuller's inexperience and production constraints. Dialogue-laden scenes are typically constructed from a master shot and inserts, and the use of optical close-ups attests to the overall lack of coverage. While Fuller often staged scenes this way in his later films, *I Shot Jesse James* features none of the intricate blocking and camera movement that bring dynamism to his long takes in *Pickup on South Street*, *Forty Guns*, or *The Crimson Kimono*. The lack of camera movement and close angles are also felt in the film's primary fistfight, captured by a high-angle, extreme long shot that diffuses the kineticism of the characters' actions. More successful is the short fight between the marshal and Frank James, staged as an exchange of point-of-view shots: first the marshal punches into the camera in a medium close-up, and then Frank James recoils in an opposing medium close-up. Here the camera optically situates the viewer in the middle of the action, and the effect of the marshal's punch is more fully felt.

The visual preferences that define Fuller's later work are most apparent in the film's opening and closing scenes. The opening is a largely wordless montage organized around character glances that depict an unfolding bank heist by Jesse James and his gang. The final image of the credits sequence, a poster announcing "$10,000 Reward For Jesse James Dead or Alive," swish pans to the beginning of the scene, a close-up of an unidentified man we conclude to be James. The scene then cuts to an opposing close-up of another unidentified man, then back to James, whereupon the camera tracks out to a medium shot of the two men, revealing James to be holding a gun on the other man. By opening on the shot–reverse shot close-ups, Fuller immediately begins raising questions in the viewer's mind: who are these men, and what is the conflict between them? The fourth shot in the scene answers these questions by presenting a long shot of the entire space: a bank robbery is in progress, and James is holding a gun on the head bank teller. Subsequent shots provide medium angles of the men, analytically dividing the space and creating eyeline matches between the tellers and the robbers, all motionless except for Bob Ford, stuffing money from the safe into a bag. The disorienting opening shots and lack of immediate exposition in *I Shot Jesse James* preview the similarly opaque beginnings of *The Steel Helmet, Pickup on South Street,* and *The Naked Kiss,* displaying an early iteration of Fuller's penchant for keeping viewers guessing even as they expect to be clearly introduced to a new narrative.

As with the first part of *I Shot Jesse James*'s opening scene, the second segment is constructed like a tense intake of breath, everything held in suspension, until the sounding of the alarm prompts a sudden, fast release. Fuller develops the suspense of the robbery in a series of intercut close-ups of (A) James, (B) the head teller, and (C) the teller's foot inching toward an alarm bell. The slight movement of the teller's foot draws the viewer's eye in contrast with the static, impassive close-ups, while the evenly paced editing draws out the teller's movement and heightens our anticipation of the alarm, still unbeknownst to the James gang: ABCBC/B/ABCBC (alarm sounds). The subtle contrast between stasis and motion introduced in the first two segments of the scene becomes overt in the third, as the sound of the alarm bell spurs every man into action. Fuller returns to the medium shots of the men, their movements forming rhythmic patterns and developing graphic contrasts across the scene, providing a sudden burst of kineticism: Jesse looks offscreen right, then Bob looks offscreen right, then the bank tellers point their guns to the right; a gang member turns to the left and shoots, then another gang member

James Ireland as Bob Ford (left) in a publicity still from the opening scene of *I Shot Jesse James*. Much of the scene is organized through eyeline matches—juxtaposing shots of characters' glances with shots of what the characters are looking at. *Photofest*

shoots to the left. The return to the establishing shot completes the editing pattern that doubles the first segment of the scene and finally clarifies the escape of the James Gang.

The piecemeal construction of space, development of eyeline matches, contrast between stasis and motion, and rhythmic and graphic editing patterns utilized in this scene are early examples of some of Fuller's favorite stylistic techniques, designed to emphasize conflict and motion within the frame. These same techniques are also brought to bear on the film's closing scene, the final confrontation between Bob Ford and the marshal. Shot in depth and largely in darkness, the scene begins with an extended sequence that intercuts (A) a deep-space shot of the marshal, static in the foreground, first facing Bob, then turned away, and (B) a medium shot of Bob, advancing on the marshal with a drawn gun from the background, producing an editing pattern of ABABABABABA. In a reversal of the prototypical western showdown, the tension in the scene hinges on the marshal's *refusal* to fight; by turning away from Bob, he dares him to again shoot a man in the back. Similar to the strategy he used in the second segment of the opening scene, Fuller extends the situation through repeated cuts back and forth between the depth shot of the marshal on the street and Bob, contrasting the marshal's stasis in the frame with Bob's advance into the foreground, causing the latter to loom ever larger in the frame. Here, however, the depth staging, chiaroscuro lighting, and violent yelling of Bob Ford create a darker, more chaotic feel. The staging of this sequence presages the showdowns at the end of *Forty Guns* and *Dead Pigeon on Beethoven Street,* each utilizing rhythmic and graphic editing patterns and contrast between stasis and movement to heighten the scene's dynamism and suspense.

The response to *I Shot Jesse James* exceeded Fuller's and Lippert's expectations, launching the film into top first-run houses, where it played steadily as the headliner from February through May of 1949 before moving to neighborhood theaters.[16] *Variety* accurately noted, "Physical values are about usual level of Screen Guild releases, giving it the dressing for top playing time in houses buying sturdy action product."[17] In April the film debuted at the Palace in New York City, a 1,700-seat, first-run Broadway theater, a first for a Lippert picture. By August, Lippert estimated grosses for the film at an exceptionally high $800,000, although actual returns were probably lower. Regardless, *I Shot Jesse James* established Fuller as a director of offbeat action fare and gave Lippert the confidence to entrust an even larger budget to Fuller's next picture.

*The Baron of Arizona* reveals both Lippert's and Fuller's increased ambitions. Lippert's announcement of its 1949–1950 slate in *Variety* signaled its desire to move into more "epic" productions, as it planned three top-budget films, several intermediate and medium-priced pictures, as well as its usual budget westerns. Early trade notices placed *The Baron of Arizona* in Lippert's top tier with a projected cost of $300,000, enabling Fuller to mount a historical costume picture with an extended shooting schedule, a ninety-minute running time, and increased production values.[18] Fuller's real coup was in attracting the services of legendary cinematographer James Wong Howe (*Air Force* [1943], *Body and Soul* [1947]), who agreed to work for a fraction of his regular fee. Again produced by Hittleman, the film is loosely based on the true story of James Addison Reavis, who planned an elaborate swindle in the 1870s to claim the territory of Arizona using a forged Spanish land grant. *The Baron of Arizona* introduces motifs and themes that will become characteristic of Fuller's work, while its visual style features a richness and complexity only intermittently apparent in *I Shot Jesse James.*

*The Baron of Arizona* begins in 1912, as a group of tuxedoed dignitaries are toasting the admission of Arizona into the Union. One man, later revealed to be John Griff (Reed Hadley), a forgery expert, offers a toast to Reavis (Vincent Price), who recently celebrated his thirtieth wedding anniversary. Griff then begins to tell Reavis's tale, prompting a flashback to 1872, when Reavis arrives outside Phoenix at the house of an adolescent girl named Sophia. Reavis tells her guardian, Alvarez (Vladimir Sokoloff), that Sophia's real name is Peralta, and a Spanish land grant reveals she is the heir to the first baron of Arizona. Reavis summarily joins the makeshift family, molding Sophia into a young baroness and creating the physical evidence of her ancestors' existence in Arizona. Despite Sophia's reluctance to part with him, Reavis sails to Spain, where he spends several years disguised first as a monk and then as a gypsy in order to modify all the copies of the actual Spanish land grant. By the time he returns, Sophia has grown into a young woman (Ellen Drew), and the two marry, thereby giving Reavis complete control over her ancestral estate.

The second half of the film concerns Reavis's attempts to defend Sophia's claim and develop their land, while the federal government and local landowners contest his control. Griff arrives to lead the government's investigation and put Reavis on trial, and Reavis, suddenly guilt-stricken, confesses his forgery to Sophia. Sophia stands by Reavis when he gives himself up to Griff, and he explains that his love for his wife is what made him confess. The film comes to a climax as an angry mob attempts to lynch Reavis. With the noose around his neck, Reavis convinces the mob that he must testify in court in order to ensure their land rights, and a newspaper insert announces his sentence of six years in prison. The epilogue portrays Reavis's release from jail, when he finds Sophia and Alvarez waiting for him in the rain, loyal to the end.

*The Baron of Arizona* offers more examples of characteristically Fullerian story elements than the writer/director's first feature, marking it as an early iteration of his emerging narrative tendencies. Here we see for the first time characters named Griff and Gunther; the gratuitous name-dropping of historical and literary figures, such as Pulitzer, Aristotle, and Cain; Fuller's beloved bust of Beethoven, a signifier of high culture; and a character wielding a cigar. Fuller's tremendous interest in history and the joy he took in research surfaces in a detailed fashion throughout the film, in scenes concerning the process of document forgery, the significance of the land grants to property holders, and the territory of Arizona. His dialogue writing also becomes more confidently campy, producing such gems as "Your claim is a cheap cigar wrapped in a rich Spanish leaf," "I feel like Caesar's wife before he was murdered," "I don't want a dead baron, I want a live husband," and "It is not death but dying that alarms me. It is not your crime but your weakness that alarms me." And a brief scene of comic relief with a gypsy dwarf presages all the oddball bits Fuller inserts in later narratives that play absolutely no role in advancing the plot.

Despite its prototypical narrative elements, *The Baron of Arizona* has received scant critical attention over the years and is among Fuller's lesser-seen pictures. Combining aspects of a costume picture, crime film, thriller, and romance, the movie is admittedly hard to categorize, and the complexity of Reavis's forgery plot can leave first-time viewers resigned to confusion. Two aspects of the narrative, the frame story and the characterization of Reavis, pose particular difficulties for the film's reception, as the first gives the plot away and the second challenges plausibility.

Griff's summary of the story in the opening scene and his subsequent voice-overs describing how Reavis falsified history serve as a frame for the primary plotline, helping to clarify the great leaps across time and space in the first half of the film and to explain why Reavis is running about chiseling on rocks and wooing a Spanish marquessa. Yet Griff's stiff introduction is both pedestrian and overly revelatory, and his voice-overs disappear following the marriage of Sophia and Reavis. The end result is awkward at best and inadvertently highlights that the exposition is half the film's running length. At the time of the film's release, the *Motion Picture Herald* review noted that the opening scene "mitigated against suspense" and "reportedly will be eliminated," but no such change was ever made.[19] Interestingly, the revised final shooting script contains neither Griff's initial scene nor his voice-overs; instead, the script begins with Reavis arriving at Alvarez's house, and Griff first appears halfway through as the government's investigation gets underway.[20] This version appears more typically Fullerian, opening as it does on a scene of confrontation that is rendered in tight close-ups. The revised final shooting script leads one to suspect that the framing scene and voice-overs were added once it became clear to Fuller, Hittleman, or both, that viewer comprehension of the narrative necessitated additional connective tissue to weave together the intricate plot.

The conclusion of the released film creates additional problems for some critics, who complained that Reavis's recognition of his love for Sophia and subsequent disavowal of the barony appear undermotivated.[21] The redemptive power of love is a theme that appears in various forms in a number of Fuller pictures, but rather than figuring as a substantive plotline, here it seems merely tacked-on. Although Griff's introduction of the story in the opening scene informs us that Reavis has been married for thirty years, as soon as Reavis arrives onscreen the film presents him as nothing less than a cad, an unrepentant liar and manipulator of all those around him. Price's spirited performance as Reavis, full of raised eyebrows and knowing glances, radiates his character's delight in criminal activity. His smoldering declaration, "I've known many women before, but with you, I'm afraid" becomes a motif, a sign of Reavis's false nature, as he repeats it first to the gypsy girl Rita, then to the Spanish marquessa, and finally to Sophia. For three-quarters of the film, Reavis's every onscreen move is motivated by greed; once he appears close to being beaten by Griff, he converts to a repentant husband in only two scenes. But it is hard for viewers to forgive a man they have grown to mistrust; they remember what they have seen (Reavis as a criminal, lying all the way), rather than what they initially heard (Reavis has been married for thirty years). The narrative's detailed focus on how Reavis attempts to steal Arizona leads viewers to wonder how he almost gets away with it rather than how he is eventually redeemed. Fuller revisits the theme of the power of love to save a criminal to greater effect in *Pickup on South Street,* with a redemptive woman that is not quite so pure and a criminal who is not so thoroughly redeemed.

It is in the style of *The Baron of Arizona* that Fuller makes his greatest advances, as he teams with James Wong Howe to produce the most classically staged and visually striking film of his Lippert career. Most likely through the influence of Howe, who was trained within the studio system to cover scenes with many shots at varied angles, Fuller moves beyond the reliance on master shots plus inserts seen in *I Shot Jesse James* and organizes scenes in a more complex manner. The vast majority of sequences include full coverage and analytical editing, as shots establish characters within space, highlight actions and emotions, and reestablish space. This exceedingly classical approach to scene construction heightens the clarity and emotional impact of the narrative in a more subtle fashion than other options adopted later by Fuller. During sequences dominated by long takes, Fuller uses character blocking, camera movement, and depth staging to create new compositions within the same shot, renewing visual interest and punctuating plot points in the absence of editing.

The primary staging strategies in *The Baron of Arizona* are illustrated by a scene midway through the film when Reavis is confronted in his office first by a railroad executive and then by landowners and a newspaperman. The three-minute, seven-second scene begins with a two-minute long take, as Gunther of Southern Railroad (Joseph Green) arrives to negotiate with Reavis for the right-of-way to run his railroad. Within the long take, five distinct compositions emerge, as the camera tracks and pans to follow the movement of the two characters around the edge of the room and into and out of depth. Pauses in camera movement, positioning of Reavis and Gunther within the frame, and their frontality (or lack of it) mark shifts in the conversation and guide the viewer's eye within the long take. After Gunther and Reavis shake hands on their

In a publicity still from *The Baron of Arizona*, the territory's men and Gunther of Southern Railroad (Joseph Green, center) question Addison Reavis (Vincent Price, foreground, right of center) about his ambitions. In this portion of the scene, Fuller uses analytical editing to highlight the men's reactions to Reavis's growing dominance. *Author's collection*

financial deal, the long take cuts to a new sequence organized analytically, as a large group of landowners barge in on Reavis and Gunther demanding to know the status of their land rights. The scene ends with a reporter telling Reavis that he is going to be written up as the man who changed geography; the camera tracks in and tilts up to capture a close-up of Reavis's reaction, as he puts his cigar in his mouth, raises his eyebrow, and beams.

The completely different staging strategies utilized in the two halves of this scene neatly divide the sequences and function in different ways. The long take that opens the scene captures two businessmen who are financial equals and reveals the breadth of Reavis's ambition as Gunther roams around the office and explores all of Reavis's financial interests. The second half of the scene unfolds as a confrontation, and analytical editing enables attention to be appropriately directed across a large number of characters. In this sequence, editing and changing shot scales provide progressively tighter or wider framings depending on the dialogue.

Reaction shots are particularly prominent, as characters digest the significance of their situations and what they have learned. Reavis's location in the center foreground of the wider shots gives him prominence within the frame and emphasizes his position of power, a stature that is reinforced by the track in to his expression of glee in the final shot of the scene. Long takes with camera and character movement and analytically edited scenes form the foundation of Fuller's visual style in *The Baron of Arizona* and remain key staging strategies throughout his career, particularly during his years at Twentieth Century–Fox.

As with the dialogue scenes, the staging of action-oriented sequences in *The Baron of Arizona* advances to a new level. The attack of the mob and attempted lynching of Reavis is the visual high point of the film and the most complicated action sequence Fuller had yet directed. Here many of the stylistic strategies utilized in the opening and closing of *I Shot Jesse James* are further developed, producing a scene of dark chaos and palpable kineticism. As in the opening of *I Shot Jesse James,* the attempted lynching scene in *The Baron of Arizona* begins in tense anticipation, as Griff, Alvarez, Reavis, Sophia, and her governess ride into an eerily quiet town square. In a series of quick cuts, Fuller reveals to the viewer what the group is unaware of: a mob of local landowners is hiding in the darkness. Fearing the mob will attack Reavis's wagon, we wait in suspense, until an offscreen gunshot breaks the silence and changes the entire mood of the scene.

As the mob runs at the wagon from all sides, Fuller orchestrates a rhythmic pattern of graphic contrasts that emphasizes the entrapment of Reavis and his loved ones. The pacing of the editing picks up as the mob runs in low angles first into the right foreground, then into the left foreground, followed by medium-close-up reaction shots of Reavis, Sophia, and Alvarez. The same pattern is repeated again, only this time the mob carries torches: the mob runs to the foreground right, the mob runs to the foreground left, then the three reaction shots. The juxtaposition of contrasting screen direction suggests a clashing of opposing forces, heightening the sense that Reavis, Sophia, and Alvarez are surrounded by danger. Their reaction shots confirm this impression, focusing attention on their fear and bewilderment as the landowners physically attack them. The rest of the scene follows Reavis, Sophia, and Alvarez as they escape from the mob and barricade themselves in Reavis's office until a battering ram breaks the door down, and the landowners attempt to string up Reavis. James Wong Howe's chiaroscuro lighting plays a dominant role in creating a mood of terror, as the flames from the torches fill the darkened frame and the shadow of the noose is cast across Reavis's wall-size map of Arizona. Mob scenes appear in a number of other Fuller pictures (*House of Bamboo, Verboten!, The Crimson Kimono, The*

*Naked Kiss*, and *Street of No Return*), providing the local community's reaction to the central events in the story, although not always in so violent a fashion. This mob scene is strikingly designed to emphasize movement and conflict within in the frame, two stylistic strategies that are central to Fuller's goal of generating physical and emotional responses in the viewer.

Although *The Baron of Arizona* was Lippert's attempt at a "prestige" release, it lacked many of the selling points that helped to insure success for a historical picture at the box office, such as an origin in a successful literary property, star power, or color cinematography. The film followed a similar distribution strategy as *I Shot Jesse James*, but the difference in the nature of the film and its lack of marketable elements doomed it to a much less successful run. *The Baron of Arizona* premiered in Phoenix in March 1950 and played first-run houses to fair returns through June, eventually limping toward a disappointing one-week run at the Palace in New York and appearing on the bottom half of first-run double bills by July.[22] While reviewers noted that the film was clearly Lippert's most expensive and ambitious effort to date, *Variety* suggested that the decision to focus on character rather than action undermined the picture's potential for success: "In so doing, it defeats its purpose in the market where Lippert releases usually play. Outlook for good returns in the general situation appears slim."[23] The box office mirrored *Variety*'s prediction, and *The Baron of Arizona* eventually was outperformed by Lippert's shorter and more moderately budgeted science-fiction effort of that year, *Rocketship X-M* (1950).[24]

Fuller publicly expressed his dissatisfaction with the way *The Baron of Arizona* turned out, especially with the supervision of producer Hittleman. While Lippert clearly intended *The Baron of Arizona* to be a more prestigious entry than *I Shot Jesse James*, the decision to distribute the two films in an identical manner failed to capitalize on the former's higher production values and aspirations as a costume drama; instead, its release pattern virtually guaranteed that *The Baron of Arizona* would disappoint audiences expecting another rousing adventure film or at least a little action. The high cost and low box-office return of *The Baron of Arizona* forced Lippert and Fuller to retrench for their next picture together, a decision that resulted in the most critically and commercially successful film of their partnership.

### *Establishing a Voice:* The Steel Helmet

With *The Steel Helmet*, Fuller had an opportunity to take the lessons he had learned from his first two pictures and apply them to a subject he was intimately familiar with: war. The result is the first picture in which his narrative and stylistic aesthetic fully takes shape. In a retreat from the epic ambitions of *The Baron of Arizona, The Steel Helmet* featured the faster shooting schedule, lower budget, and shorter length of *I Shot Jesse James*.[25] Fuller capitalized on the recent outbreak of the Korean War, quickly adapting the stories he had gathered in his diary during World War II and readying production within weeks. Rather than shooting for a low-grade A picture, as he did with *The Baron of Arizona,* Fuller mounted *The Steel Helmet* as an ambitious B. His star, Gene Evans, was an unknown and was supported entirely by no-name character actors. Without the money to film in any location resembling Korea, Fuller shot the majority of the movie in a rented studio, utilizing two sets (a forest and a Buddhist temple) and adding material from one to two days of outdoor work in Los Angeles's Griffith Park. The battle scenes consist of stock war footage intercut with shots of UCLA students dressed up as North Korean soldiers. Despite lacking anything resembling naturalistic mise-en-scene, *The Steel Helmet* nevertheless exudes authenticity due to Fuller's blunt, unsparing handling of the subject matter. Fuller knew full well the limitations inherent in depicting war on celluloid but was determined to convey the details of a footsoldier's life and the emotions of war as accurately as possible. As presented in the film, war is not noble or glorious but simply fatigue interrupted by death.

Fuller's approach to the combat film genre was very much a personal one, and he often drew the characters and situations in his war pictures directly from who he knew and what he saw during his time as a soldier. Having spent over fifteen years in journalism by the time he enlisted, Fuller seems to have approached his war service as an opportunity to gather really good copy. Although he was offered numerous opportunities to escape combat, Fuller wanted to be where the action was, on the ground with the "doggies," and he sought an assignment with the infantry.[26] He carried with him a diary that functioned much like a reporter's notebook, with descriptions of military activities, living conditions, casualties, and vacation leaves, including instructions for how real-life situations might be incorporated into future stories. When it came time to write *The Steel Helmet,* Fuller's own war experiences colored his interpretation of combat film conventions, resulting in a picture that invites us not to identify with recognizable Americans fighting for a valiant cause, but to share in the *feeling* of what it is like to be a footsoldier. When the seemingly harmless can turn deadly and a sniper waits around every corner, fear, confusion, and exhaustion reign supreme.

*The Steel Helmet* first introduces us to Sergeant Zack (Evans), a self-absorbed WWII retread who is rescued by a South Korean orphan

(William Chun) after surviving a massacre. Initially hostile to the child's friendly advances, Zack bows to his persistence and allows him to follow behind, giving him the nickname Short Round ("cause you're not going all the way"). Zack's emotional detachment protects him from the horrors of war, but he slowly starts to let his guard down and develops a fondness for Short Round. The two eventually meet up with an African-American medic, Corporal Thompson (James Edwards), and a lost patrol. Led by battle-inexperienced Lieutenant Driscoll (Steve Brodie), the patrol is made up of a strikingly oddball version of the generic "mixed platoon," including Sergeant Tanaka (Richard Loo), a second-generation Japanese-American; Bronte (Robert Hutton), who carries the hand organ of a dead priest; Baldy (Richard Monahan), a hairless radio man; Joe (Sid Melton), who manages the pack mules and doesn't speak; and a nameless soldier who will soon be blown away (Fuller regular Neyle Morrow). Zack quickly sizes each of them up, defining their competence as soldiers according to their service during WWII: while Tanaka and Thompson saw combat, Driscoll was stationed stateside and Bronte was a conscientious objector. The bedraggled group footslog through the jungle to a Buddhist temple, where Joe is killed by a North Korean major (Harold Fong) whom the remainder capture as a POW. While the others rest, the North Korean questions first Thompson and then Tanaka regarding their loyalty to a country that doesn't embrace them as equals. Zack snaps when a sniper kills Short Round, turning on the sneering POW and fatally shooting him. During an intense North Korean assault on the temple, Driscoll and Bronte prove themselves in battle and are killed, and Zack breaks down. Only Tanaka, Thompson, Baldy, and a dazed Zack walk out of the temple when reinforcements arrive.

The overarching story of *The Steel Helmet*, the title, and many of the incidents that occur in the film originated in Fuller's war diaries. On September 11, 1943, he wrote about what will become the first and last shots of *The Steel Helmet:*

Fighting in Sicily strictly an inf. war. Up & down mountains, across ravines & draws, over terrain which could be negotiated only on foot. Emphasize this in story with dedication 'to the United States infantry.' Show them on footslog— just a patrol for opening and end same way.[27]

Sergeant Zack began in Fuller's notebook as a battle-hardened veteran who hooks up with an untested patrol to capture a German operative in a monastery; when the Korean conflict broke out in 1950, Fuller quickly adapted the old plot to the new war. The title of the film came directly from another diary entry: "Everybody wants helmet with bullet hole in it for luck. Finke tells me get my own bullet hole in helmet."[28] Even one of the film's most shocking incidents was drawn from real life. Next to a diary entry, "Doggie booby trapped. W. killed examining him," is the reminder: "Remember inc. this in Finke story. Found dead American— warned—but goddam green doggie went for dog tags and blown up— body booby trapped. Use this stupid character in 'Steel Helmet' story to show what not to do."[29] As recorded in his diary, Fuller's war experiences served as a primer for the writing of his combat pictures, providing lessons in how to survive and reminders of the physical and psychological toll taken on those who do.

When sitting down to write *The Steel Helmet*, Fuller grafted his own war experiences onto a generic foundation provided by the WWII combat film, participating in a redirection of the genre toward darker themes. The opening dedication ("This story is dedicated to the U.S. Infantry"); gruff, experienced sergeant; scruffy, "mixed background" platoon; group on patrol; and defense of an outpost found in *The Steel Helmet* are all standard-issue elements in WWII combat films, as well as in later Korean War pictures.[30] By drawing on a set of characters and situations that were familiar to viewers, Fuller spared himself from having to provide detailed backstories and exposition, allowing him to focus more on the soldiers' routines and the effects of war than on how they got there and where they were going. The film's generic signposts also help to make otherwise implausible events that are not causally motivated appear more realistic to viewers.[31] Within the context of the genre, then, Zack's miraculous survival of the unseen massacre, his discovery by Short Round and their discovery of the medic, the lost patrol, and the lone Communist North Korean hiding in the temple all seem reasonable or likely, even though highly coincidental, as these are story elements that viewers recognize from previous combat pictures. The combat film genre thus provides Fuller not only with a broad outline of appropriate characters and situations, but also with a means of making the episodic events in the film appear unified and realistic.

*The Steel Helmet* takes the combat film in a new direction, however, as Fuller tweaks some conventions, abandons others, and forces the viewer to consider unpleasant truths. Apart from the retread sergeant, the film's protagonists are a bizarre collection of colorful characters atypical of the genre. It's as if Fuller said, "You want a cross representation of America? I'll show you America!" In place of the Italian from Brooklyn and the farm boy from Nebraska so often seen in earlier combat films, the "all-American" platoon of *The Steel Helmet* contains a silent mule herder and a bald man who rubs dirt on his head, both of whom provide strange scenes of comic relief. Also on the journey are an African-American and a Nisei, neither of whom would have shared a foxhole with Sergeant Zack in a WWII combat picture; along with the conscientious objector, these characters enable Fuller to address the paradoxes inherent in the choice to fight for one's country. While the white soldier, Bronte, refused to fight in the last war, Tanaka and Thompson served their country, even though their country didn't consider them as equals at the time. Even the platoon's lieutenant defies convention. Rather than being presented as an experienced leader whom the men trust, Zack and several North Korean snipers discredit Driscoll almost as soon as he is introduced, elevating combat readiness over rank in the estimation of a soldier's worth. While Driscoll redeems himself at the end of the picture, the scenario of enlisted men saddled with a green lieutenant highlights the need of soldiers to rely on themselves rather than on their officers, an emerging theme of the combat film genre that becomes particularly prominent in movies about the Vietnam War.

Fuller's representation of war is bleaker than most earlier combat films, highlighting the confusion, uncertainty, sudden death, and numbing fatigue characteristic of combat experience. From the opening sequence, which leads the viewer to anticipate Short Round will be Zack's killer rather than his savior, Zack and his fellow soldiers are presented as existing in a world where little is as it seems. Every Korean must be mistrusted; nothing can be taken for granted. Lost in a fog-wrapped jungle, the soldiers even fire on each other, mistaking fellow Americans for the enemy. The group's mission takes them into unfamiliar territory: a temple, dominated by a giant Buddha that ends up functioning in ways never intended by its builders—supporting IV bottles and protecting the men from artillery. When the soldiers have a moment to spare, they engage only in activities necessary to staying alive: eating and sleeping. No romantic subplots. No talk of Mom and God. Most of the time, they simply march and watch and wait. With only twelve minutes of battle footage in two scenes, *The Steel Helmet* presents actual warfare as a sudden break in the monotony, an intermittent obstacle to the soldiers' primary goal—survival—rather than as the centerpiece of a narrative concerned with victory or defeat, such as in *Air Force* (1943), *Guadalcanal Diary* (1943), or *Back to Bataan* (1945).

Even the final postscript of *The Steel Helmet*, "There is no end to this story," differs significantly from the sentiments expressed at the end of previous combat films. Superimposed over a shot of the bedraggled remains of the platoon, the declaration lacks any triumphant or redeeming element; instead, it suggests weary resignation, in marked contrast to the emotional note hit at the end of most WWII combat pictures in which most of the unit is killed, such as *Wake Island* (1942) ("This is not the end. There are other leathernecks who will exact a just and terrible vengeance.") or *The Story of G.I. Joe* (1945) ("I hope we can rejoice with victory . . . that all together we will try to reassemble our broken world."). In *The Steel Helmet,* the survivors march toward a mission that will repeat the patterns of the last; their replacements will fight the same battle they just fought; whoever is alive at the end will return for the next war. Fuller suggests that from battle to battle and war to war, the burdens of the footsoldiers remain unchanged.

Perhaps the most striking examples of Fuller's reworking of genre conventions are the two scenes dedicated to the question of why we fight. Rather than presenting soldiers sitting around the campfire discussing the benefits of democracy, the defense of family, or service to God and country, Fuller gets to the heart of the question: why put your life on the line for a country that has never lived up to its ideals? As the Communist North Korean POW attempts to "turn" first the African-American medic and then the Japanese-American sergeant by asking why each fights for a country that treats him as a second-class citizen, the visual presentation of each point of view remains neutral, encouraging the viewer to favor neither one side nor the other. The logical reasoning of the POW creates ambiguity concerning who is actually the more rational thinker. Although the POW has just killed the likable mule tender Joe, his perspective is not demonized; rather, his character brings to light how far America has to go in fulfilling its promise.

Both the pointed conversation and two singularly distinct visual styles differentiate these scenes from the rest of the film, setting them apart to encourage the contemplation of contemporary race relations. In his conversation with Thompson, the POW references the Jim Crow laws of the South, asking the African-American to confirm that he cannot eat with white men and has to sit at the back of the public bus. Thompson agrees, but says, "A hundred years ago I couldn't even ride in a bus. At least now I can sit in the back. Maybe in fifty years I'll sit in the middle, and some day up front. There's some things you just can't rush, buster." As Thompson is one of the most sympathetic characters in the film up to this point, you might expect his perspective on race relations to carry more visual weight than that of the POW. Yet the scene stylistically favors neither soldier. In a sequence shot, the camera tracks 180 degrees from one man to the other, unmotivated by character movement. First one soldier, then the other is favored with frontality as he states his position. With no stylistic tools emphasizing either character's speech, the viewer is encouraged to consider each in turn, perhaps to the point of acknowledging that the POW makes a certain amount of sense. Here Fuller is exposing the contradictions of America, a country still failing to live up to its credo that all are created equal. Such an explicit examination of a contemporary social problem is new to Fuller's directorial palette. While the occasion for the discussion is causally motivated by the medic attending to the POW's injury, the direction of their conversation and the singularly evenhanded yet unmotivated camera movement distance the scene from the rest of the film and mark it as a self-consciously ambiguous moment.

The POW's discussion with Tanaka, a second-generation Japanese-American, features a different visual presentation but functions similarly, again highlighting the irony of fighting for a country that denies your basic rights. Almost immediately following the scene with Thompson, the camera tilts down to frame Tanaka and the POW sitting next to each other in a two-shot. The POW notes, "You've got the same kind of eyes I have. . . . They hate us because of our eyes." Tanaka replies with a sleepy brush-off, but the POW gets his attention when he asks if Tanaka's family was among the Japanese-Americans who were interned in camps during WWII—a shameful event in American history rarely mentioned in movies of this period. The POW's question is punctuated by a cut in to an unusually tight close-up of his face, beginning a pattern of cuts between extreme close-ups of each man as he speaks. While the scene contains more conventional analytical editing than the sequence with the African-American medic, its visual construction again emphasizes both men's comments equally. Tanaka admits that his family was detained, but that he nevertheless fought in the war for the United States. When the POW questions why Tanaka fought overseas after being called a "dirty Jap rat" at home, the veteran replies, "I'm an American. When we get pushed around at home, that's our business." The scene's proximity to the POW's conversation with the medic and its evenhanded visual presentation again draw attention to the POW's argument, but Tanaka's casual dismissal of him ("Don't you guys know when you're licked?") betrays no particular concern. As before, Fuller brings front and center questions regarding what it means to be an American and to fight for one's country.

The pointed discussion of race in these scenes, their unusual visual presentation, and their singularity in the film—the POW does not question any other members of the platoon—all contribute to their self-consciousness. Set apart from the rest of the narrative, these scenes encourage viewers to think. While the POW's words are, on one level, true, we have seen the bravery and intelligence of Thompson and Tanaka and how they are respected by the rest of the men. Within the platoon, they are fully integrated, measured by their talent and experience, not by the color of their skin. In *The Steel Helmet*, it is the platoon—not the home front—that demonstrates why we fight, that illustrates the possibility of a just and equal America.

In order to provide viewers with a sense of what a footsoldier experiences during war, Fuller had to do more than rework genre conventions: he had to reconstruct how we watch a war film.

You can't make a real war picture, because the audience can get up and go buy their popcorn at any time. They're never hurt. And war means casualties. The best way would be to occasionally fire at them from behind the screen during a battle scene! No, really, I'm not joking about this. . . . If someone, once in a while, was hit, that would give the audience a feeling for the tension of war.[32]

The tension of war—the numbing anxiety evoked by unexpected out-breaks of violence, of fatigue interrupted by death—is what Fuller at-tempts to suggest in *The Steel Helmet,* structuring the episodic narrative so as create abrupt shifts in tone and alternating sequences of suspense and surprise. The opening scene telegraphs these strategies. As the film's credits come to an end, superimposed over a steel helmet with a bullet hole in it, the helmet unexpectedly tilts up, and two suspicious eyes peer out to survey the landscape. The movement takes us by surprise, as the bullet hole and the helmet's immobility previously led us to assume that the helmet's owner was dead. Our curiosity regarding the soldier's sur-vival quickly turns to suspense, however, as shots of the soldier crawling forward with his hands bound behind his back are intercut with shots of advancing bare feet and a dangling rifle. The sense of an impending threat is heightened through the heavy violin strings on the soundtrack, and we know the soldier has not escaped death yet—though he himself remains unaware. A tilt up the body of the interloper reveals a child's face, but our momentary relief is checked when he leans over the soldier with a knife. As we wonder if this child is a North Korean out to finish the job, the music comes to a halt, and the child quickly cuts the soldier's ropes rather than his throat. Fuller could have shot this scene through the perspective of the bound soldier, whom we will soon come to know as Zack, our protagonist. But by providing us at times with more infor-mation than Zack, Fuller encourages us to feel not only Zack's relief at being saved, but also the anxiety of knowing he may as easily have been killed. This play between restricted and unrestricted narration continues throughout the film, binding the viewer less to Zack's particular experi-ence than to the overall tension inherent to war.

The irony resulting from the opening sequence—a potential North Korean killer is revealed to be a friendly and helpful South Korean child—is replayed throughout the film, as sequences with perceived threats unfold harmlessly while scenes seemingly empty of threat wind up being deadly. This pattern of alternating sequences of relative calm with moments of unexpected violence becomes the dominant structural strategy in the film, constantly catching viewers off guard and teaching us to imagine the uncertainty faced by soldiers in combat. In the rest of the first act, the pattern is repeated when a group of civilians praying at an altar pull rifles from their robes and open fire on Zack and Short

Gene Evans as Sergeant Zack in a publicity still from the opening scene in *The Steel Helmet*. Fuller heightens the suspense by intercutting shots of Zack's slow crawl forward with images of an advancing Korean boy holding a gun. Note the hole in Zack's helmet—where he was shot but unharmed—and the knife in the foreground, which will be activated at the end of the scene. *Chrisam Films, Inc.*

Round; when snipers suddenly attack after Zack and Thompson initially part ways with the platoon; and then again on the road, after a protracted sequence of calm is followed by an explosion just as the rest of the men are sitting down and eating watermelon. That an American soldier is killed taking the dog tags off the corpse of a fellow infantryman makes the moment even more ironic—it is the soldier's kindness that gets him killed. As the platoon establishes an observation post in the temple during the second act, a series of comic bits with Joe, the mule driver who does not talk, again establish a carefree tone. The lighthearted mood is then undercut when the North Korean kills Joe, initiating a new line of action as the soldiers hunt for the killer. Finally, after the North Korean is caught, the third act begins with Zack, Short Round, and the POW preparing to leave the temple. It would appear that the enemy threat to the soldiers has been removed, but cutaways to a sniper setting up outside the temple suggest that the platoon is unknowingly in for a

final battle, establishing a mood of suspense. Nevertheless, even though
the shot of the sniper informs us of a threat, the offscreen death of Short
Round is deeply shocking, as the death of a child mascot, especially one
so pure and good-hearted, goes so firmly against classical Hollywood
conventions. But Fuller doesn't let up: Zack's subsequent shooting of the
POW delivers another unexpected blow, raising the specter of American
soldiers engaging in war crimes. These final acts of startling violence pre-
cipitate the massive bombardment of the temple by the enemy, the death
of most of the platoon, and the unraveling of Sergeant Zack's mind. The
sudden and ironic shifts between moments of calm and violence in *The
Steel Helmet* exemplify the stark contrasts in tone and action that per-
vade Fuller's work. The unexpected appearance of violence shocks and
surprises the viewer, who is left uncertain of when and where to expect
the next threat. The narrative structure thereby offers viewers a distant
sense of the tension felt by soldiers in war without requiring gunfire in
the theater.

Although the film's omniscient narration and Zack's off-putting personality mitigate against viewers identifying with his character, Zack's
central role within the narrative and his emergence as the most experienced and combat-smart member of the platoon position him as the hero
of the film. We root for him to survive and to protect the platoon, and as
he grows closer to Short Round, we thrill to see his awkward expressions
of sentiment. In a cruelly ironic twist characteristic of Fuller, however,
Short Round's merciful rescue of Zack at the beginning of the film proves
to be the downfall of both characters. The introduction of the two in the
opening scene highlights their significant differences: although both characters have experienced the horrors of war, Short Round remains gener-
ous and spiritual, while Zack is self-interested and suspicious. Zack's
single-minded approach to survival proves necessary in the jungle and on
the road in the first act, but upon the platoon's arrival at the temple,
Short Round's devotion to prayer highlights the basic human feeling that
has been absent in Zack for so long. Zack's attitude toward Short Round
softens, and as he slowly turns the prayer wheel, one wonders if Zack is
beginning to take seriously the spirituality he has thus far ridiculed. At
the beginning of the third act, Zack and Short Round are alone together
as the boy writes yet another prayer. Rather than making fun of Short
Round's belief in divinity, as he has consistently throughout the film,
Zack now pins the prayer on Short Round's back, a marker of his growing respect for the boy. After Short Round leaves the room, Zack crafts
"dog tags" for him, an additional sign of his growing love. Despite his
earlier aloofness, Zack has finally accepted the spiritual basis of Short
Round's loyalty to him and wants to adopt the boy into his own world—
that of the U.S. Army.

Making the dog tags is the first act of kindness and generosity committed by Zack in the entire film, and his newfound emotions prove to be his undoing. When Short Round is shot in the subsequent scene and the POW laughs at the remnants of the boy's prayer, Zack kills the POW in a fury, breaking the Geneva Convention and prompting the lieutenant to challenge him, yelling, "You're no soldier!" Recognizing his mistake, Zack calls for the medic to save the POW's life and threatens his victim, "If you die, I'll kill you!" The paradoxical nature of Zack's order underscores the ironic situation he finds himself in: his affection for Short Round caused him to forget what it means to be a soldier; now he must save the man he most wants to see dead. With both Short Round gone and his identity as a soldier in question, Zack loses his mind in battle. Without the protection of his hard-won pragmatism and emotional isolation, he leaves the temple a broken man.

The potential in the combat film for the activation of ambiguity, contradiction, death, and despair make it one of the genres most compatible with Fuller's brand of storytelling. By setting the relationship of Sergeant Zack and Short Round against the ordeals of the platoon, the narrative of *The Steel Helmet* highlights the conflict experienced by Zack between his growing humanity and his desire for self-preservation. As with most Fuller films, the construction of the narrative suggests this is a conflict that cannot be resolved. In a state of war, emotion is weakness, and compassion begets death. The killing of Short Round and the reduction of the film's hero to a mere shell of a man are shocking reminders to viewers that no one escapes unscathed from war, even those who manage to walk away.

*The Steel Helmet* establishes the character types, themes, and situations that Fuller will revisit in his four subsequent combat pictures: *Fixed Bayonets, China Gate, Merrill's Marauders,* and *The Big Red One.* All focus on a small group of soldiers rather than attempting to provide an overview of the war, and each eschews triumphalism in favor of emotional authenticity. Another Korean War film made quickly on the heels of *The Steel Helmet, Fixed Bayonets* takes the mixed platoon of its predecessor into the winter mountains and isolates the group in a cave. Fuller again utilizes unexpected violence to produce tension and surprise, as the protagonist watches his commanding officers die one by one, deeply fearing his eventual assumption of command. Produced while Fuller was under contract at Twentieth Century–Fox, *Fixed Bayonets* lacks the loopiness and ideological exchanges of *The Steel Helmet,* but these characteristics return in *China Gate,* written by Fuller as an independent Globe Enterprises release. The first American combat picture set in Vietnam, *China Gate* is also the only Fuller war film whose protagonist is motivated by something other than survival. Lucky Legs, the film's Eurasian hero, agrees to undertake a search and destroy mission in order to ensure a life for her child in America. Fuller exploits her mixed ancestry and love affair with a Communist leader for extended discussions of race and politics, making *China Gate* the most didactic of his combat pictures. Based on real events and shot on location with relatively large casts and crews, *Merrill's Marauders* and *The Big Red One* expand the scope of Fuller's combat sequences at the same time as they focus more narrowly on a single topic: staying alive. Stripped of any significant female presence or discussions of why we fight, their narratives abandon the romantic plotline and didacticism of *China Gate* to craft repetitive scenes emphasizing the unmerciful nature of war and the simple triumph of survival; in doing so, they offer perhaps the most distilled representation of Fuller's worldview. In its redirection of genre conventions, alteration of suspense and surprise, emphasis on paradoxical situations, and attempt to suggest the anxieties experienced by soldiers in war, *The Steel Helmet* anticipates aspects of each of Fuller's later combat pictures.

The topicality of *The Steel Helmet,* widespread critical praise, and its distinctly different distribution strategy helped it to attain greater financial success than Fuller's first two Lippert pictures. With its lack of stars and minimal production design, *The Steel Helmet* relied on the timeliness of its subject matter to sell the film. Newspaper advertisements exclaimed, "It's the *real* Korean story!" next to an image of Sergeant Zack's eyes peering out from below his bullet-ridden helmet. *Variety* predicted "a sure money film," and *Boxoffice* pegged it as a potentially lucrative programmer, noting the flexibility of the film's eighty-four-minute running time to play either side of a double bill.[33]

*The Steel Helmet* debuted in Los Angeles with a two-week run in mid-January 1951, topping a double bill with the Lippert western *Three Desperate Men* (1951) at the 2,100-seat United Artists theater downtown and at four smaller first run houses.[34] Strong returns, including the best trade in two years at the UA, generated momentum for the film's booking at the end of the month in New York City's Loew's State, a 3,450-seat theater that had never previously played a Lippert film. At the State, *The Steel Helmet* scored a "smash" $26,000 in its first frame, the theater's best in many weeks, and was held over for ten additional days. When the film opened in first-run theaters in five major markets at the beginning of February, it emerged as the seventh highest grosser for the week. Despite controversy surrounding the film's depiction of Sergeant Zack shooting an unarmed prisoner of war, *The Steel Helmet* eventually generated over $2 million in ticket sales and earned Fuller an award from independent exhibitors for the top-grossing drama from 1948 to 1953.[35] The film's low cost and high gross made it a model for the potential profitability of a programmer. Opening the film first in Los Angeles and New York enabled it to generate positive critical attention and to illustrate the box-office draw of its timely subject matter; during its subsequent rollout, these two factors maintained the film's status as a headliner capable of filling large houses.

Following the release of *The Steel Helmet*, Samuel Fuller was in high demand. Fuller's work at Lippert, and particularly the success of *The Steel Helmet*, demonstrated his ability to shoot quickly and cheaply and still churn out a profitable film, and soon the majors came calling. In interviews, Fuller claims to have been wooed by production executives from most of the big studios, including MGM, Warner Bros., Twentieth Century–Fox, Universal, and Columbia. Eventually he settled on Fox. Although he could not hope to gain the creative and administrative control he eventually enjoyed at Lippert from a larger studio, working for a major provided Fuller with access to stars, increased budgets, longer shooting schedules, additional equipment, better distribution, and more publicity. In leaving Lippert for Fox, Fuller temporarily left the world of low-budget filmmaking to create his only series of genuine A pictures. At the same time, he adapted his aesthetic to meet the quality controls and streamlined production methods in use at the major studios, resulting in the most refined and classically constructed films of his career.

# CHAPTER TWO

# The Fox Years, 1951–1956

uller signed with Twentieth Century–Fox at the beginning of a tumultuous decade for the motion picture industry, a period that saw the end of the studio system. Production cutbacks that began in the early 1940s accelerated in the 1950s as the studios faced declining audience attendance, rising costs, and plunging profits. In an effort to counter the lure of television, radio, and other suburban entertainment options, the major studios shifted away from producing a balanced slate of A and B pictures designed for the whole family and looked to new strategies to differentiate their product. Dramatically reducing low-budget production, the majors concentrated their resources on spectacular, big-budget films that featured color, stereophonic sound, and widescreen processes, creating an experience unable to be replicated at home. At the same time, a piecemeal decline in industry regulation and censorship beginning in the late 1940s and culminating in the 1956 revision of the Production Code enabled more filmmakers to tackle adult-oriented fare that flaunted sex, violence, and social taboos to a degree not seen in mainstream domestic filmmaking since the early 1930s. Fuller's contract with Fox enabled him to participate in many of these trends, as he had secured a job with a major studio that, at least temporarily, valued his penchant for visual experimentation and edgy material.

While Fuller's decision to sign with Twentieth Century–Fox seems largely to have been based on his fondness for Darryl Zanuck, the studio's longtime production head, Fuller's background as an action director complemented the needs of the studio. From their first meeting, Zanuck and Fuller established a close relationship that flourished through the 1950s. Fuller expressed great admiration for Zanuck's straightforwardness and commitment to strong storytelling, and Zanuck reveled in Fuller's can-do spirit and real-life adventures. Both were equally fond of cigars and explosives, once apparently firing off a nine-millimeter German Luger in an underground screening room together.[1] Although Zanuck's interest in more "realistic" material remained firm,

Twentieth Century–Fox's production chief, Darryl Zanuck (left), at a birthday party for Samuel Fuller (right) during the shooting of *Hell and High Water*. Zanuck and Fuller had a warm relationship and worked closely while Fuller was under contract at Fox. *Chrisam Films, Inc.*

when Fuller arrived at Fox in the early 1950s the production head was steering the studio toward big-picture entertainment rooted in action and sex rather than the social problem films it produced at the end of the previous decade.[2] As a director who had made a name for himself in action films but who still maintained an obsession with history and journalism, Fuller was a fine fit. All of the films he directed while under contract at

Fox—*Fixed Bayonets, Pickup on South Street, Hell and High Water,* and *House of Bamboo*—were action-oriented war, crime, or adventure stories rooted in contemporary political and social conflicts.

The classical norms embraced by the major studios as a means of ensuring clarity, coherence, and quality had a decided impact on Fuller's work. Now he was operating within a system of long-standing production practices fully ingrained in workers at every level of authority, a system that directly and indirectly influenced the choices available to filmmakers. During this period, the narratives of Fuller's films adhere to classical, generic, and cultural conventions to a degree never again seen in his career, and his visual style becomes more refined and polished. Fuller's artistic instincts are not completely buried, however. With the proper material and the support of the studio they could come very much to the fore or, alternately, they could express themselves in a more subtle fashion, achieving his favored effects while still reflecting classical norms. The proof of Fox's influence on the expression of Fuller's aesthetic is most clearly seen through comparison with his one independent project during this period, *Park Row.* If the Fox films are Fuller restrained, *Park Row* is Fuller unbound; the difference is palpable.

## The Trade-offs of Studio Filmmaking

As a director at a major studio, Fuller occupied a role defined by specific expectations, and as a director at Twentieth Century–Fox, his role was actively overseen by Darryl Zanuck. Under the modes of production utilized by the majors during the studio era, a director's primary responsibility was the coordination of actors and crew during the shoot itself.[3] The producer and studio managers typically left directors alone on set, relying on daily production reports, script supervisor notes, and rushes to confirm if a director was staying on time, on budget, and maintaining narrative and visual quality. The producer and department heads sought ideas and approval from the director during preproduction (script development, casting, set construction, wardrobe creation) and postproduction (editing, scoring), but at these stages the producer's opinion trumped that of the director. At Fox, Zanuck was the top production manager, and he exerted overt control during pre- and postproduction. Zanuck started his Hollywood career as a screenwriter at Warner Bros. during the 1920s, and as production chief he closely supervised story development.[4] He regularly selected literary properties and reviewed synopses, treatments, and scripts. When meeting the screenwriter and production team during story conferences, he dictated the direction of the conversation, offering general story ideas and line-by-line script notes. While Zanuck respected directors' autonomy on set as long as they kept to the schedule and provided acceptable footage, he re-exerted control in postproduction, watching rushes, making comments to the director and editor, selecting takes to use, and ordering reshoots. A range of entrenched institutional systems and practices thus shaped Fuller's degree of artistic control during this period, and Zanuck's influence was particularly acute.

Although Fuller lost some measure of control over his films while at Twentieth Century–Fox, his contract provided him with an opportunity to direct higher-profile pictures while still retaining the ability to work independently. The seven-year option contract, signed in April 1951, stated that Fuller would render his services to Fox for twenty-six weeks as a writer and director on an initial film and, at the pleasure of the studio, also act as a producer for the film. Subsequent contract extensions also bound Fuller to Fox for half of every year, leaving the director free to pursue one outside motion picture or television show the remaining twenty-six weeks of the extension. When Fuller notified Fox of a starting date on an outside project, the studio had the right to preempt the project by dictating its own starting date on a new film, but Fuller then had to have twenty-six weeks later in the contract in which to complete his outside work. He had the freedom to write his own screenplays and to reject assignments at will. Fuller also was not obligated to submit to Fox any literary material, and he could offer stories and screenplays to other studios before showing them to Fox; in addition, his contract specified that only he could direct his screenplays, subject to his availability.[5] Fuller's deal thus protected a number of freedoms he held dear: the pursuit of projects he cared about, regardless of studio interest; the choice of where to develop his original stories and screenplays; the direction of his own written work; and the chance to produce his own films (if Fox so desired—it never did).

Fuller's tenure at Fox introduced him to both the benefits and the restrictions of major-studio filmmaking. For the first time, his films employed stars, color, widescreen, and location shooting; he had the luxury to rehearse more, to shoot for a longer period, and to experiment with extended tracking shots and cranes. He was also assured that his films would receive wide, first-run distribution in top houses, supported by a national publicity campaign. On the other hand, Fuller no longer produced his own films, nor did he have profit participation or final cut. Most of his original screenplays were rejected by the studio, and except for *Fixed Bayonets*, he did not originate the stories for any of his Fox films. Finally, although he did write one script and a scenario for other studios while under contract, *Park Row* was the only independent film he was able to write, direct, and produce during his five years at Fox.

Executive oversight and the use of studio departments and crews led Fuller's films to adhere more closely to classical narrative and stylistic norms while he was at Twentieth Century–Fox. The screenplays for his Fox pictures fit neatly into defined genres and feature tight, causally-driven plots free of the narrative digressions, didacticism, and offbeat humor that cropped up in various Lippert films. While Fuller's dialogue remains punchy and his protagonists gruff, increased use of subjective narration, particularly in *Fixed Bayonets,* encourages greater alignment with his primary characters. Visually, Fuller's films continue to develop the diverse staging strategies previously seen in *The Baron of Arizona,* as both long takes with camera movement and analytically edited scenes enable action to be fully covered from a variety of angles and shot scales. Fox's state-of-the-art equipment, sound stages, and highly trained crews encouraged Fuller to craft intricately choreographed shots featuring extended tracking and craning as well as movement by multiple characters, shots he simply did not have the resources to attempt while at Lippert. At the same time, dialogue-heavy scenes are more likely to feature multiple camera setups and cuts from establishing shots into and out of tighter framings—conventions developed at the studios to ensure quality scene construction—rather than simply an extended master shot with inserts. The pressure to conform to classical norms during the Fox years smoothes many of Fuller's rougher edges, resulting in the most elegant films of his career. Nevertheless, given the proper encouragement and appropriate story material, Fuller was still able to craft distinctively idiosyncratic films under the studio system, films that forcefully deliver truth and emotion.

### *Return to War:* Fixed Bayonets

Fuller's first picture for Fox, *Fixed Bayonets,* functioned as a transitional film, exploiting many of the same elements as *The Steel Helmet* while introducing Fuller to production on a larger scale. Released less than a year after the premiere of *The Steel Helmet,* again set during the ongoing Korean War, and starring the same grizzly, up-and-coming actor, Gene Evans, *Fixed Bayonets* appeared positioned to capitalize on its predecessor's success. Production values were low for a Fox film but significantly higher than Fuller was used to at Lippert, and they are evident on the screen. Fuller still lacked a star-studded cast, shot the entire film on two sets on a single soundstage, and had one of the smallest budgets of any Fox picture that year; nevertheless, he enjoyed a two-month shoot and a $685,000 budget—more than triple his previous schedules and production costs—as well as access to a crane for the first time.[6] The larger cast;

swooping, intricately choreographed long-take cinematography; fake ice and snow; large munitions explosions; and realistic, functioning tanks all distinguish *Fixed Bayonets* from its lower-budgeted predecessor.

*Fixed Bayonets* follows a platoon left behind as a rear guard decoy on a snowy mountain pass as its soldiers attempt to hold off the North Korean army long enough to let the rest of the brigade escape. Leading the platoon are a lieutenant, two sergeants, and a corporal, Denno (Richard Basehart), who fears to assume command and cannot bring himself to kill. After the rest of the brigade has left, the platoon splits into two squads, one of which, led by Sergeant Lonergan (Michael O'Shea), establishes a series of observation posts and digs in; the other, led by Sergeant Rock (Gene Evans), sets mines in a pass, goes out on patrol, and holes up in a cave. In between enemy bombardments, the soldiers in the cave huddle together to keep warm, drink weak coffee, eat bad chow, massage their feet to ward off frostbite, and sleep when they can. A sniper kills the lieutenant, and Denno confesses to Rock that he is afraid of ever having to be responsible for the lives of other men. Rock tells him, "You gotta have the guts to lead." After snipers bring down Lonergan in the middle of the minefield and a medic is blown up trying to retrieve him, Denno crosses the minefield to save him, proving he has guts but failing to keep Lonergan alive. Following another enemy artillery strike, a bullet ricochets through the cave and kills Rock, leaving Denno in command with just an hour left to hold back the enemy. As the platoon packs up to retreat, North Korean scouts and a tank come through the mountain pass. Denno devises a plan to take out the tank, kills his first enemy soldier, and earns the respect of his men. As the exhausted and injured platoon rejoins the rest of the brigade, Denno remembers Rock's words: "Ain't nobody goes out looking for responsibility. Sometimes you get it whether you're looking for it or not."

*Fixed Bayonets* is one of Fuller's tightest plots and, when compared with *The Steel Helmet,* demonstrates how the classical narrative conventions championed by the major studios affected Fuller's writing style. Working from a treatment written by Sy Bartlett, Fuller drafted an original outline for the story, the screenplay, and two revisions. Zanuck worked closely with Fuller during script development, focusing the narrative on Denno's fear of command and arguing that nothing in the story must "cover or make fuzzy" this primary theme.[7] In his notes on Fuller's original outline, Zanuck suggested the plot structure, the use of voice-over, and the content of the final scene, all of which Fuller incorporated into his subsequent scripts. As a result of Zanuck's oversight, absent from Fuller's second Korean War film are the racially mixed unit, episodic plot, digressive episodes, and didactic interludes that characterized his first. In their place are more typical character types (the loudmouth from Brooklyn, the wide-eyed farm boy) and a causally driven plot that carefully guides the viewer through the story.

Every scene advances the plot in a logical fashion, beginning with the establishment of the film's theme (scene 1: "You gotta have the guts to lead."), the military decision behind the rear guard action (scene 2: "Forty-eight men giving 15,000 a break."), the effect of the decision on the rear guard (scene 3), the territory and time in which the action will take place (scene 4), Denno and his inner conflict (scene 5), and the officers that stand between Denno and command (scene 7). By the end of the first act, all of the major pieces of the film's plot are in place, and the narrative becomes a countdown of casualties leading to the moment when Denno must assume command. As is typical in classical Hollywood narratives, major turning points are neatly foreshadowed and highlighted before they occur: scene 6 introduces the land mines, scene 9 reinforces their danger, and scene 13 activates them in the death of Lonergan; scene 8 introduces the ricochet effect, scene 18 has Rock saying a ricochet would be a good tactic, and then he is killed by one; in scene 9, Rock warns that when they hear a tank, they'll know the North Koreans are coming, in scene 16 Rock says he can smell the enemy, and in scene 21 the enemy tank appears for the final showdown, and Denno remembers Rock's warning. The narrative's adherence to classical norms in *Fixed Bayonets* results in a more focused but less provocative story than that told in *The Steel Helmet;* what remains is Fuller's determination to represent honestly the experience of war from a footsoldier's point of view.

Fuller's commitment to truth telling—to depicting that which is often denied or ignored—reveals itself through his reinterpretation of generic conventions. As in *The Steel Helmet,* Fuller recasts the discussion of "why we fight" inherent to the war picture, reducing it to a question Denno asks of Rock: "What makes a guy stay in the army?" The question addresses the basic mystery at the heart of a soldier's life: why would a man volunteer to experience such horror, to make a living killing other men? Rock's reply reflects the everyday reasons motivating soldiers, reasons that offer little to invest their sacrifice with meaning: "Some of us are poor, some of us are lazy, some of us got some vanity. I wish I knew the answer." While this sequence fulfills generic expectations, it dodges an opportunity to allow viewers to feel good about sending these men off to war. As he did in *The Steel Helmet,* Fuller reminds us that soldiering is a job, one that can make a man some money, but one that has nothing to do with glory.

Fuller's interest in the daily grind of combat is displayed in a more-humorous fashion during the prototypical "what paradise awaits me when I get home" scene. As the camera pans from one man to the next holed up in the cave, each thinks in voice-over of what he most wants. One hopes to open a bowling alley when he gets home, another just to lie all day in a swimming pool, a third to become a doctor. These desires are interspersed, however, with unexpected thoughts: One man denies the chance to hope, cynically thinking, "Who cares?" Another hopes Denno doesn't die, as then *he* would have to assume command. The sequence reaches an absurd climax when the obsessions of the final three soldiers are revealed: the first wishes he had a pair of dry socks, the second hopes the first doesn't know he *has* a pair of dry socks, and the third hopes the second doesn't know that he's *stolen* his pair of dry socks. While the sequence begins by carrying out the generic norm of the soldier dreaming of home, it ends by trumping dreams with reality; as Rock says earlier in the film, and as reinforced in the many scenes involving foot care, "There's only three things you gotta worry about in the infantry: your rifle and your two feet." This insistence on showing what is *really* important to soldiers is characteristic of Fuller's approach to the combat film genre, and it transcends the constrictions of convention.

Similar to *The Steel Helmet, Fixed Bayonets* is structured to provide the viewer with a sense of what a soldier's life is like, but the latter film makes greater use of subjectivity to link the viewer's perspective with that of the platoon. Subjective voice-over narration most closely aligns the viewer with Denno, tying the effects of the rear guard's situation to his personal conflict. We first hear Denno's voice-over in scene five, as he agonizes over his inability to shoot the enemy. His thoughts and visual perspective provide the viewer with access to the same experience that every new soldier has to go through: killing a man for the first time. Thereafter the narrative returns sparingly to Denno's voice-over, using it to build suspense during parallel sequences capping the deaths of the platoon leaders. When first the lieutenant, then Lonergan, then Rock dies, the newly anointed leader steps up and orders the soldiers to "Strip [the dead man] of everything we can use. Roll him up in a blanket. Bury him . . . and mark him." Denno's voice-over follows the recurring ritual, noting how many men stand between him and platoon leader. When Rock finally dies and Denno assumes command, the initial line of suspense is dissolved and a new tension emerges: can Denno lead? This shift in the narrative is marked by the reappearance of Denno's voice-over as he considers if he has "what it takes." The narrative suggests that Rock's legacy is what carries Denno through, as Denno's inner worries are replaced in voice-over by his memories of Rock's advice, first when the tank shows up, then at the close of the film. Denno's voice-over functions as a key structuring element in the narrative, helping to mark turning points and build suspense. At the same time, it provides viewers with access to the fears and memories of an everyman protagonist who illustrates what few films of the era were willing to admit: that ambivalence about warfare does not make you a coward.

In order to convey both the chaos and the boredom of war, Fuller employs a range of stylistic strategies that foreshadow how his visual style will develop at Twentieth Century–Fox. Fuller's excitement at having access to a crane is visibly palpable, and *Fixed Bayonets* exhibits his first systematic use of a moving camera. Kinetic crane shots follow the soldiers in long takes as they clamber up hillsides, cross over ridges, and slide down embankments, while tracking and panning shots, including one 360-degree pan, are frequently in use within the cave. In the absence of camera movement, Fuller tends to pack the frame with four to eight men, particularly within the cave, using multiplanar staging and eyelines to direct the viewer's attention. During artillery sequences, percussive editing assaults the viewer, as a series of quick, causally-driven shots repeat and vary to demonstrate the shifting tide of battle. First the enemy artillery will fire, the shell will explode, the soldiers will run, and the enemy will fire again; then the soldiers will fire, the shell will explode, and the enemy will run. While all these visual strategies are highly efficient—they rely on relatively few camera setups—they nevertheless take full advantage of the resources on the Fox lot, showing off the size of the winter mountain set, the large cast, and the lifelike artillery and tank explosions. As significant, however, are the different ways they involve the viewer in the action. A camera rushing headlong up and down a mountainside instills a propulsive energy, while tightly packed frames encourage us to compare actions and reactions within the same shot, and fast, montage-based sequences pound us into submission. Each staging strategy pulls viewers into the experiences of the soldiers in the story, heightening our emotional involvement with the film.

The scene that most vividly draws the viewer into the emotional experience of the film's characters is Denno's rescue of Lonergan. Lonergan lies wounded in the middle of a minefield, and an explosion has killed the medic who tried to save him. The knowledge that every step Denno takes could also trigger a bomb shifts us to the edge of our seats, as we wait to see what happens each time he puts his foot down. The scene intercuts only the most basic elements, each of which raises and answers different questions for the viewer: tight shots of Denno's slowly advancing feet (will he step on a mine?), close-ups of Denno's anxious face (how is he holding up?), tight shots of the wounded Lonergan (is he still alive?), and close-ups of soldiers looking down from the mountainside (will Denno make it?). Only ambient sound accompanies the action, the silence occasionally broken by the sound of snow crunching under Denno's feet, his heavy breathing, or Lonergan yelling. The increasingly tight shots of Denno's feet intercut with reaction shots and the absence of an accompa-

A production still taken during the shooting of *Fixed Bayonets* on Twentieth Century–Fox's largest sound stage. Fuller sits on the camera crane (center, wearing a baseball hat backwards) to watch the take. Fox's production resources enabled Fuller to use the crane extensively, a first for his films. *Chrisam Films, Inc.*

nying score focus the viewer's attention on all that really matters: what happens each time Denno puts his foot down. Fuller stretches Denno's walk through the minefield across thirty-five shots—over two-and-a-half minutes of screen time—prolonging the duration of the action and further increasing the tension. Once Denno reaches Lonergan and hoists him on his shoulders, he then retraces his footsteps, consuming another minute and a half onscreen. By the time Denno steps out of the minefield and is surrounded by the other soldiers, we feel the force of his accomplishment. This man *does* have guts! But as is his wont, Fuller snatches triumph away: Lonergan died en route, and Denno didn't even know it. He risked his life for nothing. This is war, Fuller says, the frustration of our best intentions.

The reception of *Fixed Bayonets* benefited from the film's release during truce talks for the Korean conflict, as well as from Twentieth Century–Fox's distribution strategy. Fox released *Fixed Bayonets* widely to first-run theaters in a concentrated period of time and supported the film with "plenty of bally." Promotional materials lauded the film's realism, comparing Fuller to Ernie Pyle and Bill Mauldin—fixtures of WWII journalism—and noted the casts' "nineteen casualties, ranging from bayonet stabs and broken legs to minor wounds."[8] Reinforcing Fuller's commitment to authenticity, the press kit relayed one incident in which he berated Gene Evans for cleaning his fingernails before a date, then failing to dirty them when returning to work. Said the director: "We're not going to have romance interfering with the war we're fighting here!"

*Fixed Bayonets* had its East Coast premiere November 20, 1951 at the Rivoli in New York, followed by premieres in Toronto and in Los Angeles at Grauman's Chinese theater.[9] On December 5, the film opened in flagship houses in nine major cities, elevating the film to number two at the box office for the week. While the *New York Times* continued its trend of dismissing Fuller's work for its "affected realism and rather obvious theatricality," both *Variety* and *Boxoffice* noted *Fixed Bayonets*'s box-office potential due to its ability to tie into the Korean truce talks. Trade critics expected the film to do well in action houses with predominantly male fans but predicted that its lack of feminine presence or comic relief would make a broad sell more difficult.[10] When the total box office came in, the film grossed $1.45 million—more than double its production cost but ranking it only eighty-fourth for the year; internationally, it grossed approximately $375,000, considered by Zanuck a disappointment.[11]

### *Complete Independence:* Park Row

Immediately following completion of his work on *Fixed Bayonets*, Fuller exercised his right to work on an outside project and made his first enthusiastic stab at independent production: *Park Row,* the admiring story of a crusading newspaperman in New York City in the 1880s. Fuller originally brought the property to Zanuck at Twentieth Century–Fox but remembers Zanuck insisting the story needed stars, color, and CinemaScope: "With unknown actors in a black-and-white picture, your period piece is a loser, Sam."[12] Rather than make the picture a color musical as the production head advised, Fuller decided to produce it himself, completely self-financing the $200,000-or-more budget from his *Steel Helmet* profits. He cast Gene Evans alongside other virtual unknowns and hired many of the crewmembers he worked with during the Lippert years for the sixteen-day shoot.[13] Most of the budget went into building a realistic, four-story replica of Park Row, the street that housed all of New York's newspaper giants, testifying to Fuller's nostalgic desire for authenticity, if not his cost consciousness.

In his autobiography, Fuller explains his reluctance to compromise his vision of the film by insisting, "Goddamnit, Park Row *was* me!"[14] And indeed, Fuller's romantic tale of newspaper heroism exhibited many of the personal traits of its creator: tremendous energy, a passion for history, a dedication to truth, a fighting spirit, and an optimistic belief in the ability of one man to enact change. The film concerns the efforts of an idealistic, muckraking journalist, Phineas Mitchell (Gene Evans), to create a newspaper that truly serves the people. Fuller writes Mitchell as the kind of newspaper editor he would have liked to have been: a man driven to reveal the unvarnished facts, fighting for the people with two fists, if necessary. Mitchell sets up shop with a venerable old reporter, Josiah Davenport (Herbert Heyes), lines his office with photos of the heroes of journalism, and dubs his new daily *The Globe*. His efforts put him in direct competition with Charity Hackett (Mary Welch), the publisher of a wealthy rival paper, who is blessed with beauty and brains but few ethics. As Hackett sets in motion a series of crooked ploys to put *The Globe* out of business, Mitchell and his team report on Steve Brodie's jump from the Brooklyn Bridge, witness the invention of the linotype, invent the newsstand, and inaugurate the drive to fund the base of the Statue of Liberty. Romantic sparks fly between Hackett and Mitchell, with Mitchell attracted to Hackett's power but repulsed by how she uses it. After Hackett's minions bomb *The Globe* office and cripple a child, she gives in, agreeing to help Mitchell publish his paper. The resolution confirms a dictate uttered earlier in the film: "The press is good or evil according to the character of those who direct it."

*Park Row* is the one film on which Fuller truly operated without oversight, free as he was of studio interest, the pressures of a producer, or the demands of a financier. His vision was bound only by the limitations imposed by his available resources. It is no surprise, then, that Fuller's general narrative and stylistic tendencies are exaggerated to an excessive degree. In *Park Row*, Fuller returns to an episodic plot that relies on coincidence to heighten situations. The narrative frequently digresses from the primary plotline in order to provide lessons in journalistic history, terminology, and processes, while also telescoping historical events into a limited time span and manipulating the characters into a violent conflict. Newspaper history is presented as war as Fuller seeks both to educate the viewer about the responsibilities of the press and to entertain through action-oriented set pieces. Even the love affair between Mitchell and Hackett is expressed through competition and violence, a dynamic Fuller revisits in *Forty Guns, Shark!*, and *Dead Pigeon on Beethoven Street*. At the same time, however, Fuller's deep reverence for the newspaper business and its history imbues the film with an overt sentimentality only intermittently present in his previous work. The result is a jarring juxtaposition of competing moods and tones, an aesthetic trait that Fuller repeated and refined over the course of his career.

Fuller's production freedom during *Park Row* allowed him to commit his energies where he wanted, and the film reflects both the most anemic and the most exciting techniques within his visual repertoire. *Park Row* is the film in which Fuller demonstrates his greatest reliance on the long-take master shot, containing an average shot length of thirty-six seconds—well above the Hollywood average of eleven to twelve seconds normative during the period and the longest of Fuller's career. Some of the master shots, particularly those of the scenes set in O'Rourke's bar, suffer from flat, two-dimensional staging and little to no movement of any kind, forcing the creation of optical cut-ins to provide some dynamism in the image. Scenes set in *The Globe* office, however, frequently contain well-choreographed long takes with high-contrast lighting, deep-space staging, and cut-ins to extreme close-ups for emotional emphasis, a style Fuller first adopted to great effect in *The Baron of Arizona*. Even a relatively simple shot can become highly expressive, as when Mitchell and Hackett first kiss. After the two lock lips, the camera curves to the right to partially obscure their embrace behind dark, vertical bars; the camera holds on the ominous composition for a few moments, then reverses direction and tracks left, setting up Mitchell's rejection of their "merger" and Hackett's forceful response.

Fuller's most experimental sequence takes place after Hackett's men begin destroying *Globe* newsstands. Mitchell tears out of O'Rourke's bar and races down the street to halt the destruction of the newsstands, confronting Hackett and dealing out two-fisted retribution along the way. Two free-wheeling, medium-long-shot long takes recorded with the camera strapped to the body of the cameraman heighten the propulsive nature of the scene. The camera quickly leads Mitchell through the action, bounding ahead of each new attack, providing the viewer with a physical sense of his fury. As Mitchell clobbers a perpetrator at the base of the statue of Benjamin Franklin, the long take quickly tracks out, then cuts to a series of shorter, tighter shots of the fight. The change in duration and shot scale enables Fuller to maintain the intensity of the sequence through fresh means, focusing viewer attention on Mitchell's expression of rage. With its contrasting use of long takes and rapid editing, this sequence is a microcosm of Fuller's visual aesthetic, and its extreme kineticism looks forward to the action choreography in *Pickup on South Street*. More significantly, the narrative and stylistic exuberance of *Park Row* and its uninhibited sincerity provide a preview of the aesthetic exhibited by Fuller's films during his next period of independence, when he operated under his own Globe banner.

*Park Row* is a visual embodiment of Fuller's passion for journalism and history and of his excitement at the freedoms afforded by independent production. While it has come to be loved by fans who view it as Fuller's purest cinematic statement, it was challenged by a lack of marketable elements at the time of its release. In order to hedge his bets against big-budget competitors, Fuller ingeniously mounted a massive exploitation campaign aimed at garnering press support by writing to the editors of over 1,700 American daily newspapers, holding a special preview screening at the American Newspaper Publishers Association convention, and taking out ad space in *Editor and Publisher*, the trade paper of the news industry.[15] When opening night arrived at Grauman's Chinese in Los Angeles, a working printing press met the audience in front of the theater, churning out papers with the *Globe* masthead—just as in the movie. Fuller even dedicated the film to the nation's papers, superimposing the dedication over a scrolling backdrop of newspaper mastheads. Lacking stars, color, and glossy production values to sell the film, Fuller relied on the press to provide him with ballyhoo.

While Fuller's promotional campaign garnered *Park Row* widespread publicity and reviews in major national magazines, it could not turn a low-budget love letter to journalism into a grade-A hit. Fuller released the film through United Artists, which was then in the midst of refashioning itself as the premier distributor of independent product. *Park Row* debuted on September 1, 1952 with Republic's re-edited drama *Tough Girl* (1952) at the Chinese and two smaller first-run houses in downtown Los Angeles. While the film was held over for two to three days at each theater, exhibitors rated it "disappointing after a nice take-off."[16] United Artists rolled the film out slowly, one to two cities at a time, over the next four months. By October, *Park Row* began appearing on the bottom half of first-run double bills. Despite the initial press excitement, the film received mixed to negative critical notices, with many reviewers speculating that Fuller's enthusiasm for the subject matter drove him to integrate too many historic facts and dramatic events into one movie. Robert Hatch's biting review in *Theatre Arts* summarized the consensus, arguing that the film's pretensions could not successfully mask its low-budget origins: "How much of this gaslit, beer-spattered history is accurate I don't know and I don't care—it is pitched at a level of amateur enthusiasm with which one can easily sympathize but which never succeeds outside a high school auditorium."[17] Without a substantial first run as a headliner, *Park Row* failed to make back its production costs and wiped out Fuller's savings.[18]

*Park Row* demonstrated both the difficulty of selling a film as a headliner without stars, production values, or a reliable gimmick and the dan-

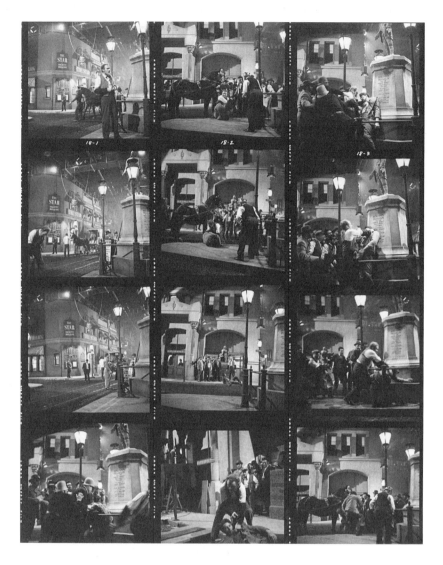

A contact sheet of images taken by the unit photographer of *Park Row* during the scene in which Phineas Mitchell attacks a lackey of rival newspaper *The Star*. Gene Evans (Mitchell) rests between takes in the upper left, while Fuller crosses tracks laid in the street for moving camera shots below. The center and right columns depict images of the fight, which culminates at the base of a statue of Benjamin Franklin. *Chrisam Films, Inc.*

ger of self-financing independent production. While the failure of *The Baron of Arizona* robbed Fuller only of a possible profit share and the relative disappointment of *Fixed Bayonets* cost him nothing at all, *Park Row*'s disastrous box office almost bankrupted the director and prevented him from ever completely self-financing a film again. If Twentieth Century–Fox had not picked up the next option on his contract, he would also have been without a job, severely crippling his ability to secure financing and distribution for subsequent independent films. In order to make independent programmers successfully again, Fuller needed to increase selling points through the acquisition of stars, higher budgets, or exploitable subject matter, a lesson he put to use later in the decade during his Globe Enterprises years. In the meantime, Fox did renew his contract, although Fuller did not advance any of his other independent projects past the preproduction stage for the next four years. After returning from *Park Row*, Fuller's subsequent three films at Fox continued to increase in prestige, featuring larger budgets, rising stars, and eventually color, CinemaScope, and overseas location shooting—as well as greater adherence to classical conventions.

### *Brutality:* Pickup on South Street

*Pickup on South Street* combined the assets of Fox and the inclinations of Fuller to produce one of the director's most accessible yet most brutal pictures. The film originated as a courtroom drama by Dwight Taylor, but Fuller rewrote the script into the story of a pickpocket who accidentally steals government secrets from a Communist courier. Production records, screenplay drafts, and Production Code Administration (PCA) files reveal that both Zanuck and Production Code regulations influenced the development of the script and its visual realization. Zanuck specifically recruited Fuller to rewrite and direct *Pickup on South Street,* hoping to infuse the film with an intensity and raw realism that would raise it above its genre origins. Fuller's rewrite pushed the limits of acceptable representations of crime and violence under the Code, but negotiations enabled the film to retain a surprising amount of objectionable material, perhaps because of the support of Zanuck and the anti-Communist leanings of PCA administrator Joseph Breen. In this instance, Fuller's talent for translating the clipped language and hard-hitting morality of the criminal underworld to the screen complemented the aims of the studio and benefited from lax enforcement of the Production Code, enabling *Pickup on South Street* to emerge as one of the most shockingly violent films of the mid-1950s as well as one of Fuller's most singular achievements.

The script of *Pickup on South Street* that went into production in September 1952 was the result of a calculated attempt by Twentieth Century–Fox executives and Fuller to produce a rough, unconventional crime picture. Dwight Taylor's original story, *Blaze of Glory,* provided the basic narrative outline of the film and was faithfully adapted by Harry Brown into a first-draft continuity script in March 1952. In Brown's script, a criminal named Skip steals a wallet containing government microfilm and is hunted by a police lieutenant and the FBI. In the wallet is the address of Helen Courtland, a gorgeous, good-hearted woman, with whom Skip falls in love. In order to clear her from being implicated in the spy ring, Skip decides to turn himself in. Secondary characters include a priest, Father Dodd, who mentors Skip's redemption, and the landlady at Skip's boarding house. At the story conference for Brown's continuity script, Zanuck discussed the project with producer Fred Kohlmar and director Henry Hathaway, the same team behind Fox's noir *Kiss of Death* (1947). Hathaway had also directed the successful pseudodocumentary spy thriller *The House on 92nd St.* (1945), but the realism associated with that project is precisely what Zanuck found lacking in Brown's script.

The basic story is excellent but [Brown's] is a very conventional treatment of the idea. This is a formula treatment where it should have been an unorthodox treatment. Alan Ladd treatment vs. Humphrey Bogart treatment. Illustrated by relationship with girl—should have been a hard-hitting Richard Widmark kind of thing—tough, dirty, full of authority. Are we going to take this idea and treat it with guts and realism?[19]

Zanuck's language when comparing the Brown treatment to the ideal treatment—formula vs. unorthodox, Ladd vs. Bogart—reveals his desire for a darker, harder-edged approach to the material that would challenge convention. In particular, he cites as a model for the protagonist the kind of character frequently played by Richard Widmark, then best known for a series of edgy, tough-guy roles in *Kiss of Death, The Street with No Name* (1948), *Night and the City* (1950), *Panic in the Streets* (1950), and *No Way Out* (1950)—all gritty films noir. For Zanuck, guts and realism required a writer with intimate knowledge of underworld scum, someone who could inject action and "authority" into the script. *Blaze of Glory* required someone like Sam Fuller.

    With Zanuck's encouragement, Fuller rewrote *Blaze of Glory* and punched it full of enough grit and guts to set it on a collision course with the PCA. Fuller finished a new story outline by June, reworking all but the basic configuration of Skip, the microfilm, the detective, and the woman. His new synopsis stressed the authentic details, rough-and-tumble protagonist, and shady love affair that Zanuck yearned for during the first story conference:

The central figure in this story is a veteran pickpocket, a three time loser, who is both fascinating and terrifying in his own little crooked world. This habitual criminal knows the jargon and manners of pickpockets and he knows what makes the world of ex-cons tick. He is full of sentimental urges as well as cold blooded ferocity. He meets a girl oozing sex—the kind who lives to get love, cheap to get it. And for this girl the pickpocket violates the Baumes [three strike] law, is convicted of a fourth offense, and gets life.[20]

Fuller tossed the landlady, the priest, and the redemptive woman in favor of an isolated waterfront shack, a weary tie-selling snitch named Moe, and Candy, a former prostitute. He begins the story outline with the same detailed subway heist that eventually opens the film, highlighting from the start the techniques and manners of the professional criminal. By emphasizing criminal methods, "cold blooded ferocity," and prostitution, Fuller knowingly ran the risk of substantial PCA editing but initially hedged his bets by playing up the patriotism and sending his protagonist to jail. At the conference for Fuller's initial story outline, however, Zanuck suggested toning down Skip's patriotism.[21] Fuller's writer's working script and first-draft continuity, both completed at the beginning of August, lose not only the patriotism but also the jailhouse, as Skip is permitted to walk out into the streets at the end of the film with Candy on his arm, betting the police caption that he will never be caught again. By drafting a cynical, knowing look at the moral codes of the criminal underworld and highlighting the methods and violence of its men and women, Fuller simultaneously realized Zanuck's story goals and provided himself with a narrative highly conducive to a visceral stylistic approach.

*Pickup on South Street* is one of Fuller's best screenplays, both a model of classical clarity and representative of his own narrative voice. The plot is exceedingly tight and causally driven, with each scene advancing the story. The film opens with a subway sequence: two FBI agents trail Candy (Jean Peters), an unwitting courier for Communist spies. While appearing to flirt with Candy, Skip (Richard Widmark) steals her wallet and the microfilm inside. Realizing she has lost her "package," Candy contacts her handler, Joey (Richard Kiley), who tells her to hit the streets and find the thief; meanwhile, the FBI agents go to the police, who call in Moe (Thelma Ritter), a seller of neckties and underworld information. Moe gives up Skip's name in order to feed her "kitty," but he has already discovered the microfilm and hidden it. When the police and FBI agents confront Skip at his shack, he taunts their appeals to his patriotism and decides instead to sell the microfilm back to the Communists. Candy arrives at Skip's shack seeking the microfilm, only to end up in his arms. Through a series of flirtations and fights Candy starts to fall for Skip, but his sole motivation remains money. Nevertheless, Candy, hoping to keep Skip out of jail for theft, knocks him cold and returns the microfilm to Joey. But Joey viciously attacks her when he discovers a frame is missing from the microfilm, prompting Skip to acknowledge Candy's sacrifice, forget about the money, and seek revenge. Skip sets upon Joey in a crowded subway station, and after beating him to a pulp, captures the spy and clears his name, much to the chagrin of local law enforcement. As Skip and Candy stroll arm-in-arm out of the police station, the captain predicts Skip will be arrested again within the month, to which Candy replies, "Wanna bet?"

Fuller's lurid portrait of the criminal underworld immediately raised eyebrows at the PCA and sparked three rounds of script revisions. Breen found Fuller's first-draft continuity script "unacceptable by reason of excessive brutality and sadistic beatings, both of men and of women."[22] In addition to assorted fights and sexually suggestive situations, Breen particularly objected to the method and level of violence in three sequences: Skip and Candy's lovemaking scene, Joey's beating of a half-naked Candy, and the final fight between Joey and Skip. Any mention of slapping, kneeing, kicking, or slugging someone with a gun invited charges of excessive brutality and PCA recommendations to shake, push, or attempt to choke instead. Fuller's final script toned down the physical violence between Skip and Candy, but still sparked criticism for Joey's beating of the bathrobed Candy and the final fight sequence.[23] Subsequent revised pages cleared the film with the PCA, but Zanuck allegedly also had to deal with the input of the FBI. As was standard for any film depicting FBI personnel, the PCA recommended that Twentieth Century–Fox consult the Bureau for technical advice. According to Fuller, J. Edgar Hoover objected to Skip's lack of patriotism, especially his order to the FBI agents: "Don't wave that goddam flag at me." Fuller recalled Zanuck agreeing that the profanity should be removed from the line, but resisting Hoover's efforts to censor anything unpatriotic about the flag. Zanuck's argument: Skip's statement reflected his character, something Hoover had no jurisdiction over.[24] The line remained in the film. Zanuck's move to protect the dialogue reflected his desire to produce a different sort of spy thriller, one in which the heroes were not patriotic officers of the law but selfish criminals who helped the government only when it helped them.

Despite the revisions made to placate the PCA, Fuller, too, never lost sight of Zanuck's aim, adopting for the film a visual style that highlighted the brutal physicality of its script. Though *Pickup on South Street* lacked the stature of the CinemaScope and Technicolor extravaganzas on the rest of Fox's slate, it brought Fuller together with an experienced crew led by veteran cinematographer Joe MacDonald, a favorite of directors John Ford, Henry Hathaway, and Elia Kazan. MacDonald shot the film in black and white, utilizing high-contrast noir lighting to add an air of menace and uncertainty. Fuller completed the gritty New York story entirely in the Fox studio and downtown Los Angeles in less than a month, with one week of rehearsal.[25] *Pickup on South Street*'s $780,000 budget was slightly larger than that of *Fixed Bayonets*, yet its shooting schedule was half as long; like its predecessor, it fit comfortably into the rough-and-tumble genres that were quickly becoming associated with Fuller.

Fuller adopted a range of staging strategies for *Pickup on South Street,* and with the help of MacDonald achieved a polished visual style that anticipated the elegance of *House of Bamboo* even while punching up the sex and violence. Although Fuller uses close-ups and eyeline matches to establish spatial relations and build tension in the opening scene—much as he did at the beginning of *I Shot Jesse James*—he relies less on constructive editing in the rest of the film than on fluid master shots intercut with select inserts. The introduction of Moe in the police station offers a useful example. The nearly six-minute-long scene contains just six shots and four camera setups: a master shot, an alternate version of the master shot, and two reaction-shot inserts. Throughout the master shots, Fuller orchestrates camera and actor movement to create new compositions even while maintaining the same take. Lengthy master shots also typically ground his fight sequences, allowing the action to play out in a defined space and real time and emphasizing movement within the frame.

The visceral nature of Fuller's aesthetic dominates *Pickup on South Street,* inflecting scenes oriented around both romance and action. The mise-en-scene and blocking directly emphasize the brutality at the core of Skip and Candy's relationship, establishing a motif of violent love that links the picture with *Park Row* and subsequent Fuller films featuring combative couples. For example, Skip's initial visit from Candy in his shack begins with a wallop, as Skip knocks her to the ground in the darkness, mistaking her for an intruder. After Skip pours a beer over Candy to wake her up, he interrogates her about breaking into his shack. In a shot–reverse shot exchange of medium-close-up and close-up two-shots, Candy winces from the bruise developing on her cheek, prompting Skip to "helpfully" wrap his hand around her face and massage the bruise. Although Candy does not pull away, the massage appears more painful than soothing, and Skip's open hand works just inches above Candy's throat. The staging leads the viewer to anticipate that at any minute Skip may strangle her, while the dark shadow covering Candy's face prevents the viewer from registering her emotional response. The visual style thus heightens the ambiguity of Skip's action, suggesting a violent undercurrent to his ministrations. The reverse angle confirms this impression, as a large iron chain and hook dominate the foreground in the left third of the frame, partially blocking Skip and Candy from view. While there is a narrative motivation for framing the chain and hook—they suspend the container that holds the microfilm Candy is searching for—their dominant placement in the composition further injects an air of menace into the couple's embrace. The shot–reverse shot pattern continues, with the camera tracking to an extreme-close-up two-shot as Skip dives in to kiss Candy, his action repeated in the reverse angle as the camera tracks left to rereveal the chain and hook in an even closer foreground framing. The visual association of Skip and Candy's union with tools of bondage and pain illustrate the sadistic aspect of their relationship, one seemingly grounded in a strange intermingling of violence and lust. The shot–reverse shot pattern is broken by a quick track out as Skip pushes Candy away, wraps Moe's tie around her neck, and slings her toward the door. The same dance of extreme intimacy and brutal rejection is replayed in their subsequent meetings on the dock and in the shack, as Skip continues to throw Candy around while she slaps him in the face and cold cocks him with a beer bottle. Theirs is a relationship defined by violence—violence that is both directly represented and suggested through mise-en-scene—entirely contrary to the dictates of the Production Code.

The PCA's efforts to reduce the excessive brutality in Fuller's script are also undermined by how the film's action sequences are staged. While there is indeed no kneeing, kicking, or slugging with a gun in the final film, the sequences that most alarmed Breen remain largely intact, their violence heightened by staging, lighting, camera movement, and sound. Fuller's stylistic choices emphasize the conflict and kineticism within the frame, physically conveying to the viewer the impact of each blow. This is bruising cinema at its best, designed to leave the viewer much like Skip and Candy at the end of the film—battered, yes, but thrilled to have made it.

Joey's vicious beating of Candy after he discovers the missing microfilm frame is a prime example of how Fuller managed to communicate the script's physical violence despite strong cautions from the PCA. In the first and second rounds of script review, Code administrators objected both to the excessively sadistic attack and to the suggestion in the script that Candy falls out of her bathrobe and is naked during the assault. When reviewing the final script, the PCA warned, "As we advised you before, this brutal beating of a half naked woman is entirely unacceptable and could not be approved in the final picture."[26] While Candy does remain fully zipped in her robe during the attack in the film, the sequence retains its power to shock due largely to a visual and sonic presentation that heightens its visceral impact.

A publicity still of the first clinch between Skip (Richard Widmark) and Candy (Jean Peters) in *Pickup on South Street*. The high-contrast lighting and framing of the couple between hooks and pulleys reflect the scene as shot, emphasizing the violent nature of the characters' attraction. *Courtesy of the Academy of Motion Picture Arts and Sciences*

Shot primarily in a long take using only diegetic sound and a moving camera, the staging and camerawork during the scene coldly illustrate Candy's inability to escape Joey's rage. The long take begins as Joey corners Candy coming out of the bathroom and demands the microfilm, grabbing her by the collar of her robe, shaking her, and twice banging her head against the bathroom door. As throughout the scene, the staging emphasizes that Joey has Candy trapped, his hulking torso looming over her in the foreground. After Joey grabs the microfilm from her, he turns to face the camera and examine the film, but discovers a frame is missing. Swinging back to Candy, he pulls the hood of her robe down, grabs her arms and shakes her, throwing her against the rear wall and knocking a lamp over. No nondiegetic music accompanies the sequence; instead, only Candy's cries, the thudding of furniture, and the crashing of lamps give voice to the assault, providing immediate punctuation for each blow. The camera tracks in to follow Joey as he advances on Candy, his back dominating the bulk of the frame while only Candy's frightened face, lit from below, can be glimpsed over his shoulder.

This pattern of Candy's futile retreat followed by Joey's menacing advance is repeated and varied throughout the long take, with camera movement and blocking emphasizing the physical nature of the attack. Joey demands to know where Skip is, grabbing Candy and swinging her away from the door. She tries to flee toward the camera, but Joey pulls her back, the camera tracking rapidly backward as he slaps her. Unlike in most of the scene, where the camera reframes, pans, and tracks to follow the action, here the camera retreats from the slap, perhaps as a concession to Code administrators who feared the explicit depiction of brutality in this scene. Again, however, the stylistic choice functions not to diminish the violence but to heighten it, as the camera's sudden, quick movement in anticipation of the slap adds a kinetic intensity to the sequence. As Candy bolts to the right, trying again to escape Joey, the camera continues to track back into an extreme long shot, enabling the camera operator to follow the entirety of the action by reframing and panning. Joey again grabs Candy, throws her into a table, and overturns a lamp, then repeatedly slams her against a bookcase and knocks over another lamp, his cries of "Where does he live?" rising above the clatter of the falling furniture and Candy's wails. The left-to-right trajectory of the action now moves toward the camera and into the foreground, as Candy pushes Joey backward over a chair and falls down herself, then runs left in the midground toward the door, the camera panning left to follow. A close-up insert of a gun firing interrupts the one-minute, twenty-second long take; a return to the wide angle clarifies that Joey has shot Candy as she falls to the floor, taking yet another table and vase of flowers with her. With its diegetic clatter punctuating the collapsing figure movement, Candy's final fall completes the series of retreats and advances that structure the entire sequence.

Although the sequence does not contain the emphatic nondiegetic music, close-ups, matches on action, and shot–reverse shot patterns that often punctuate a fight scene, the staging and use of sound in the long take nevertheless heighten the brutal physicality of Joey's relentless attack on Candy. Rather than merely illustrating an exchange of blows in the middle of a room, the staging brings the characters into contact not only with each other but also with the surfaces of the apartment itself. Every slap or shake is but the first of a series of blows, followed by a collapse into a wall or table or lamp or sometimes all three. The staging thus multiplies the kinetic force of each action, as Candy struggles to maintain her footing and escape in some direction—any direction. The camera movement in the long take further heightens the chaotic energy of the fight, often paralleling or opposing the trajectory of characters in motion. In the absence of nondiegetic music, the sounds of the crashing furniture adopt a more emphatic function on the soundtrack, acting in unison with Candy's cries to loudly punctuate Joey's blows. Finally, the duration of the long take itself grounds the assault in real time and extends the seemingly never-ending attack. The staging, sound, and lack of editing thus create a fight sequence that is not only intensely physical and brutal, but is also disturbingly immediate.

Staging, camera movement, and sound function in a similarly visceral fashion during the final fight between Skip and Joey, producing a kinetic explosion that releases Skip's pent-up rage. Although the scene lacks the kneeing and kicking that Breen initially objected to in the script, Joey's collisions with various objects, including Skip's fists, create yet another unrelentingly brutal sequence. Unlike the earlier sequence that relied on a long-take master shot, over half of the shots during the climax are unique camera setups. Camera movement and match cuts enable the action to remain legible from shot to shot even as Skip and Joey careen from one corner of the subway station to the next and finally land on the train tracks.

The character and camera movement heighten the freneticism of the scene, while a series of match cuts emphasize the bone-crushing physicality of the fight in a direct and visceral manner. The camera aggressively tracks and pans to follow the action, framing Joey's head bouncing down the cement stairs, his torso slamming into the bars of the subway gate, and the turnstile swinging into his gut. As with Candy's earlier efforts to evade Joey, Joey's attempts to escape from Skip only result in further injury. Though utilizing a crowded subway platform rather than an empty apartment, the staging of Skip and Joey's fistfight recalls Candy's earlier beating and emphasizes the real motivation for the confrontation—not Skip's desire to capture a traitor, but his desire to avenge Candy.

Also as in the earlier assault, the climactic showdown utilizes strictly diegetic sound. The cries of the crowd, the sound of the punches, and the characters' verbal responses to being hit heighten the chaos of the sequence and mark each moment of impact. Stripped of the layer of distance provided by nondiegetic sound, the soundtrack functions in a more immediate fashion to punctuate the physical injuries suffered by the characters. This effect is most apparent after Skip follows Joey onto the tracks. With the crowd presence diminished and the wind in the tunnel the primary ambient sound, each punch, groan, and gasp resonates more fully. Staging and mise-en-scene again promote a sense of realism as a subway car passes across the foreground, permitting intermittent glimpses of Skip pummeling Joey in the background during a long take. In a final cut in to a medium shot, Skip stands in front of a niche in the wall delivering an unending series of blows, each punch to the stomach propelling Joey's face into the light and back again into

darkness. Staging, sound, and mise-en-scene all work together to intensify the physicality of the fight and document the punishment delivered
to Joey.

Fuller's rough, hard-hitting visual approach to *Pickup on South Street*
put an "unorthodox" spin on the sort of pseudodocumentary spy caper
that Zanuck and Fox had tasted success with before, emphasizing sex
and violence in order to appeal to a more mature audience. Zanuck encouraged Fuller to do what he did best, and Fuller delivered. As the film
blew into the market before the 1956 revision of the Production Code
tightened the regulation of crime and violence, it benefited from the
PCA's loose standards during reviews of both its script and visual presentation. While the PCA suggested Fuller revise dialogue and details in the
script in order for the film to pass the Code, it nevertheless enabled
*Pickup on South Street* to have an amoral, unpatriotic, and criminal protagonist stay one step ahead of law enforcement and walk away scott-
free at the end, his revenge-driven assault on a spy apparently enough
moral compensation for his crimes. In addition, Breen apparently made
no move to request cuts in the completed film that might limit the intense
violence of the scenes between Candy, Skip, and Joey, likely buckling
during negotiations with Twentieth Century–Fox and desiring to keep
the picture's physical attack on Communism intact. Zanuck and Fuller's
shared intention to produce a crime picture differentiated by its grit and
visceral impact thus remained largely unaltered, producing a prime example of how working within a major studio did not necessarily neuter
the artistic impulses of a filmmaker. Today, many critics describe *Pickup
on South Street* as a quintessential Samuel Fuller picture, yet it is also
very much a product of the Hollywood studio system.

*Pickup on South Street*'s strong selling points brought Fuller the kind
of box-office success he had not seen since *The Steel Helmet*. The film
premiered in Los Angeles at the end of May 1953 and in June rolled into
first-run theaters throughout major cities. By the end of the month,
*Pickup on South Street* had grossed the third highest national box
office.[27] Reviews for the picture were largely unfavorable due to its lurid
subject matter and excessive violence, with only MacDonald's photography and Thelma Ritter's performance receiving stand-out notices.[28] Nevertheless, the film grossed $1.9 million domestically, ranking in the top
half of Twentieth Century–Fox's releases for the year, and won the
Bronze Lion of St. Mark at the 1954 Venice Film Festival for best direction, the only award at the festival granted that year to an American
film.[29] While *Pickup on South Street* brought Fuller to the attention of
European film cultists, its tremendous box-office success at home swept
him into the ranks of Fox's top action directors. Fuller next wrote two
westerns, *Run of the Arrow* and *Woman with a Whip*, both of which

Zanuck declined to produce. Fuller returned to directing action films, the westerns temporarily put on hold.

### Classical Style: Hell and High Water *and* House of Bamboo

Fuller's last two films as a contract director for Twentieth Century–Fox, *Hell and High Water* and *House of Bamboo,* signaled his ascension into the ranks of big-budget, A-picture film directors. *Hell and High Water* kept Fuller firmly within the action camp while providing him with the opportunity to direct his first Technicolor and CinemaScope picture, the fifth such release for Fox. *House of Bamboo* continued Fuller's work in color and widescreen while enabling him to shoot for the first time overseas. Both films reflect an industry-wide trend within the action genre toward epic adventure yarns featuring large casts, international locations, color, and widescreen; both films also demonstrate Fuller's ability to adhere fully to classical norms. While *Hell and High Water* is so conventionally shot it barely seems like a Fuller production, *House of Bamboo* reveals a more dynamic integration of classicism and Fuller's personal aesthetic, resulting in his most elegant, subtly striking picture.

By far the most expensive film of his early career, *Hell and High Water* demonstrated Fuller's ability to make the transition from shooting quickly and cheaply to managing a larger production and a longer shooting schedule. An implausibly sensational submarine story, the film reteamed Fuller with Richard Widmark and cinematographer Joe Mac-Donald while providing him with a technical challenge: his first Cinema-Scope production. Zanuck encouraged Fuller to move the bulky Cinema-Scope camera within the cramped submarine set as he would on a normal interior; Fuller responded by packing the elongated frame with rows of bodies and utilizing short camera moves to heighten the sense of claustrophobia. Fuller's active style of shooting led to numerous on-set injuries and press reports of a "jinx," but he completed the film on time in sixty days at a budget of $1.87 million.[30] With more than double the budget and three times the shooting schedule he enjoyed on *Pickup on South Street,* Fuller had the resources and the time to craft a high-quality Hollywood action film; in all likelihood, he also experienced the increased production oversight afforded big-budget spectacles. The end result is Fuller's least personal film, featuring a few signature narrative elements but defined by strict adherence to classical stylistic conventions.

Fuller had little to work with in the "misfits on a mission" screenplay, which he partially rewrote from a version by Jesse Lasky, Jr., but as usual he managed to open with a bang: in this instance, an atomic bomb blast. A voice-over that speciously intermingles fact with fiction declares the blast came from behind the Iron Curtain in the North Pacific, and the film will explain what happened and why. According to the narrative, the story begins when a distinguished group of international citizens organizes a scientific expedition to explore rumors that an atomic installation is being built in the North Pacific. The group hires a mercenary former Navy man, Adam Jones (played by Richard Widmark with his customary scowl), to captain the submarine with his handpicked crew. Also on board are a team of ideologically driven nuclear scientists: the renowned Professor Montel (Victor Francen) and his young, attractive daughter, Denise (Bella Darvi). Denise provides an early source of onboard friction, as the all-male crew questions her presence on the submarine; only after she proves her intelligence and linguistic ability is she accepted, prompting one man to declare, "That's no female, that's a scientist!"

The conflict between Jones's financial motivation and Montel's interests in science and peace, as well as the presence of a female scientist on board, were added to the original scenario during the scriptwriting process. The character of Jones emerges from the revisions as less likable and more of an antihero in the vein of *Pickup on South Street*'s Skip: he's on board not because the expedition is the right thing to do, but because it pays well. More so than in the earlier film, however, Widmark's character undergoes a conversion over the course of *Hell and High Water;* his growing attraction to Denise and Montel's self-sacrifice move him grudgingly to admit there may be a reason to risk your life that has nothing to do with money. Here we see the self-interest indicative of Fuller's crime and war film protagonists leavened with a conversion story: the resistant hero decides to support the larger cause, a strategy popular within wartime narratives as it directly appeals to the viewer's own sense of patriotism. The character of Denise also contains typically Fullerian elements while functioning in a conventional way. A great admirer of women, Fuller likes his female characters smart and tough. (Even when they're working girls who regularly get beat up, as in *Pickup on South Street* or *Underworld, U.S.A.*, their resolve never wavers.) Denise deflects the submarine crew's resentment and unwanted sexual attention through her intelligence and resiliency; like Lucky Legs in *China Gate*, she proves she can contribute to the mission without pretending to be "one of the boys." At the same time, however, her presence enables a romantic plotline, a Hollywood norm that broadens the film's appeal beyond the male action fan. While the characters of Jones and Denise reveal parallels with other Fuller protagonists, the bulk of the narrative is strictly generic, organized around a series of action-oriented set pieces.

Over the course of the film, tensions between individual expedition members continuously bubble up, only to be quashed by the need for communal action to defeat the enemy. The first challenge emerges on the trip north, when the expedition engages in an underwater cat-and-mouse game with a Chinese Communist sub. Meanwhile, Montel and Jones battle for command of the expedition, Montel loses his thumb in a hatch accident, and Jones and Denise share several sweaty embraces. After a brief skirmish on the original island destination, Montel orders the expedition to a new island; reconnaissance by Jones and Denise uncovers an American bomber and the presence of radioactive material. A captured Chinese prisoner provides an explanation: the Chinese Communists plan to drop an atomic bomb on Korea and frame the United States. Jones volunteers to go ashore and warn the expedition when the plane will take off so the submarine can surface in time to shoot it down; unbeknownst to the captain, Montel departs for the island instead. The plane is successfully shot down and crashes into the island, killing Montel and allegedly producing the atomic blast from the opening of the film.

Out of all of Fuller's pictures, *Hell and High Water* is the one that most consistently adheres to conventional staging and editing. Rather than organizing scenes around extended master shots and select inserts—as in *I Shot Jesse James*—or a mix of long takes and sequences reliant on editing—as in *The Baron of Arizona*—here Fuller shoots complete coverage and edits scenes analytically: wider establishing shots introduce the environment and confirm the characters' spatial relationships; cut-ins to medium shots isolate significant characters and action; close-ups and shot–reverse shot sequences punctuate important dialogue while also foregrounding character reactions and cueing viewer responses. When one line of narrative action is closed, a return to the original establishing shot resituates the characters in the scene and signals a new direction in the narrative. Classical scene dissection is so ubiquitous it is invisible to most audiences, so even momentary divergences can disrupt the viewer's immersion in the story and produce a startling jolt—the kind of jolt Fuller typically liked to create. Such visually arresting, signature moments are largely absent from *Hell and High Water,* however. Instead, this is a film that demonstrates Fuller's mastery of classical norms, a sharp repudiation to any who suggest his frequent disregard for visual conventions was the result of "primitive" instinct or spontaneous intuition rather than deliberate choice.

Fuller's most conventional film was also one of his most commercially successful. *Hell and High Water* opened big in February 1954 at the Roxy in New York.[31] Backed by a substantial marketing campaign that highlighted its action, large cast, and stunning use of CinemaScope, the film received solid box-office returns, holdovers, and exhibitor ratings of "strong," "big," and "huge" while rolling across the rest of the country. *Variety* again predicted healthy box office from the action trade, and reviews generally applauded the film's technical mastery and entertainment

A publicity still showing the interior of the submarine in *Hell and High Water,* with Richard Widmark (center) as Captain Jones and Cameron Mitchell (lower left, glancing at Widmark) as sonar operator Ski Brodski. The submarine's cat-and-mouse chase sequences are among the most suspenseful set pieces in the film. *Courtesy of the Academy of Motion Picture Arts and Sciences*

value while recognizing its farfetched and formulaic storyline.[32] *Hell and High Water* came through for Fuller, landing as the thirty-third highest-grossing film of the year and the tenth highest for Fox; with a $2.7 million domestic return, it earned the largest box office for any Fuller film except *The Big Red One.*[33] With Twentieth Century–Fox quickly moving toward an all-color, all-CinemaScope production slate dominated by action-adventure, the success of *Hell and High Water* seemingly secured Fuller a role in the future of the studio.

Fuller's next two assignments for Fox continued his involvement in big-budget action pictures. Following *Hell and High Water,* Zanuck assigned Fuller to rewrite *Saber Tooth,* an A-grade science-fiction adventure originated by Philip Dunne and intended for CinemaScope. Brought in as a cowriter with Dunne, Fuller drafted a new version of the script for Zanuck in the fall of 1953 and continued with rewrites through the following April, although Fox did not promise him the chance to direct the picture.[34] In April 1954, Fuller requested his twenty-six weeks for an out-side picture and delved into preproduction work on *The Story of Esther Costello,* a tale about a teacher who brings a deaf, blind, and mute Irish woman to America to learn how to communicate.[35] While Fuller was in Europe scouting locations for *The Story of Esther Costello,* Fox picked up his next option and offered him a job directing *House of Bamboo,* the story of an American officer who infiltrates a circle of ex-GI gangsters in occupied Tokyo.[36] Unable to start shooting before his twenty-six weeks outside the studio were up, Fuller abandoned *The Story of Esther Costello* in October and jumped on board *House of Bamboo.* Fuller's work for Twentieth Century–Fox in 1953 and 1954 suggests that despite his desire to make films independent of the studio, he was willing to drop outside commitments in order to direct properties for Fox that suited his interests and expanded his palette as a director. By helming overseas ac-tion-adventure stories with high production values and major stars, Fuller could solidify his status as an A-grade director.

The opportunity to direct Hollywood's first-ever film shot in Japan was an extraordinary coup for Fuller. Support for his overseas debut came from veteran producer Buddy Adler, who previously oversaw Fox's Hong Kong–based *Soldier of Fortune* (1955). Headlining the pic-ture were established stars Robert Ryan and Sessue Hayakawa and rela-tive newcomers Robert Stack and Shirley Yamaguchi. Even with the overseas travel, the film's $1.38 million budget was one of Fox's least expensive of the year.[37] Fuller filmed all exteriors in Japan and com-pleted production in forty-six days, spending half the time on location in Tokyo and the other half in the studio. Working again in Technicolor and CinemaScope with cinematographer Joe MacDonald, Fuller utilized the sort of careful compositions and lush production design that critics rarely associate with his work.

*House of Bamboo* was written by Harry Kleiner as an adaptation of his earlier Fox script *The Street with No Name.* Kleiner took the prem-ise of an FBI agent who goes undercover to infiltrate the mob and trans-posed it to postwar occupied Japan, with the mob in question now a gang of ex-American servicemen who use their military training to build a criminal empire. During preproduction, Fuller actively partici-pated in story conferences concerning Kleiner's screenplay drafts where Zanuck emphasized the need to differentiate the two films through the addition of a romantic subplot.[38] In *House of Bamboo,* an army police-man named Kenner (Stack) arrives in Japan posing as Eddie Spanier, an old friend of a dead gang member and the holder of an impressive rap sheet. After attempting to extort money from a series of pachinko par-lors, Eddie catches the eye of Sandy Dawson (Ryan), the disciplined leader of the gang, and quickly joins his unit. The suspicions of Griff

(Cameron Mitchell), Sandy's "ichibon" (number one man), force Eddie to enlist the help of Mariko (Yamaguchi), the secret widow of the dead gang member; Mariko agrees to pose as Eddie's "kimono girl" and cover for his absences, though cohabitating with an American brings her personal shame. As Eddie and Mariko grow closer, they work together to feed the police information about an upcoming heist. When the robbery goes haywire, Sandy believes it was Griff who betrayed him and plugs him in a steam room tub. A reporter tips off Sandy to the true mole, and Sandy sets up Eddie to take a fall during the gang's next robbery. Eddie catches the double cross in time and, along with the cops, chases Sandy up to a rooftop amusement park, setting in motion a cat-and-mouse game among the rides that culminates in a shootout on a Saturn-shaped Ferris wheel.

During production and reshoots, Fuller reworked Kleiner's script to craft a more elliptical, hard-boiled narrative and a stronger love story, earning a writing credit for additional dialogue.[39] First-act exposition is greatly condensed, with quick voice-overs providing pertinent information while largely dialogue-free scenes visually convey the gang's train robbery, the arrival of Eddie, and his subsequent search for Mariko. Fuller develops suspense by initially withholding Eddie's true identity and playing up his rough-handed ways, encouraging the viewer to share Mariko's caution toward him. Once Eddie reveals himself to Mariko and viewers are invested in their partnership, we see first a gang member and then the reporter threaten their ruse, further heightening our concern for their welfare. Scenes developing Eddie and Mariko's relationship are one of Fuller's primary contributions to the narrative, enabling him to increase Mariko's involvement in the action while also adding humor and contributing to the film's exotic appeal. Fuller provides the character of Mariko with much more agency than in the script, revising the scene in which she agrees to front for Eddie to make Eddie's request more indirect and Mariko's choice more her own; additionally, Fuller adds the intrigue involving Mariko contacting the police about the last caper and subsequently being questioned by Sandy. Both scenes highlight Mariko's personal motivations for wanting Sandy's gang out of commission—her loyalty to her dead husband and to Eddie—as well as the price she may pay in return—losing her reputation and possibly her life. These changes transform Mariko from a convenient "kimono girl" into the most sympathetic character in the film and likely contributed to the standout notices Shirley Yamaguchi received for the role. Other additions more directly evoke cultural stereotypes, including Eddie and Mariko's first "morning after" scene, in which differences in bathing and breakfast etiquette are played for laughs, and an elongated bathhouse scene, the basis of the print ad's image of Yamaguchi in nothing but a towel. Fuller's contributions to the narrative add depth and complexity as well as local color, reflecting his interest in both gripping the viewer's emotions and revealing cultural differences. Nevertheless, like the script itself, the completed film at times falls prey to stereotyped and anachronistic depictions of the Japanese, a problem Fuller more effectively avoids in *The Crimson Kimono*.

*House of Bamboo* represents the most nuanced blending of Fuller's visual aesthetic with the classical stylistic conventions that governed the high-quality, A-picture output of the major studios. Though shooting ran six days over schedule, daily production reports suggest that Fuller was not dawdling, as the crew completed most shots in one to two takes, a habit Fuller maintained throughout his career.[40] The film predominantly features classical scene dissection, although its average shot length of 14.4 seconds—the second longest for Fuller, behind *Park Row*—points to the significant usage of long-take master shots, as does the appearance of eight sequence shots across the film. Mise-en-scene, cinematography, and sound can be expressive, but scenes are staged and edited for maximum clarity and coherence. Balanced compositions, smoothly choreographed staging, naturalistic acting, analytical editing, and richly detailed mise-en-scene attest to the dominance of classical norms in the film. Still, Fuller takes full advantage of Technicolor, CinemaScope, and the graphic possibilities inherent in the Japanese architecture and landscape, creating redundant visual cues that highlight contrasts and movement within and between shots, thereby heightening the story's emotion and producing visceral thrills.

An analysis of two scenes from the film illustrates how Fuller achieved his preferred effects within the classical paradigm. In a bedroom scene when Mariko grapples with whether or not to stay with Eddie, mise-en-scene and music emphasize graphic conflict and movement within the frame, while cinematography and editing mark shifts in tone. Fuller's characteristic stylistic strategies appear in a relatively subtle form, supporting emotional beats and shifts in the narrative without calling attention to themselves. In the film's most elaborate scene, the climactic chase through the rooftop amusement park, mise-en-scene, music, and cinematography not only highlight contrasts and movement, but also produce pictorial compositions abstracted from the narrative. Here Fuller's visual style appears in its most overtly expressive form, harnessing color, motion, and sound to heighten the impact of the chase. *House of Bamboo* illustrates Fuller's ability to construct a beautifully photographed film in the classical tradition that still bears the stamp of his unique aesthetic vision.

During the second time Mariko visits Eddie in his shack, the narration marks the couple's first kiss and Mariko's fateful decision to cast her lot with Eddie through dramatic changes in music, mise-en-scene, and editing. The resulting graphic contrasts and tonal shifts encourage viewers to invest themselves emotionally in the scene and align with Mariko and Eddie against Sandy and his gang. The scene is organized around a long-take master shot and cut-ins to a close-up and a medium shot. In a one-and-a-half-minute master shot, the scene begins with Mariko kneeling in a medium shot facing the camera; in front of her is the bamboo screen she hangs between herself and Eddie at night to divide their sleeping space, an attempt at preserving her honor so flimsy it can be seen through. The curve of Mariko's red kimono stands out sharply against the blue squares of the room's rear wall, creating graphic contrast within the frame that makes her image pop. With her eyes gazing offscreen left at Eddie, Mariko tells him that she can't stay with him anymore due to the shame. The camera punctuates the end of her confession with a track out to a medium long shot, revealing Eddie lying face up on a tatami mat in the foreground in front of the bamboo screen. His face is softly lit, drawing the viewer to search his expression for a reaction, while his blue bedding and dark blue wrap provide a horizontal balance to the vertical blocks of blue on the rear wall. Centered in the composition, Mariko, too, balances the frame, yet the clashing color of her kimono underlines her contention that she does not belong. Eddie tells Mariko to go, that their arrangement was a bad idea from the start. He then literally turns his back on her, rolling toward the camera and hiding his face. As Mariko leaves, the camera tracks back to a long shot; as with Eddie's change in position, the camera movement subtly marks the dissolution of their bond. In Mariko's absence the frame remains still; the shot holds for several seconds in a pregnant pause, the wide angle and lack of a cut prompting the viewer to anticipate that someone will come through the door. In this segment of the scene, color and blocking produce contrast within the frame that highlights the conflict between the two characters. Although the low flute score that has accompanied the scene continues, the final composition suggests that something is about to change.

Mariko's unexpected return through the door and desperate lurch from background to foreground diagonally across the frame creates a sudden shift in both tone and action. Mariko's change of heart is highlighted not only by the contrast between the stasis resulting from her departure and the kinetic intensity of her return, but also by subsequent figure movement, the score, and editing. The music rises to a crescendo as she throws off her wrap and violently raises the bamboo screen—an abrupt and daring change of behavior given her previous admission and the couple's breakup. Eddie rolls over and begins to sit up, now silhouetted against the blue wall, but Mariko pushes him down and leans over him, ordering him to hold her. The master shot then cuts on their action to a medium close-up of the two kissing, an activity desired by the characters but previously denied. With their kiss, the status quo of Eddie and Mariko's relationship has irrevocably changed. This shift in the narrative is punctuated stylistically on several levels: by the rising score, the elevation of the bamboo screen, and the cut in from the distanced, master-shot long take that has dominated their nighttime domestic scenes. The sequence continues with typically classical analytical editing, cutting back to the reestablishing master shot as Griff opens the door and stands in the doorway to deliver a message from Sandy, thereby revealing the cause of Mariko's hasty retreat. Fuller initiates a shot–reverse shot sequence, with the medium close-up of the couple, a closer medium shot of Griff, and a return to the medium close-up. The closer shots highlight Mariko's shame at being seen by Griff and Eddie's protective stance toward her, as well as Griff's leering enjoyment of interrupting their kiss. The visual presentation and construction of this scene is entirely normative, featuring a redundancy of stylistic cues and classical analytical editing. Yet within the conventional staging, mise-en-scene, cinematography, sound, and editing produce the visual contrasts and abrupt shifts in tone and style that are characteristic of Fuller's work. The net effect binds viewers to the union of Mariko and Eddie, emphasizing both their shared loyalty and their shared vulnerability.

The scene in *House of Bamboo* in which Fuller uses stylistic techniques in the most self-conscious fashion is the climactic cornering of Sandy by Eddie and the police on the department store roof. The scene is divided into three sections: Sandy trying to escape the roof, the evacuation of the crowd from the amusement park, and Eddie sneaking up on Sandy on the Saturn-shaped Ferris wheel. In the absence of much dialogue or a score, visual cues provide the primary means of expressing the scene's tension and amplifying suspense. Within each section, mise-en-scene, cinematography, and editing highlight graphic contrasts, foreground movement, and punctuate shifts in the action, while the final section is most notable for its extreme pictorialism. Given a literal fun park to exploit, Fuller's aesthetic preferences burst through, assaulting the viewer in an exciting and often playful manner.

In the first section of the scene, aspects of mise-en-scene create visual conflict within the frame that helps to make Sandy stand out from the crowd, while framing and camera movement emphasize the kineticism of the chase. As Sandy bursts through the roof door and begins searching for a way out, he finds himself in a packed crowd but completely unable to blend in. His tall, thin figure, gray suit and fedora, and Caucasian features visibly contrast with the Japanese people around him. Most are women and children, and thus are of a much smaller stature, causing

Sandy's chest and face to rise above them wherever he goes. The majority of the parkgoers wear anachronistic kimonos and ceremonial garb, their bright hues of red, orange, and yellow encircling Sandy's gray suit and isolating him. Sandy's figure movement also clashes with his surroundings, as he frantically dashes through the crowd, climbing over benches and pushing through people in order to find a door or stairwell that will take him to safety. The Japanese adults, on the other hand, slowly stroll through the park, look around, or stand completely still, while the children hold balloons and cheer. Differences in color, volume, and movement within the frame thus separate Sandy from his environment and identify him as an interloper. Diegetic sound further contributes to the narrative tension produced by the graphic contrasts, as the languid carnival music playing over the loudspeakers ironically clashes with Sandy's desperation, while the cheers emanating from the children seem to express delight in his frustration. While other Fuller films employ visual and aural contrasts in a more shocking, assaultive manner, here conflicting elements appear in a graceful, integrated, yet expressive fashion, clearly apparent yet fully motivated.

As the segment continues, blocking and camera movement highlight motion within the frame, visually demonstrating that Sandy is being chased even though his pursuers have not yet arrived on the roof. Panning shots following Sandy as he runs through the crowd amplify his movement, while a run-in with a miniature train eventually enables the camera itself to chase Sandy, further heightening the segment's visceral nature. When Sandy jumps inside the track of the miniature train ride, he is literally followed by the children as he is forced to flee in front of their oncoming train. A cut then places the camera *on* the train, tracking forward in pursuit of Sandy. The children and their balloons sit facing away from the camera in the mid-ground, while Sandy runs from the train into the background, wildly looking behind him as he seeks to escape his pint-sized pursuers. Here Fuller has a laugh at Sandy's expense, positioning viewers as one of the children merrily chasing a strange-looking man. Yay! If only we had balloons! Motion within the frame is further emphasized as the train turns to the left and the camera pans to the right, following Sandy as he leaps over benches to safety. This portion of the segment playfully heightens the kineticism of the scene, visually illustrating Sandy's desperation while ironically involving harmless children—and even the viewers—as Sandy's pursuers.

The second segment begins after Sandy has climbed the Saturn-shaped Ferris wheel and again features movement and graphic contrasts that underscore a change in narrative action. Now Sandy has the upper hand, and the civilians who previously terrorized him become potential target practice. In an extreme long shot of the entire rooftop amusement park, the police swarm out of the central stairwell and the carnival music stops, punctuating the sudden shift in tone; the police begin to wave the crowd down off the roof, recognizing that they are sitting ducks for Sandy. A cut to a bird's-eye view of a single officer waving and yelling at the crowd rushing by him suggests Sandy's optical perspective when looking down from the wheel above. The dramatic change in shot scale, angle, and character size from shot to shot radically alters the viewer's perspective of the action, emphasizing the narrative reversal of power. High-angle shots continue as the dominant visual motif of this segment, highlighting the vulnerable position of the crowd as mothers and officers grab children and rush them offscreen to safety. A long shot of Sandy with his gun out, looking at the crowd from the horizontal Ferris wheel, cues the viewer to suspect that he may yet shoot, while extreme long shots of the entire park build suspense by revealing how many people are still running toward the exits. Where the graphic conflicts and kinetic effects in the previous segment illustrated Sandy's fear and confusion, the cinematography and figure movement in this segment return him to a position of power, conveying the vulnerability of the crowd and the police officers below.

After Eddie receives permission to go up to the roof and the final segment of the scene begins, the wheel ride becomes a key participant in the unfolding action; it is a jungle gym on and around which the characters play, an element within the CinemaScope frame that offers the potential for dynamic graphic play. The wheel ride is shaped like the planet Saturn, with a central globe surrounded by a horizontal, ring-like walkway; the globe and the walkway each rotate in opposing directions. Fuller exploits the width and depth of the widescreen frame to maximum effect, creating balanced and often symmetrical compositions of the interior globe that Sandy hides behind and the arc of the walkway that encircles it. Eyelines connect the space of Eddie and an officer hiding behind a guardhouse with that of Sandy on the walkway, and a cut into a medium closeup of Eddie—the closest shot of the scene—cues the viewer to suspect that he has an idea. Eddie begins to flank Sandy, preparing to jump onto the walkway on the opposite side of the globe. The composition and blocking in a subsequent shot amplify the suspense by graphically highlighting the opposition of the men. The shot begins slightly above and behind the ride on the roof, the foreground in the left-hand third of the frame dominated by the walkway rotating right while the inner globe rotates left. In the background lower-right corner of the frame Eddie is on the roof running left; as he runs, the camera pans left, the ride eventually obscuring Eddie but the pan revealing Sandy on the other side of the ride. The movement and compositional elements within the frame direct the viewer's gaze through space, from right to left, background to fore-

Samuel Fuller, chomping on a stogie, climbs down from the Saturn-shaped Ferris wheel that is the site of the climactic shoot-out at the end of *House of Bamboo*. The Ferris wheel—perched above an amusement park situated on a Tokyo rooftop—features a central rotating globe and a walkway that circles the globe in the opposite direction. *Chrisam Films, Inc.*

ground, lower corner to upper corner, and Eddie to Sandy; the ride itself becomes a graphic division, adding to the contrasts within the frame as it rotates in opposing directions. The visual conflicts developed in the mise-en-scene and cinematography from the very beginning of the scene unite here in one virtuoso shot, reinforcing the narrative tension between Eddie and Sandy.

The opposing directions of the globe and wheel rotations and the use of offscreen space transform Eddie's confrontation with Sandy into a visual game of hide and seek, culminating in one of Fuller's most pictorial shots. When Sandy ducks behind the globe clockwise, Eddie hops on the walkway heading in the opposite direction. As Eddie crawls toward Sandy, who is now unwittingly backing up toward him, the camera is behind Eddie on the rotating wheel. The effect is oddly disorienting, as the globe continues to rotate clockwise inside the walkway to the left of the frame while the rest of Tokyo appears to rotate around the walkway in the opposite direction above and to the right. The composition is weighted toward Eddie, who is crawling to the center of the frame from the lower right. The viewer expects Sandy to appear from the other side of the globe at any second, thus heightening suspense even as there is very little action within the frame. When Sandy finally appears shooting offscreen left at the police, Eddie shoots him from behind (Fuller never cared much about fighting fair) until Sandy slumps over the side of the walkway. Music rises on the soundtrack to punctuate the moment, but the emotional triumph of the narrative climax is undercut by its visual presentation.

As Eddie hops off the wheel, Sandy's limp body rotates past him, setting up a shot of the ride that functions solely as a pictorial image. In an extreme low-angle shot from beneath the ride, the globe is centered in the frame, rotating to the left, while the underside of the walkway arcs above in a perfect semicircle, rotating to the right and slowly carrying Sandy's dangling, gray body up and over and down the other side. The symmetry of the composition, grace of the movement, and opposing directions of the spinning, circular globe and ring become a pleasure in themselves, reducing Sandy to a compositional element and distancing the viewer from the killing. A pictorial distillation of the carefully crafted visual style that dominates the film, the final shot is a serene end to a scene in which graphic contrasts and movement within the frame are central components in the creation of tension and suspense. With the stylistic change evident in the last shot, Fuller again provides a visual counterpart to the narrative action: the plot's central conflict is resolved and the tension diffused, returning peace and harmony to the onscreen world as illustrated through the order, balance, and symmetry of the composition.

As indicated by these sample scenes, *House of Bamboo* is one of Fuller's most subtle yet visually rich films, utilizing cinematography and mise-en-scene in unexpected and delightful ways. While largely adhering to classical stylistic conventions, Fuller characteristically strives to emphasize conflict and kineticism and to mark shifts in tone and action; these strategies complement the development of the narrative and increase the viewer's emotional and visceral engagement with the film. *House of Bamboo* thus exemplifies Fuller's ability to adapt his aesthetic inclinations to varying production circumstances. With his previous experience shooting in Technicolor and CinemaScope and enthusiasm for the film's genre and location, Fuller had the creative confidence and control necessary to produce his most visually arresting studio picture.

Although *House of Bamboo* was an artistic triumph for Fuller, featured the same production values and action-based plotline as *Hell and High Water,* and even boasted an exotic locale and upper-tier stars, its release enjoyed only mixed success. *House of Bamboo* opened July 1, 1955 in New York City at the Mayfair, a 1,700-seat Broadway house, as well as in six other major cities, receiving above-average exhibitor ratings in all but one locale.[41] While noting its standard undercover cop storyline, reviews for the film in the trade and popular press were almost uniformly positive, especially focusing on the striking cinematography and Shirley Yamaguchi's performance.[42] Vincent Canby summed up trade predictions when he suggested *House of Bamboo* would "satisfy the action fan as well as the armchair traveler."[43] The film ranked tenth in box office its opening week, however, and stayed near the bottom of the top twelve the following three weeks during its initial wave of first-run debuts.[44] The following month brought moderately strong openings in additional cities, but by then the film had dropped off the list of top box-office winners. While *House of Bamboo* appeared to draw well initially, it did not have enough staying power for successful holdover runs. By October, it returned to Los Angeles on the bottom half of a double bill at two Fox West Coast theaters, a testament to the film's difficulty in finding an audience. *House of Bamboo*'s reported domestic gross of $1.7 million thus stood well below the receipts for Fox's other overseas extravaganzas in 1955, and foreign response to the film was also lukewarm, especially in Japan.[45] Barely earning more than its production cost, *House of Bamboo* was one of Fuller's greatest box-office disappointments. A beautifully shot film with action, stars, high production values, and the support of solid distribution and widespread publicity, it lacked only public interest.

*House of Bamboo* proved to be the beginning of the end of Fuller's association with Twentieth Century–Fox and studio filmmaking. Immediately following the film's completion, Fox exercised Fuller's next option; Fuller agreed to accelerate his start date and waive his right to work on an outside project in order to commence the screenplay for *Tigrero,* an original story about a tiger hunter involved in a love triangle in the jungles of South America that Fuller hoped would star John Wayne.[46] Following the failure of *House of Bamboo* and Fuller's scouting expedition for *Tigrero* through the Brazilian jungles, Fox notified Fuller in September 1955 that it was postponing the production of *Tigrero* due to insurance fears.[47] The day after his work finished on *Tigrero,* Fuller sent notice to Fox that he had received and accepted an outside offer made by

Columbia Pictures; in keeping with his contract, this commitment was limited to twenty-six weeks and would end in March 1956.[48] The actual existence and nature of Fuller's proposed commitment to Columbia remains unknown, as there is no evidence that he completed a script for the studio or made any deals for distribution of independent product with it before 1959. Fuller may simply have been claiming his right to time outside of the studio, regardless of whether he had an actual "outside commitment" or not, or he may have suggested an outside project as a bargaining chip, in order to demonstrate to Fox continued demand for his services by other studios.

In any event, when the end of his outside term arrived in March, Fuller requested a leave of absence for six months without compensation. While this move extended the length of Fuller's current contract with the studio, the parties agreed that Fuller would finish out the contract only by working on *Tigrero,* and if Fox did not desire to reassign him to the project or if he was unavailable at the requested time, then the balance of Fuller's unused term would be canceled.[49] Clearly signaling to Fox his desire to return to the studio only to complete his own projects, Fuller established his independent production company, Globe Enterprises, during his leave of absence, beginning preproduction on *Run of the Arrow* in April and setting up a distribution deal with RKO. In early August, before the end of Fuller's six-month leave, Fox notified the director that it would neither recall him for additional work on *Tigrero* nor exercise his next option.[50] That same summer, Darryl Zanuck followed Fuller's leave and left Twentieth Century–Fox to become an independent producer. While Fuller's departure from Twentieth Century–Fox was not the result of a particular wave of payroll cuts, it was in keeping with general trends toward studio downsizing in the 1950s, as well as Fuller's desire to direct his own scripts.[51]

Fuller's split from Twentieth Century–Fox in 1956 marked the end of his early involvement with big-budget filmmaking and the continuation of his quest for production control. The factors contributing to the termination of his employment suggest both possible studio impatience with Fuller and a conscious effort by the director to escape his contract. Perhaps responding to Fox's lack of confidence in *Tigrero* and its rejection of *Woman with a Whip* and *Run of the Arrow* or perhaps frustrated by the difficulty of juggling studio films with outside work, Fuller seems to have consciously decided to throw his eggs in the independent production basket.

While at Fox, Fuller demonstrated an ability to craft tightly plotted, beautifully photographed A pictures, but his own desire to devote more energy to his personal projects eventually pulled him back into lower-budget filmmaking. His tenure at Fox had increased the size and scope of his pictures and had raised his stature within the industry, providing him with a steady paycheck and a largely positive track record of tough, action-oriented films that could bolster his ability to form financing and distribution deals as an independent. Leaving Fox meant temporarily leaving behind major stars, higher production values, and overseas shooting, but Fuller appeared willing to move back into the world of programmers if he could both direct and produce the movies he wrote— something he was entirely unable to do at Fox.

# CHAPTER THREE

# The Globe Years, 1956–1961

●●● n the five years following his departure from Fox, Fuller pro-
 ● duced films through Globe Enterprises, an independent com-
●●● pany in which he had a 50 percent stake and complete control
over production.[1] Fuller served as producer, director, and writer of his
Globe pictures and signed single and multiple picture contracts with
RKO, Twentieth Century–Fox, and Columbia for financing and distribution. Fuller had big plans for Globe, hoping the company would
eventually branch out into television and produce six films a year by a
variety of directors.[2] During this period Fuller stretched his aesthetic
muscles, completing projects such as *Run of the Arrow* and *Forty Guns,*
which were terminated while he was under contract at Fox, and freeing
himself from the classical "quality controls" that so shaped his studio
releases. His narratives were more loosely constructed, often contained
politically or socially charged content, and featured jarring tonal shifts
and offbeat displays of humor. His visual style was likewise more varied, combining extended long takes during conversation scenes with
rapid editing during action. Conflict and kineticism came to the fore,
often in sensationalistic ways.

While Globe provided Fuller with much greater control over his own
material than he had at Fox and saddled him with less financial risk than
he carried making *Park Row,* he still relied on steady box office returns
in order to attract financing and distribution agreements. In the late
1950s, as the market for programmers continued to constrict, steady box
office was difficult to find. Producers were primarily making action-
oriented films as blockbusters with big budgets, major stars, exotic locations, color, and widescreen, while low-budget filmmaking became increasingly dominated by exploitation pictures designed to appeal to the
youth market. Television became the new home for inexpensive genre
narratives that could appeal to the whole family. Fuller responded to
these industrial trends by largely staying the course, producing offbeat
action films from original scripts while ratcheting up the sex and violence. Although both Twentieth Century–Fox and Columbia appear to

have contemplated four Fuller releases each, poor box office led to only two films being distributed by each company, while RKO completely dissolved during the production of *Verboten!* and neither of the television pilots shot by Fuller were picked up. By 1961, Globe Enterprises was effectively finished.

## The Challenges of Independence

As it became less expensive and less risky during the 1950s for the major studios to finance and distribute films made by outside producers, the centralized production of the studio system gave way to individually packaged films, increasing the number of "independent" pictures and multiplying the power of talented directors, agents, and stars. Under the new system, a producer brought together a story, financing, cast, crew, production facilities, and materials, relying on the major studios only for financing and/or distribution. A significant amount of time went into developing each project, as producers no longer relied on the studios to provide all the talent and equipment—now the means of production had to be assembled fresh for each film. The difficulty of orchestrating all of the necessary elements of production meant that films frequently collapsed before they were ever shot, forcing producers to develop multiple projects simultaneously in order to maintain consistent output.[3]

Although independent producers faced common responsibilities and challenges, their administrative power and creative freedom varied widely. Independent producers made a single feature or at most a few films a year; they had no direct corporate relationship to a distributor, although they might have had an ongoing distribution contract.[4] While many variations of independent production flourished in the 1950s and 1960s, a 1957 article in *Motion Picture Herald* identified three main types of indies based on their financing arrangements.[5] Total independents financed their own productions with their own money and enjoyed the most complete autonomy. Because few had the long-term careers of men like Samuel Goldwyn or Walt Disney, however, this form of independent production was the most rare. The second group of indie producers invested some of their own money into production, along with the advance granted by the distributor of the film. Members of this group had widely varying degrees of autonomy depending on the level of their investment and contract stipulations. The third arrangement, and also the most common, included independent producers who obtained their entire financing from distributors and who therefore were bound by whatever controls the distributor stipulated. These producers shouldered the least financial risk but also wielded the least power.

Because of financing and contractual arrangements, the actual independence of independent producers could be quite circumscribed.[6] When considering loan requests for independent productions, banks considered the track record and fiscal responsibility of the producer, the experience of the director, the reputations of the cast and crew, and the box-office potential of the film. Banks required a distribution contract and completion bond even before negotiations began and often reserved approval of the script, cast, and budget.[7] As a result, film packages with untested directors, unknown casts, or highly controversial subjects typically had a difficult time receiving financing. In addition, independent producers had to adhere to distributor contracts that specified preferred running times, PCA requirements, and the right of the distributor to re-edit the film for television or foreign exhibition; some contractual arrangements granted distributors even further creative control and the final cut. The financing and distribution system for independent productions therefore rarely resulted in big-budget films that operated outside of classical norms; more offbeat fare required the producer to assume a greater share of the financial risk and to demonstrate a viable market for the film.

Independent producers thus found long-term survival in the marketplace quite risky and were often forced to spend more time securing financing than actually making movies. While indie producers gained some flexibility and creative control, most nevertheless still relied on the banks and major studios for cofinancing, production resources, and access to distribution and first-run exhibition. In addition, since independent producers usually deferred their salaries in return for up to 50 percent of the profits, they only made money if their films made money—and over half of all films did not. Directors who functioned as their own producers, as Fuller frequently did, therefore found themselves more reliant on box-office success as an independent than most were accustomed to as contract directors for studios or smaller independent outfits. A series of films that failed as A features or proved too expensive to return a profit through distribution as Bs could cost an independent producer financing and distribution for subsequent films.

Despite the reduction of B releases by the major and minor studios, the need to fill double bills maintained the market for very low-budget films into the early 1960s. Programmers, rather than true Bs, faced the greater challenge at the box office, both at home and abroad. The studios' move toward blockbuster films with high production values made it more difficult for "in-betweeners" to compete as A product—especially within action-adventure genres, now tracking toward the epic—while the flat rental rates awarded to the programmer demoted to the bottom half of the bill virtually guaranteed a profit loss.[8] As the market in the mid-1950s increasingly split into high-budget and very low-budget tracks, Columbia, Universal, and United Artists released a handful of highly successful low-budget films, and by 1956 Twentieth Century–Fox, MGM, Republic, and Allied Artists also began producing or distributing a limited number of inexpensive black-and-white pictures.[9] Typically featuring CinemaScope for added production value, these films fit neatly into the western, horror, crime, and science fiction genres, as well as the fastest-growing genre of them all, the teenpic.

Rapidly becoming a powerful presence in the consumer marketplace, teenagers formed the target audience for budget filmmakers in the 1950s and 1960s. In response to the astonishing success of producer Sam Katzman's *Rock Around the Clock* (1956), low-budget outfits such as American International Pictures (AIP) cranked out topical movies for the youth market in genres indebted to traditional B films. Recognizing the difficulty in turning a profit by distributing B pictures for a flat rental fee, AIP bundled inexpensive action-oriented films into same-genre double bills and sold them to states' rights franchises as a unit for a percentage of the box office. Arguing that the market for mid-budget films had dried up, the company positioned itself to fill exhibitor needs in between screenings of blockbusters.[10] The sensational advertising used by AIP and like-minded producers prompted *Variety* to categorize their product as teen exploitation: "These are low-budget films based on controversial and timely subjects that make newspaper headlines. In the main, these pictures appeal to 'uncontrolled' juveniles and 'undesireables.'"[11]

The difficulty of surviving in the low-budget market without appealing to teens is illustrated by the struggles of director Robert Aldrich's independent production company, Associates and Aldrich, during the late 1950s. The financial success of his first pictures as a director, *Apache* (1954), *Vera Cruz* (1954), and *Kiss Me Deadly* (1955), enabled Aldrich to form Associates and to continue his involvement with United Artists, the distributor of his first three films.[12] After its retrenchment in 1951, UA began an aggressive campaign of offering independent producers complete production financing, creative autonomy, and profit sharing in exchange for distribution.[13] Aldrich's proven ability to deliver profitable films on time and under budget convinced UA to finance and distribute the Associates and Aldrich productions *The Big Knife* (1955), an adaptation of a scathing Clifford Odets's play about Hollywood, and *Attack* (1956), a grim World War II combat picture, both budgeted for less than $500,000. Neither film made money, however, and after a disastrous three years spent clashing with Harry Cohn while under contract at Columbia, Aldrich found himself nearing bankruptcy by the end of the decade.[14] When UA pulled financing for his dream project, *Taras Bulba*, a Nikolai Gogol adaptation slated to star Anthony Quinn, Aldrich was forced to direct television dramas and to freelance in Europe. Despite his desire to produce more artistic projects, Aldrich's slide from box-office success to near bankruptcy in the 1950s convinced him to pursue a production strategy in the 1960s geared toward generating secure returns and guaranteeing his ability to make the next picture. "If I weren't wearing both hats, I'd like to make a picture that would free Angela Davis," he said. "But I don't want the producer part of me to lose so much money that he can't make the next one."[15] By recognizing his reliance on box-office returns and developing multiple properties at a time, Aldrich kept his independent production company afloat for seventeen years and fourteen films, eventually making multimillion dollar action-adventures such as *The Flight of the Phoenix* (1965) and *The Dirty Dozen* (1967). Although his films did not directly appeal to the teen market, Aldrich's hard-headed realism kept him working when many of his postwar low-budget contemporaries, including Fuller, struggled to complete pictures.

By the early 1960s, the market for low-budget B films was increasingly restricted to the bottom half of the few remaining double bills at first-run theaters and to the secondary-run and drive-in circuit. Programmers and medium-budget films continued to be made but were rapidly becoming "a vanishing breed."[16] The examples of Associates and Aldrich and AIP suggest that in order to find bookings and make a profit, smaller companies and independent producers either had to craft accessible films with guaranteed returns or had to stay one step ahead of the major and minor studios through exploitation of gimmicks and cutting-edge cultural trends. If producers competed directly with the studios in popular genres, then stars, larger budgets, and higher production values were necessary for success. In addition, films that appealed to teens through the use of youth-oriented actors, genres, or humor—as demonstrated in those pictures released by AIP—sported an advantage in the low-budget market, both due to the high percentage of youth in the moviegoing population and to their preference for double bills and drive-ins, now the primary homes of low-budget material.[17] As Fuller ventured into independent production in the late 1950s, his best bets for box-office success were thus glossy, star-filled blockbusters or lower-budget, topical teenpics; instead, he largely took the middle path, producing programmers for adults despite the limitations of the market.

### *No Holds Barred:* Run of the Arrow, China Gate, Forty Guns, *and* Verboten!

Fuller's first Globe picture, *Run of the Arrow,* originated as a script Fox declined to produce; it went into production with RKO in the summer of 1956, even before Fuller's option contract with Fox was officially termi-

nated. RKO greatly reduced studio output during the 1950s and was relying heavily on independent product to keep itself afloat. In his autobiography, Fuller describes pitching RKO studio head William Dozier, who
greenlit *Run of the Arrow* subject to approval of the principal cast. Although Dozier lobbied for Gary Cooper to play the lead, a Yankee-hating
Southerner who heads west after the Civil War, Fuller fought hard for up-
and-comer Rod Steiger, as his "sour face" more accurately suggested the
character's status as a "sore loser."[18] Fuller shot *Run of the Arrow* in
Technicolor and masked widescreen for five weeks on location near
St. George, Utah, with a budget of $1 million, his highest for any Globe
production.[19] The film teamed Fuller with cinematographer Joseph Biroc,
a veteran of Robert Aldrich and John Ford films, and editor Gene Fowler,
Jr., who previously cut for Fritz Lang; both men continued to work with
Fuller on his Globe pictures for Twentieth Century–Fox, *China Gate* and
*Forty Guns*. As was his tendency, Fuller grounded his ideas for *Run of the
Arrow* in substantive research, seeking to portray the Sioux in a more re-
spectful and realistic fashion than was the norm in Hollywood. The
official press release differentiates the film from others in the genre by describing it as "an epic Western which has nothing to do with cowboys,
rustlers, dishonest sheriffs or pretty schoolteachers. . . . [I]t is one of the
few motion pictures to bring to the screen American Indian life with complete authenticity."[20]

With its unified plot structure, focus on the legacy of the Civil War
and Sioux culture, and mediating female character who is a romantic
helpmate, *Run of the Arrow* does in fact engage genre conventions—particularly those circulating in post–Civil War cavalry and American Indian pictures like John Ford's *Fort Apache* (1948)—and it does so more
fully than Fuller's other westerns. The film begins with O'Meara
(Steiger), a Confederate soldier, firing the last shot of the Civil War before he hears of Lee's surrender. O'Meara merely wounds the Union soldier, Driscoll (Ralph Meeker), and bitterly holds onto the warped bullet,
an ugly reminder of what he views as the South's capitulation. Refusing
to live under Yankee dominion, O'Meara heads west to the frontier,
where he meets an aging Sioux army scout (Jay C. Flippen) who teaches
him the ways of his tribe. The two are set upon by a young Sioux war-
rior, Crazy Wolf (H. M. Wynant), who challenges them to the run of the
arrow, a footrace in which a barefoot runner is given a head start equal
to the length of an arrow in flight. The Sioux scout collapses during the
run, but O'Meara outpaces Crazy Wolf and is ultimately hidden by Yellow Moccasin (Sarita Montiel), a Sioux maiden. O'Meara and Yellow
Moccasin marry, and O'Meara is welcomed into the Sioux community
by its chief, Blue Buffalo (Charles Bronson). When the United States and
the Sioux sign a peace treaty, O'Meara is hired as a scout attached to an

army fort. He finds Blue Buffalo's wisdom and tolerance mirrored in Captain Clark (Brian Keith), the soldier in command of the army detachment, but Clark is killed by Crazy Wolf, leaving O'Meara's Civil War nemesis, Lieutenant Driscoll, in charge. O'Meara forces Crazy Wolf to answer for Clark's death through the run of the arrow, but hotheaded Driscoll interferes with the run and shoots Crazy Wolf, prompting the Sioux to attack the army fort. The Sioux burn the fort and proceed to skin Driscoll alive, until O'Meara responds by putting a bullet in the lieutenant's head—the same bullet he tried to kill Driscoll with at the beginning of the film. Rethinking where his loyalties lie, O'Meara heads east with Yellow Moccasin at the close of the picture, accompanied by the final title: "The end of this story can only be written by you."

*Run of the Arrow* is one of Fuller's most overt explorations of identity and allegiance and makes strong use of motifs and parallels to structure narrative meaning. O'Meara attempts to enact the myth of the frontier as an opportunity for renewal and reinvention, but his past proves difficult to shake. Though he finds love and purpose among the Sioux, he hesitates with the question they repeatedly ask him: "Would you kill an American in battle?" As is typical of Fuller's female helpmates, Yellow Moccasin figures it out first, telling O'Meara: "You will always be unhappy as a Sioux. You were born an American." O'Meara is left unable to deny the values that have shaped him; he embraces the ritual nobility of the run of the arrow, but draws the line at flaying a man alive. Fuller carefully charts O'Meara's struggle through the motifs of the run and the bullet, each of which appear twice in the narrative. During the runs of the arrow, O'Meara is first victim of the Sioux and then defender of Sioux honor; as the assailant of Driscoll, O'Meara shoots initially in anger and finally in pity—he is not Sioux, after all, but American. The pairings of Blue Buffalo–Captain Clark and Crazy Wolf–Driscoll underline O'Meara's ultimate choice as one based not on an assumption of cultural superiority, but rather on the recognition of innate identity: both the Sioux and the Americans are capable of producing men of reason and men of hatred. With his open-ended epilogue, Fuller reminds viewers that it is up to us to champion reason over hatred, to heal ourselves as a step toward healing our own nations.

*Run of the Arrow* marks a return to a less classical visual style for Fuller, and he adopts a variety of stylistic strategies to provoke viewers both intellectually and emotionally. Gone is the tendency, most evident in *Hell and High Water*, to construct scenes with full coverage, cutting from establishing shots to medium shots and in to close-ups for emphasis. Instead, Fuller intercuts shots of varying distance from the camera in more unusual scene dissection. Six scenes contain extreme long takes of over a minute and a half, a length far exceeding Hollywood's widescreen average shot length of nine to twelve seconds. As with the exceptional four-minute, forty-two-second shot of Captain Clark telling O'Meara why it is important to fight for the United States, these lengthy takes tend to be largely static and reserved for weighty discussions that explore the film's central themes. By stripping the frame of movement and competing points of interest, Fuller forces the viewer to focus on the conversations at hand; his confidence in his message seems to outweigh any fear of viewer boredom. Long takes are balanced throughout the film by visceral sequences more reliant on editing, a dynamic last seen in *Park Row.* The constructive editing Fuller used in the openings of *I Shot Jesse James, The Steel Helmet,* and *Pickup on South Street* becomes central to his presentation of the run of the arrow, while the most brutal sequence in the film, the skinning of Driscoll, relies heavily on montage to represent indirectly that which cannot be explicitly shown.

The presentation of Crazy Wolf's pursuit of O'Meara and the old Sioux scout during the first run of the arrow is a prime example of Fuller's ongoing tendency to use constructive editing, match cuts, and graphic contrasts in order to create dynamic sequences of expressive motion. Fuller intercuts tracking medium shots of each man, framed from the waist down running from right to left. Each pair of legs is centered in the frame, producing a series of matching shots and making the identity of each man ambiguous. Rather than clarifying who is who and how far away the men are from each other—a logical choice during a chase scene—the editing and framing primarily function to create pairs of legs that are mirror images and to emphasize motion itself. Fuller was especially fond of depicting disembodied legs running or walking, and similar sequences appear in *The Steel Helmet, Fixed Bayonets, Forty Guns, The Crimson Kimono, Underworld, U.S.A.,* and *Dead Pigeon on Beethoven Street.*

In addition to the two runs of the arrow, the most heavily edited scene in the film is the attack on the army fort and the skinning of Driscoll. Here Fuller utilizes visual ellipses, constructive editing, quick cuts, and offscreen sound in order to address PCA objections to the scene's brutality while still exploiting its sensational impact. PCA administrator Geoffrey Shurlock objected to the torture and death of Lieutenant Driscoll in the script of *Run of the Arrow* as "a justification of mercy killing" and claimed it was too much "dramatized": "It is one thing to establish this inhuman torture and another thing to revert constantly to close-ups of Driscoll's face showing the excruciating agony of the man."[21] The sequence as it appears in the film obligingly avoids constant close-ups of Driscoll, while nevertheless featuring editing and sound that actually intensify the suspense and thrills of the sequence. The scene immediately highlights Driscoll's torture and impending execution by opening with a

Samuel Fuller directs (left to right) Rod Steiger as O'Meara, Ralph Meeker as Lieutenant Driscoll, and Chuck Roberson as a cavalry sergeant on location in St. George, Utah, for *Run of the Arrow. Author's Collection*

high-angle shot that cranes down as the Sioux tie Driscoll to a stake and rip his shirt open. A cut to a medium-close shot focuses attention on Driscoll's face as Crazy Wolf slices the lieutenant's throat, producing a stream of Technicolor blood. Driscoll screams, cueing a series of cutaways to O'Meara and the Sioux. O'Meara repeatedly turns away in close-up, with Driscoll's agonized cries echoing across each shot. O'Meara finally takes out his bullet, silently loads his gun, and shoots; in an extreme close-up, Driscoll's sweaty, bloodied face recoils as a whiff of smoke marks the entry of the bullet into his head. The entire sequence lasts nearly a minute and a half, with Driscoll's wailing covering two-thirds of the sequence.

By cutting away to O'Meara's reaction shots as well as those of Blue Buffalo watching O'Meara watching Driscoll, the sequence actually prolongs Driscoll's agony, encouraging the viewer to speculate how he is being tortured. While close-ups of Driscoll's face would have underlined his pain, emphasizing O'Meara's reaction more effectively suggests a torture of unspeakable dimensions, one so heinous that it prompts O'Meara to break his pledge of loyalty to the Sioux and take pity on a man he despises. The final close-up of Driscoll, quite graphic in its specificity, further underlines the horror of the torture—if putting a bullet in a man's forehead is an act of pity, then the alternative must truly be foul. As enacted in the film, Shurlock's suggestion neither softened the brutality of the sequence nor toned down the mercy killing; if anything, both points were intensified by the alternatives Fuller chose. Because of its use of stylistic techniques that heighten the impression of extreme suffering, this sequence is an excellent example of how Fuller's films often bypassed PCA restrictions through indirect representation in order to retain their visceral impact. Critics duly noted the shocking power of the violence, with *Variety* describing the film as "pretty rough at times, especially for the squeamish."[22]

*Run of the Arrow* was the best positioned of all of Fuller's Globe pictures to achieve box-office success. The cast, use of Technicolor, and location photography lent the film top-flight production values, while its promotional campaign stressed its originality. In addition, the film enjoyed an extended release accompanied by a national advertising campaign indicative of its intended status as an A picture. With steady first-run distribution by Universal-International on behalf of RKO, the film played a range of downtown houses, drive-ins, and neighborhood theaters from July to November 1957. During its initial month of release, full-page ads ran in *Look* and *Life,* and a national billboard campaign targeted sixty-nine major markets in support of a saturation booking strategy.[23] The film modestly premiered first-run in two small seaters and two drive-ins in Kansas City, booked with a pair of second-run RKO releases. Exhibitors reported that the box office "looks good," and critics gave *Run of the Arrow* acceptable and even enthusiastic reviews, particularly noting the Technicolor bloodletting and the film's appeal to the outdoor market.[24] The film opened the following week at the 1,700-seat Palace in New York City and subsequently played across the country, consistently screening solo or at the top of first-run double bills but meeting with mixed response.[25] During the week of August 21, *Run of the Arrow* reached its highest position in national box office, ranking thirteenth despite only fair reports from major exhibitors. Absent from *Variety*'s list of films grossing more than $1 million in 1957, *Run of the Arrow* in all likelihood did not break even.[26] While the film received steady distribution, its expensive price tag set the box-office bar too high for a western lacking star power, thereby effectively ending Fuller's access to million-dollar budgets as an independent producer.

After Fuller completed postproduction on *Run of the Arrow,* he made a financing and distribution deal that reteamed him with Twentieth Century–Fox and Robert Lippert. In the mid-1950s, Fox began increasingly to rely on independent producers for its product and to reconsider the value of low-budget filmmaking. With double bills continuing and location shooting leaving studio sound stages bare, Fox contracted with Lippert in August 1956 to supervise the production of seven black-and-white 'Scope pictures budgeted between $100,000 and $110,000 under the banner of Regal Films, Inc.[27] Lippert's first Regal title, *Stagecoach to Fury* (1956), made a healthy profit and demonstrated the potential of the low-budget film during an era dominated by multimillion-dollar extravaganzas. In January 1957, Fox extended Lippert's contract for an additional sixteen pictures "with exploitation angles" budgeted between $125,000 and $250,000, including two by Fuller at the high end of the scale.[28] Under the terms of the contract that applied to Fuller, the entire negative costs of the Regal films would be covered by loans from the Bank of America; the net receipts for each film would go half to Regal and half to Fox in perpetuity. The agreement also stipulated that Fox "may make such modifications, additions, or deletions in the picture[s] as it may deem necessary or desirable," and required all films to adhere to the Production Code and receive an A or B rating by the Legion of Decency, a Catholic ratings organization.[29] Finally, Fox reserved the right to approve story and cast and requested the films be shot on Fox studio property, using some studio equipment.[30] The Regal agreement thus provided Fox with B pictures that filled the bottom half of double bills and made efficient use of studio resources, much like Bs during the studio era.

In 1957, Fuller produced two Globe films for Regal that were distributed through Fox: *China Gate* and *Forty Guns;* they were the most expensive films covered by the Regal-Fox agreement, falling into the programmer category. Under Globe's production and distribution deal with Regal, Globe received a share of Regal's percentage of a film's net profits, less a $25,000 advance and any costs associated with profit participation or screenplay purchase.[31] According to the agreement covering *Forty Guns,* for example, of the 50 percent share of the net profits owed to Regal, Globe received 80 percent of the first $100,000, 75 percent of the next $50,000, 70 percent of the next $50,000, etc.; for anything in excess of a million dollars in profits, Globe would receive a flat 50 percent of Regal's net receipts. Out of Globe's percentage of the profits also came repayment of the $25,000 advance, the $46,500 cost of purchasing the screenplay from Fox, and Barbara Stanwyck's 2.5 percent profit participation.[32] Fuller's agreement with Regal and Fox provided him with complete financing, distribution, and a share of the profits, as well as access to Fox's backlots and soundstages, equipment, and technical personnel. In exchange, Fuller agreed to lower budgets, major cast approval, and the potential for distributor meddling.

After directing A pictures with substantial production resources, Fuller returned to comparatively low-budget filmmaking with *China Gate*. A war adventure set in Vietnam but shot in black-and-white CinemaScope on Fox sound stages, *China Gate* went into production in January 1957 with a budget of $285,000, less than a third of the cost of *Run of the Arrow*.[33] The cast included singing sensation Nat "King" Cole and two relative newcomers, Gene Barry and pre–*Rio Bravo* (1959) Angie Dickinson. *China Gate* finds Fuller revisiting the war genre with the story of a biracial woman who leads a group of French Foreign Legion soldiers to destroy a Communist ammunition dump in Vietnam. Drawing on narrative elements reminiscent of *The Steel Helmet*, Fuller continues his exploration of race and the promise of America while incorporating more tonal discontinuity than seen in *Run of the Arrow*. With stunning widescreen cinematography second only to *House of Bamboo*, *China Gate* illustrates the primary visual strategies adopted by Fuller as he transitioned back into low-budget filmmaking.

As in *Hell and High Water* and *House of Bamboo*, *China Gate* opens with expository narration designed to situate the film's fictional action within historical fact. Stock footage sketches the rise of Ho Chi Minh in Vietnam and the threat produced by the Communist underground arsenal located in the northern region known as the China Gate. A hundred miles south lies a bombed-out village that "fights as it starves," the home of our protagonist, Lea (Dickinson), and her young son. Half Caucasian and half Chinese, Lea runs a saloon and is friendly with both sides of the conflict; her son's father, Brock (Barry), is out of the picture, an American soldier in the French Foreign Legion who married Lea but repudiated their child when he was born with Chinese features. Legion officers approach Lea to lead an expedition to the China Gate and blow up the ammunition dump that is fueling the Viet Minh's efforts; her friendship with the Communist fighters and their leader, Major Cham (Lee Van Cleef), will help smooth the way. Lea accepts their offer in exchange for getting her son to America; the only catch is that her son-of-a-bitch husband is coming along, his disdain for her and their son balanced by the loving attention of Goldie (Cole), an African-American veteran of the Big Red One. The expedition group makes its way north, hiding under the cover of Lea's cognac smuggling and dodging Viet Minh patrols and booby traps. At night, the men reveal their backstories, while Lea and Brock fight their continuing attraction and Brock his lingering racism. At the China Gate, Lea visits Cham, a former schoolteacher who was once her lover and now has his eye on the Viet Minh Politburo. Cham proposes to Lea and offers to take her child to Moscow for schooling; he takes her on a tour of the ammo dump to show her "why it is logical you should marry me." Lea responds by

Brock (Gene Barry, center) and Lea (Angie Dickinson, glancing over Brock's shoulder) lead French Foreign Legionnaires through the Vietnamese jungle in a publicity still from *China Gate*. The love affair that rekindles between Lea and Brock is haunted by Brock's racism. *Author's Collection*

shoving Cham off a balcony and revealing the location of the dump to the French expedition. Brock has a change of heart and tells Lea he wants them to be a family again, but when the expedition's munitions fail, Lea sacrifices herself to set off the explosion. Brock, Goldie, and the dying French captain barely manage to escape, and the picture closes with Cole crooning the film's melancholy theme song as Brock walks into the distance, holding hands with his young son.

In its narrative structure and thematic development, *China Gate* is best viewed as an extension of *The Steel Helmet* and *Run of the Arrow.* As with *The Steel Helmet, China Gate* is the story of a military patrol on a mission, newly differentiated by its female protagonist, her personal motivation, and the relative newness of the Vietnam conflict to American fiction film. Both films are structured with alternating sequences of action and reflection, but in *China Gate*, rather than emphasizing what his characters learn through warfare—the harsh lessons of *The Steel Helmet*—Fuller focuses more on what characters learn through conversation—the paradox of America that carries over most directly from *Run of the Arrow* but was present even in *The Steel Helmet*. Fuller offers several images of America: the innate bigotry of Brock that is redeemed by love, the tough-yet-caring wisdom of Goldie, and Lea's dream of a place where her child has a chance. As in his earlier pictures, Fuller suggests that America does not always live up to its ideals, but the fight for those ideals is what is most important. His pro-American stance becomes that much more explicit in *China Gate* through the contrast provided by Major Cham and the alternative life he offers Lea and her boy. As is true of the North Korean major in *The Steel Helmet*, Cham's arguments are dictated by logic, but it is a logic that kills. Moscow's gifts to the Vietnamese are bombs and death; by sacrificing herself to send her boy to America, Lea opts for the promise of life.

While Fuller's attraction to irony runs continuously through his works, his use of unexpected contradictions to create dark humor reemerges in several lively instances in *China Gate* after being put on temporary hold during *Run of the Arrow*. These moments of dark humor occur at the dialogue level—as when, recalling lines from both *Pickup on South Street* and *The Steel Helmet*, a dying soldier tells his comrades, "Let there be a heaven, for it would kill me to have to come back here again"—and also on the level of plot and style. A vivid example occurs when a soldier entertains his fellow Foreign Legionnaires one night with stories from his life in France, acting out his old job as a traffic policeman. Nondiegetic sound effects of him stopping and starting the traffic add to the lighthearted tone of the scene. Just as the soldier happily explains that he stays in the Legion because "this is the way to live," he is riddled with bullets by an unseen sniper. Upbeat comedy and joy quickly turn to surprise and horror. The soldier's last words, already ironic due to his job—killing for survival—attain an additional layer of irony as they mark the moment of his death. By juxtaposing elements that sharply contrast in meaning or tone, Fuller's scripts shock viewers in thrilling and often disturbing ways, prompting us to do a mental double take. Similar scenes that use contradictory dialogue and tonal contrasts for dark humor multiply in Fuller's subsequent Globe releases.

The visual style of *China Gate* likewise expands upon Fuller's previous work while anticipating the strategies that become dominant during his subsequent low-budget phase. After *House of Bamboo*, *China Gate* features Fuller's most stunning use of CinemaScope. In scenes such as the introduction of Lea's village, Brock's visit to Lea at home, and Chan's unveiling of the ammunition dump, Fuller and cinematographer Joseph Biroc skillfully arrange multiple points of interest across the frame in the foreground, midground, and background, using blocking, lighting, frontality, and movement to direct the viewer's gaze and emphasize the emotional beats within the narrative. In their ability to visually summarize the conflict inherent in a scene, these shots recall the work of James Wong Howe on *The Baron of Arizona* and Joe MacDonald on *Pickup on South Street* and *House of Bamboo*. Also contributing to the emotional expressivity of scenes is editor Gene Fowler, Jr.'s insistence on squaring Fuller's economical shooting practices with classical editing conventions. Fowler aggressively incorporates optical zooms and close-ups into Fuller's long-take master shots throughout the film during moments of emotional significance, while constructing sequences featuring a limited number of camera setups in a manner that emphasizes the development and resolution of narrative action. These strategies explain the absence of the one-minute-plus long takes that slowed the narrative pace of *Run of the Arrow,* and they remain a part of Fuller's aesthetic even after Fowler leaves his team.

Although *China Gate* was top-heavy with neither stars nor production values, its ninety-six-minute running time and the promotional push and strong first-run distribution orchestrated by Fox suggest that its producers and distributor intended it to be a breakout "in-betweener." Fox provided the film with a $125,000 budget for a national publicity campaign—more than twice the ad budget for other Regal films—including a San Francisco premiere at the 4,700-seat Fox Theater, personal appearances by Gene Barry and Nat "King" Cole, and print, radio, and television ads.[34] While the film opened "strong" in its premiere frame and played solo or at the top of the bill in prime houses in eighteen key cities throughout its month-long first run, box office was underwhelming and holdovers rare.[35] An exhibitor report from *China Gate*'s opening-week booking in Minneapolis summarizes the consensus: "Nothing in cast names or too much otherwise to bring 'em in. Poor." Reviews appear to have helped little, with favorable notices for the action scenes and central performances but widespread criticism of the contrived plotline and didactic, dialogue-heavy passages.[36] By September, *China Gate* was screening in Buffalo at the bottom of the bill. While *China Gate*'s impressive cinematography, Vietnam setting, female protagonist, and blatant anti-Communism distinguished it from other action offerings, content alone was not enough to sell the film. Once again, *China Gate* demonstrated the difficulties of producing a successful programmer in the late 1950s.

Fuller's follow-up, *Forty Guns,* was his most audacious assault on classical and generic conventions up to this point in his career, and its originality of conceit, freewheeling narrative, and sensational visual style anticipate the direction of his subsequent pictures. The film concerns a Wyatt Earp–like federal marshal who becomes personally and professionally entangled with a land baroness; both have younger siblings whose hijinks further complicate the relationship. The plot juggles sev-

eral romances, grudges, behind-the-scenes corruption, and enough action to result in four murders, a suicide, and a serious maiming. At the
core of the narrative is another of Fuller's impossible conflicts: the marshal and the land baroness love each other, but the marshal has cracked
down on the baroness's empire and threatened the younger brother she
has vowed to protect. *Forty Guns* was originally written during Fuller's
tenure at Fox, and Darryl Zanuck's notes on the rejected script pinpoint
some of the difficulties Fuller encountered when attempting to adapt his
character and narrative interests to a studio western. The script's larger-
than-life female protagonist, criminal elements, multiple plotlines, and
romantic rivalry threaten classical and genre conventions at every turn.
Although in his autobiography Fuller describes his honest intention to
dramatize America's fascination with guns and violence,[37] *Forty Guns*
contains none of the didacticism of *Run of the Arrow* or *China Gate*. Instead, the film is loopy and visceral entertainment—astonishing, funny,
and triumphantly Fuller.

Fuller first wrote *Forty Guns* as *Woman with a Whip* in 1953, his
third original screenplay delivered to Twentieth Century–Fox as part of
his option contract. Fox's production head, Darryl Zanuck, wrote detailed notes on Fuller's first-draft continuity but set aside the decision of
whether or not to develop the script until Fuller completed his writing
and directing assignment on *Hell and High Water*. Immediately after *Hell
and High Water* wrapped production, Fox declined to purchase *Woman
with a Whip*.[38] Fuller began resurrecting the screenplay almost immediately after finishing shooting *China Gate*. Regal purchased the script
rights from Fox for Globe, and Fuller convinced Barbara Stanwyck to
star alongside Barry Sullivan. While *Forty Guns* was originally budgeted
at $353,000, its production costs rose to $429,000 due to an increase in
cast size and unforeseen expenses, making it by far the most expensive of
the Regal-Fox pictures.[39]

Zanuck's original notes suggest several reasons why Fox may have decided not to produce *Woman with a Whip*. The studio was in the middle
of unrolling its first slate of CinemaScope pictures, and all of the films to
be shot in 1953 had already been selected and their budgets assigned.[40]
In addition, Zanuck had problems swallowing the overall plot of
*Woman with a Whip*, the multiple villains, and the characterization of
Alamo, the land baroness. The original treatment Fuller provided
Zanuck outlined a story about conflict between the legendary Earp
brothers. Zanuck found this basic theme greatly diffused in the first-draft
continuity, overshadowed by subplots involving Tombstone's sheriff,
Alamo's crooked dealings and political power, and gratuitous violence.
In particular, Zanuck considered the character of a "strong woman"
who runs not only a big ranch but also a corrupt empire to be "phony,"

an artificial construction that detracted from the realism of the Earp brothers and their "simple human problem[s]."[41] He suggested eliminating the subplots involving Alamo's financial and political empire and focusing instead on the problems Alamo and Earp have with their younger siblings and on the love stories between Wyatt Earp and Alamo and Morgan Earp and Louvenia:

This is real, honest-to-goodness stuff, and you can't mix it with hidden dynasties and fabulous castles where thirty people dine at long, lace-covered tables. . . . I think you will be surprised to see the change that comes almost as a result of drastic elimination and supplying realism to replace contrivance.[42]

Rather than investing in substantial rewrites on a western property that did not fit well into Fox's proposed slate of CinemaScope blockbusters, Zanuck reassigned Fuller to work on the script for *Saber Tooth*, a science fiction adventure story that originated with Philip Dunne. Zanuck's notes on *Woman with a Whip* and his eventual rejection of the script highlight the importance of maintaining clarity and plausibility in scripts written for the major studios, as well as adhering to social norms and generic expectations. Multiple and diffused story lines, overly powerful women, and castles and caviar simply had no place in a Fox western; in a Globe Enterprises western, however, these unruly elements found a home.

   A comparison of the March 1953 first-draft continuity script rejected by Twentieth Century–Fox and the February 1957 revised script produced by Globe reveals very few fundamental changes. The Globe script opens with federal marshal Griff Bonnell (Barry Sullivan) and his younger brothers Wes (Gene Barry) and Chico (Robert Dix) arriving in Tombstone to deliver a warrant for mail theft against Howard Swain (Chuck Roberson), a deputy sheriff under the employ of Jessica Drummond (Stanwyck), leather-wearing land baroness and "boss" of Cochise County. In town, Griff chats with his old friend John Chisum (Hank Worden), the local marshal who is going blind. While the Bonnell boys enjoy a scrub at Barney Cashman's bathhouse, Brockie Drummond (John Ericson), Jessica's unruly younger brother, challenges Chisum and kills him. Griff subsequently faces down Brockie with an imposing walk down Main Street, disarms him, and puts him in jail, though Jessica quickly rides into town with her forty guns and releases her brother. Jessica then takes away Brockie's guns and scolds him for killing Chisum and getting a girl pregnant. Back in town, Wes, who acts as Griff's second gun, gets friendly with Louvenia (Eve Brent), the daughter of the local gunsmith, and decides he'd "like to stay around long enough to clean her rifle." Chico, the youngest Bonnell, resists his brothers' decision to put him on a stagecoach for California, as he'd rather be a gunman than a farmer. Griff visits Jessica at her mansion to deliver the warrant for Howard Swain, and the two initiate a loaded flirtation; impressed by what she sees, Jessica offers Griff the job of local sheriff, currently held by Ned Logan (Dean Jagger). Logan, carrying an unrequited torch for Jessica, has Charlie Savage shoot Swain in jail to keep him from implicating Jessica in his crimes. When Jessica and Griff tour her property she reveals her past to him, again asking him to team up with her. After a suspiciously allegorical tornado nearly blows them away, Jessica and Griff enjoy a roll in the hay. Logan and Savage set up Griff to be killed in town, but Chico surprisingly saves his brother from the ambush. Logan just won't give up, though, and sets upon Griff in Jessica's house; Jessica pays off Logan and pledges her love to Griff, prompting Logan to hang himself. Wild man Brockie reenters the picture at Wes's wedding to Louvenia, killing Wes minutes after the ceremony and driving a wedge between Jessica and Griff. Jessica pledges to stand beside her brother, though it means losing her empire; in the end, the judge and jury can't be bought, and Brockie is sentenced to hang. Hearing the news from Jessica, Brockie grabs his sister and uses her as a shield to escape jail. Griff confronts them in the street and shoots through Jessica to Brockie, who falls with an incredulous "I'm killed!" Griff walks past the injured Jessica and intones, "Get a doctor. She'll live." Though Griff fears Jessica will never forgive him, the wounded woman runs after him on his way out of town, and the two drive off together.

When revising his Fox script for Globe, Fuller changed the names of the principal characters so they sounded less mythical and more naturalistic, making the Earp brothers the Bonnell brothers and renaming Alamo as Jessica Drummond. Fuller also apparently heeded Zanuck's advice regarding the outsized characterization of the land baroness: rather than living in a castle guarded by Apache Indians, she now lives in a mansion protected by hired guns. One character is eliminated— Nellie, a hotel owner, whose lines are adopted by Barney the washtub operator—and two sequences are dropped: a scene in which Griff and Jessica walk off in search of water after the tornado has died down and are seen kissing in a stream by Griff's brothers and a sequence in which Virgil/Chico wounds both Brockie and Griff in an attempt to avenge the murder of Morgan/Wes, his older brother. The first cut sequence would have added little new information to the narrative, while the second simply created another diversion from the final showdown between Griff and Brockie. Dialogue is also tightened in the revision, and additional double entendres increase the sexual humor. All in all, however, the revised script maintains the bulk of the plot structure and details Zanuck objected to four years prior. Fuller's newfound independence provided him with the creative freedom to produce offbeat projects like *Forty Guns* that challenged the storytelling conventions embraced by the major studios.

Interestingly, the end of the plot, in which Brockie uses Jessica as a human shield, Griff shoots through Jessica to injure Brockie, and a healed Jessica runs after Griff, is exactly the same in the script rejected by Fox, the script produced by Globe, and in the completed film. In many interviews and in his autobiography, Fuller alleges that his original script ended with Griff walking away after killing Brockie and mortally wounding Jessica, but Fox insisted that the star of the picture survive to ride off with the hero into the sunset.[43] If Fox executives did demand this change, they must have done so between Fuller's submission of the treatment and the completion of the first-draft continuity, as the latter contains Griff's same dismissive "She'll live" as the film. It is curious, however, that Fuller did not revise the ending to fit his original vision when he rewrote the script for the Globe production. While it is possible that representatives of Fox, the Globe film's distributor, again insisted on keeping Stanwyck's character alive, the "happy" ending remains inexplicable and discordant with a story that builds toward a very unhappy—but typically Fullerian—resolution. Only the lyrics to the theme song that is playing at the end—"A woman with a whip is only a woman after all"— and a few stray lines of dialogue concerning the power of love and forgiveness provide glimmers of motivation for Jessica's survival and re-union with Griff. On the other hand, Jessica's death would have efficiently captured the impossibility of her love affair with Griff, as Griff's decision to place his job and his loyalty to his brothers above his love for her would have resulted in her complete elimination. In its denial of an unequivocally positive resolution to the double plotline, such an ending would be more consistent with the majority of Fuller's work. As it is, Jessica's survival and sudden change of heart graft a classically tidy and triumphant ending onto a very untidy and problematic plot.

Indeed, the plot's disregard for coherence and clarity in favor of maximum emotional punch is one of the most vivid examples of Fuller's aesthetic at work, and well illustrates his melodramatic sensibility. Some plot developments, such as the pregnancy of Brockie's girlfriend, arise and vanish immediately, never to be mentioned again, while others, such as Jessica losing her empire, are referenced but not fully explained. At least two plotlines—the Bonnell sibling conflict and the romance between Wes and Louvenia—come to a premature and abrupt end, while two others—the Drummond sibling conflict and the romance between Griff and Jessica—involve dramatic character reversals in the third act. The lack of tight causal construction in *Forty Guns* prompted critics to complain that the film was "unnecessarily confusing," with a "cluttered"

plot that "explodes rather than develops."[44] While it might seem haphazard on the surface, much of the narrative development in *Forty Guns*
functions to intensify steadily the pressure on Jessica and Griff's relationship. The causal factors leading to the seemingly impossible conflict between the two are quite clear: Jessica and Griff love each other but are
also protective of their siblings. When Jessica's brother kills Griff's
brother, Griff must bring him in to be hanged, but Jessica swears, "I'll do
everything I can to see him live." The sibling and corruption plotlines
both enable Griff and Jessica's romance to blossom and create a series of
obstacles to their successful union. Genre conventions aid in providing
narrative motivation for random plot developments, while each additional obstacle builds toward a showdown between Griff and Jessica that
cannot be resolved in a mutually beneficial way. The sudden, often audacious twists and turns in the narrative repeatedly raise the stakes for the
protagonists, producing the plot "explosions" denigrated by the critics
but embraced by Fuller.

Just as Fuller abandons the coherence of classical narrative conventions in an effort to heighten the impact of the central conflict, he also
plays fast and loose with the western genre to produce humorous and
shocking thrills. The most overt example of his generic play is the script's
uproarious use of analogies linking sex and western iconography. Jessica
berates Brockie for beating his pregnant girlfriend with, "If you can't
handle a horse without spurs you've no business riding," while she later
tells Griff about a cabin, "I was bit by a rattler in there when I was
fifteen." He replies dryly, "Bet that rattler died." Louvenia's job as a gunsmith is an easy source for sexual humor, as when Wes tells his brothers
about her: "She's built like a 40/40," and she asks him after they kiss,
"Any recoil?" An even more explicit exchange occurs after Jessica asks
Griff to be sheriff: "I'm not interested in you, Mr. Bonnell. It's your
trademark. Can I feel it?" When she reaches out her hand for his gun,
Griff replies, "Uh-uh. It might go off in your face." These verbal
conflations of animals, guns, and sex take some of the underlying
metaphors found in westerns and exaggerate them for comic effect, involving the viewer in a knowing wink at a convention of the genre. This
use of dialogue is distinctly different from references to Chico as a "wet-
nose" or Brockie as a "calf" who needs to be "broken." The latter usage
functions as a sort of western patois, the equivalent of a pickpocket
being called a "cannon" in *Pickup on South Street*. Fuller's dialogue increasingly contains colorful analogies and absurd references as his Globe
career progresses, imbuing his films with additional self-consciousness.
The outrageousness of the dialogue provides campy comic relief from
narrative situations designed for maximum tension.

Fuller's play with generic elements in *Forty Guns* extends beyond the narrative and into the realm of the visual, transforming three western conventions—the showdown, the wedding, and the funeral—into highly stylized sequences. The initial confrontation between Griff and Brockie after the killing of Chisum primes the viewer to anticipate a classic shootout: Brockie is standing in the middle of the town's Main Street, wildly waving his gun and yelling, while Griff approaches from the opposite end of the street, covered by Wes and his shotgun. The typical western script would have Griff stop fifty yards or so away from Brockie, say a few words, and pull out his gun. Instead, Griff simply keeps striding toward Brockie, each step punctuated by increasingly loud musical chords. Dun, dun! Dun, dun! As the music continues, the long shot of Griff's walk is broken down into repeating tight shots of his face, his legs, and his shifting point of view of Brockie. Here Fuller reduces the showdown to its most basic elements: Griff's calm determination, his destination, and the feet that will take him there. As Griff and Brockie are not shown in the same shot until the end of the sequence, the actual space between the two is abstracted, and the viewer is not quite sure when Griff will reach his target. Suddenly, Fuller varies the initial pattern he established: an extreme close-up appears of Griff's eyes, shifting up and down to reflect his movement, intercut with gradually tighter point-of-view shots of Brockie. This cut never fails to elicit gasps when *Forty Guns* is projected in a theater—imagine, eyes bigger than your body bobbing up and down on the gigantic CinemaScope screen! This is the boldness of Fuller. The repetition of images in this sequence builds tension and suspense, while the unnatural size of Griff's eyes in the Cinema-Scope frame, the extreme changes in shot scale, and the musical score contribute an element of hysteria.

Typically, strength and skill are illustrated in a showdown by who draws first and shoots most accurately; it is the bullets that close the distance between the two opponents and mark one as triumphant and the other as unworthy. In the showdown at the beginning of *Forty Guns*, however, Griff himself traverses the street and attacks Brockie, his mastery over all others demonstrated by his eyes, his walk, and his ability to transfix and dominate his opponent even when unarmed. The walk reimagines the standard western shootout, providing significant characterization of Griff in an unusually intensified and startling fashion. When Griff again faces Brockie on Main Street at the end of the film and decides to shoot *through* the woman he loves in order to kill the man he hates (another deromanticized break from genre tradition), his actions thereby appear entirely in character; the walk has already presented Griff as a man of great confidence and control who is capable of anything.

1

2

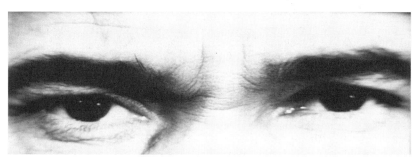

3

4

Frame enlargements of Griff Bonnell's (Barry Sullivan's) walk down Main Street to subdue
Brockie Drummond (John Ericson) in *Forty Guns*. Rhythmic editing between the images,
punctuated by the percussive score and the sudden changes in shot scale, injects tension
into Fuller's reimagination of the classic western showdown.

Fuller's presentation of Wes and Louvenia's wedding is equally daring, as he turns the communal celebration of the couple's nuptials into the prologue of a funeral. The wedding itself is never seen; instead, the scene begins with an extreme high angle of the crowd outside the church, waiting for the couple and their family and friends to emerge for photos. The moment is joyous, with the playful, upbeat score from the previous washtub scene (Fuller loves those washtubs!) carrying over into "Here Comes the Bride." As Louvenia, Wes, and their families, beaming, pose in a medium close-up for a picture, Wes asks his brother, "Aren't you going to kiss the bride, Griff?" The music lulls to a stop, Griff leans past his brother to kiss Louvenia, and a gunshot is heard. Whoa! The viewer is as startled as the characters. After an insert of Brockie on his horse, gun in hand, two over-the-shoulder close-ups favoring first Wes and then Louvenia are intercut at an increasing rate, following the groom as he collapses into his bride's arms and onto the ground. The rapid, repeating close-ups extend the duration of Wes's fall, heightening the impact of the murder. The scene's euphoria has turned to shock and despair. In a wide shot the crowd converges around the prone couple, and Louvenia's gasping wails are heard like the cry of a wounded animal: "Wes! Wes!" A high-angle close-up looks down on the bride, struggling on the ground under the weight of her dead husband's body. It is all too unnerving. Wes and Louvenia, the high-spirited, double-entendre-trading couple, were married for all of thirty-two seconds—one of the most extreme tonal shifts in all of Fuller's work.

A slow dissolve then segues into Wes's funeral, as visually stylized and abstracted as the showdown and the wedding. Typically, western funerals emphasize communal mourning and the vulnerability of settlers on the untamed frontier. In *Forty Guns,* Fuller leeches all sentimentality from the ritual until only its iconography remains. In the first shot, Louvenia stands on a hilltop in widow's weeds, and the camera tracks left past a hearse and in on Barney, singing "God Has His Arms Around Me." Following a brief cut in to a close-up of Barney, the third shot of the sequence reverses the first, tracking back out and to the right, past the hearse and settling again on Louvenia. The three-shot scene reduces the funeral to its barest elements: the widow, the dead man, and the act of mourning. The slow pace of the sequence, its camera movement, and lack of cutting contrast with the end of the previous scene, in which rapidly cut, static close-ups of Wes falling on top of his new bride heighten the horror of his murder. Together, the wedding and funeral compress the married life of Wes and Louvenia into only a little over three minutes of screen time, serving as one of the most expressive examples of how Fuller's films exploit stark contrasts in tone and action in a jarring, ironic, and often unsentimental fashion. While *Run of the Arrow* respectfully acknowledged the tropes of the cavalry-and-Indian western while attempting to expand their application through a unified, coherent narrative, *Forty Guns* picks key generic situations, stands them in a row, and gleefully blows them up.

Despite its narrative pleasures and formal inventiveness, *Forty Guns* received less promotional fanfare and a more tentative first-run release than its predecessor and struggled at the box office. The picture opened in September 1957 at the Fox Theater in Detroit on the bottom half of a double bill with Twentieth Century–Fox's *Sea Wife* (1957), though in subsequent weeks it headlined in other venues, often paired with another Regal picture.[45] Reviews for the film were generally positive, finding the fast-paced action and pairing of Barbara Stanwyck and Barry Sullivan particularly ideal for the drive-in market.[46] Fox's decision to book *Forty Guns* on the bottom half of the bill in the largest major-market first-run houses, as well as only in secondary runs in New York City, reveals the distributor's lack of faith in the film as an A-grade contender. As critics suggested, the film was well suited for drive-ins, yet cost too much to make a profit without a successful first run as a headliner. Reaching as high as number twelve only once on the weekly box-office list, *Forty Guns* proved to be another in-betweener that could only make it as a B.[47] While an August 1957 memo from Fox suggests that the studio was considering an agreement for Fuller and Regal to produce two additional action pictures at a cost of $300,000 each, after the lackluster showings of *China Gate* and *Forty Guns* this proposal never came to fruition.[48] Following *Forty Guns*, Fuller ended his associations with Lippert and Twentieth Century–Fox and further lowered his budgets for subsequent Globe pictures.

Fuller retrenched in 1958 by producing a true B movie, *Verboten!*, with financing from RKO.[49] By this time, RKO had turned over its handling of prints, billing, and other administrative work to the J. Arthur Rank Association and unveiled a plan to make the studio a key source of financing for independent producers. According to the plan, RKO would provide financial support on either a short-term or long-term basis, with no restrictions on cast or distributor and no unloading of studio charges or other overhead.[50] *Verboten!*, the story of a GI in Germany who falls in love with a local woman and subsequently works for the American military government after WWII, features no stars and little production value. Fuller shot the film entirely in Los Angeles during approximately two weeks, and intercut his footage with stock images of artillery and aerial warfare, Nazi atrocities, and postwar Germany to increase the realism.[51] Efficiently staged and sensationally presented, *Verboten!* is, like *Park Row,* a product of Fuller's passions. What it lacks in polish it makes up for in strength of purpose.

The film begins in Germany during the last days of World War II. Sergeant David Brent (James Best), part of a U.S. Army patrol weeding out snipers in the remains of a bombed-out town, is wounded and taken in by Helga Schiller (Susan Cummings), a German who protects him from retreating soldiers. Helga nurses Brent back to health, arguing that she will show him "the difference between a German and a Nazi," and he in turn protects her and her family when U.S. forces occupy the town. Brent falls in love with Helga, and when the war is over he arranges to stay behind in Germany as a civilian, work for the American military government, and marry Helga. Meanwhile, Helga's neighbor, Bruno (Tom Pittman), arrives back in town, disillusioned by the German surrender but still faithful to the Nazi party line. Helga tells Bruno she views her new husband as a "meal ticket," a good source of otherwise scarce food, clothes, and nylons. Bruno becomes a leader of the Werewolves, underground remnants of the Hitler Youth intent on disrupting the American occupation, and induces Helga's younger brother, Franz (Harold Daye), to join. Bruno uses his job at the U.S. Army headquarters to provide intelligence to the Werewolves and manages to get Brent fired as the result of a Werewolves-organized food riot. Brent confronts Helga after Bruno reveals to him her motives for marriage, and though Helga swears she now loves him, Brent fails to believe her. Helga discovers Franz is a member of the Werewolves, and in an effort to redeem them both, takes him to the Nuremberg trials to confront the Nazi legacy. Shocked by what he sees, Franz helps bring a fiery end to the Werewolves, while Brent recognizes Helga's true love and the two reunite.

Though at times the integration of its disparate elements threatens to come apart at the seams, the emotional effect of *Verboten!* builds as it goes along. The film contains both a subjective tale of moral transformation and an objective rendering of Germany after WWII, a love story and historical intrigue, a fictional film and documentary footage—all interwoven with a single goal: to inform and arouse the viewer. Working again with cinematographer Joseph Biroc, Fuller constructs his scenes with the utmost economy, consistently relying on camera movement to redirect attention and create new compositions within long-take master shots; shots lasting two to five minutes are not uncommon amongst the original footage. The end result can be a bit stagy, and as these sequences primarily depict the romance, viewers are more likely to feel they are witnessing the love affair than becoming emotionally invested in it. With the arrival of Bruno and the shift in the narrative toward the Werewolves subplot, however, the use of stock footage increases and the pace quickens. Brent, previously the site of viewer alignment, recedes into the shadows while Franz emerges at the center of the story, his close-up re-

Eric (Sasha Harden, lower center), a young neo-Nazi "Werewolf" in post–World War II Germany, leads a food riot to disrupt the American occupation in a publicity still from *Verboten!* Fuller, who occasionally worked as a cartoonist in his youth, did the drawings and lettering on the English-language posters. *Author's Collection*

action shots hinting at his significance. The consistent use of stock footage throughout the film primes the viewer for the impact of the Nuremberg trail scene. Lacking the resources to fully depict the world of the story, Fuller cunningly integrates stock footage and his own fictional footage within the same scenes, using eyeline matches and other devices to suggest the images are all from a unified space and time. The result can be disorienting, as differences in the content, quality, and texture of the footage call attention to themselves. Rather than highlighting the narrative's lack of verisimilitude, however, the documentary nature of the stock footage influences our understanding of the rest of the film, consistently suggesting parallels between the real world and the fictional world that lend credibility to the narrative. In the Nuremberg trial scene, stock footage not only fills in the blanks of the story world (images of the courtroom, the judges, the defendants, etc.), but also presents a film within the film: footage from the actual trial seen within the story by Franz, footage that becomes the source of his character transformation.

*Verboten!*, like Fuller's other cinematic explorations of identity, nationalism, and the struggle for survival, testifies to his optimistic belief that "with film, we can make progress and history and civilization."[52] During the Nuremberg sequence, we see the transformative power of film in action. Fuller opens the scene with original footage of Helga, Franz, and others filing into courtroom pews intercut with documentary footage of the arrival of the actual trial's judges, prosecutors, and defendants, suggesting that both are inhabiting the same space. Initially, voice-over narration read by Fuller assumes the role of a court commentator, setting the stage for the events of the trial. The camera tracks in to frame Helga and Franz in the last row, and cuts back and forth between the siblings and a frontal close-up of Franz, still skeptical of the proceedings. Now assuming the voice of the American lead prosecutor, Fuller's voice-over narration announces, "We will show you the defendants' own film. You will see their own conduct" over a stock shot from the rear of the Nuremberg courtroom—as if from the point of view of Franz and Helga—of a man at a lectern in front of a blank projection screen.

The voice-over then narrates what the siblings are presumably seeing onscreen, the film within the film: a history of Nazi atrocities, beginning with those against fellow Germans and ending with the Final Solution. As the narration repeats the Nazi party propaganda that led to the incidents onscreen, the scene cuts back three times to a close-up of Franz superimposed over flashbacks to Bruno's Werewolf rhetoric, suggesting that Franz is connecting the past to the present and cueing us, the viewers, to do the same. As the documentary footage becomes increasingly graphic, the pace quickens and the inserts of Franz's close-up are more frequent. The close-ups and point-of-view editing structure align us with Franz's viewing experience: we see what he sees as he sees it, and we see the effect it has on him. After horrific images of gas chambers and piles of skeletal bodies, the narration culminates with the declaration "This was genocide" over a final shot of a corpse being unceremoniously tossed into a pit; Franz breaks down next to his sister, sobbing, but she turns his face toward the screen: "You've got to look. We'll look together. Everyone should see." This is Fuller, prodding us: we have to face the past in order to affect the future. In encouraging Franz to watch the Nuremberg footage, Helga opens his eyes to activities he had indirectly fostered but had long denied. After watching the film, the boy recognizes his own complicity and guilt. He runs to Brent, crying, "I saw film. I didn't know! I didn't know," and promptly confesses his association with the Werewolves. The process of viewing the footage implicates Franz, the viewer made manifest in the film, and forces him—and by extension us—to fully confront the horror of the Nazi crimes. This is what *Verboten!* has been working up to: an honest depiction of the past, of a moral transformation, and of the need to take responsibility and enact change. The sequence is gut-wrenching and powerful. For Fuller, learning the truth is essential, and cinema has a role to play.

Although critics reacted well to the film's sense of conviction, *Verboten!* received only spotty promotion and distribution, the most uneven of any Fuller picture from this era. *Verboten!* was the last film made before RKO's collapse, and the studio had ceased operating by the time it was completed. Rank initially took over distribution for RKO, and in March 1959 booked *Verboten!* into the Palace in Milwaukee and the Fox in Detroit, where it held on for two weeks. Rank dropped out of U.S. distribution later that month, and Columbia picked up *Verboten!* as part of its four-picture deal with Fuller.[53] When the film finally returned to theaters in the second half of 1959, it appeared largely in secondary run and on the bottom half of first-run double bills. Playing in only eight major cities in first run, *Verboten!* did not open in New York until July the following year.[54] Most reviews found *Verboten!*'s theme and use of documentary footage both authentically gripping and exploitable. In the *New York Times,* Eugene Archer gave the film an uncharacteristically strong notice for a low-budget picture, describing it as "intriguing evidence that the offbeat and interesting American "B" picture, often considered a thing of the past, has not quite disappeared from the screen."[55] But, with its spotty distribution, positive reviews could do little to help *Verboten!* generate box office. Nevertheless, Fuller continued to formulate ambitious plans in 1958.

After finishing *Verboten!*, Fuller moved into preproduction on *The Big Red One,* a story about his old infantry outfit that he had been developing since World War II. He announced in *Variety* that he had secured a contract with Bantam for a novelization of the film, had the cooperation of the Defense Department, and was seeking permission to shoot in Czechoslovakia.[56] Warner Bros. was backing the project, an unsurprising move given that Fuller had written a scenario and a screenplay for the studio earlier in the decade.[57] At the same time, Fuller also revealed in *Variety* that he was looking for a financing-distribution deal to enlarge Globe into a six-films-a-year production unit, plus television work, though he did not intend to produce and direct every film.[58] Although none of these plans materialized, Fuller did shoot *Dogface,* a pilot for CBS, under the Globe TV Enterprises banner in March 1959. Fuller produced, wrote, and directed the half-hour pilot about American GIs in World War II and shot it on Columbia's ranch in the San Fernando Valley. A month later, *Variety* reported that Globe would develop a second series for CBS, a western entitled *Trigger-happy,* although it is unclear whether or not Fuller actually advanced these plans. As with over 80 percent of pilots shot for television during the period, neither Fuller project was picked up, likely resulting in the loss of hundreds of thousands of production dollars for Globe.[59]

Fuller's attempt to enter television was a logical outgrowth of his low-budget film production, given the similarities in budgeting, casting, scheduling, and content between very low-budget films and television shows. Television was commonly viewed in the industry as the last refuge of the B films that were being squeezed out of movie theaters and, if picked up by CBS, Fuller's pilots would have provided him with a hedge against the shrinking market for his brand of low-budget action film. Yet Fuller's long-take visual style and nontraditional narrative interests left him ill-suited for the intimacy and family orientation of broadcast television. While he would find work directing for TV during the 1960s, Fuller's chances to produce his own series ended in 1959.

### Sensational Style: The Crimson Kimono and Underworld, U.S.A.

After *The Big Red One* was put on hold by Warner Bros. in late 1958, Fuller signed a four-picture distribution deal with Columbia Pictures.[60] Earlier that March, Columbia had moved to a new, indie-friendly format after failing to find a production chief following the death of Harry Cohn. *Variety* reported Columbia's interest in financing and distributing packages brought in by outside producers, acquiring properties to attract top talent for profit-participation deals, and offering staff producers the chance to set up independent companies on the lot. By the end of the year, Columbia had more contracts with independent producers than any other major studio, including deals with producer-directors such as Otto Preminger, Stanley Donen, and William Castle.[61] Contractual arrangements with independent producers varied; the producer could utilize Columbia facilities and personnel or receive a minimum of direct help during production.[62] At the same time as it sought new, independent blood, the studio switched from an emphasis on programmers to a reliance on blockbusters, citing a trend against smaller pictures, especially overseas. The low-budget action picture had been a staple of Columbia's production slate, but now the studio suggested it would only carry low-budget films that could be exploited for top, stand-alone dates both domestically and abroad.[63]

Although little definitive information exists regarding the budgets and shooting schedules of Fuller's two Columbia pictures, *The Crimson Kimono* and *Underworld, U.S.A.*, it seems probable that they were completed for $1 million or less after shooting for a month or under based on reports in *Variety*, cast lists, number of sets, and use of locations. Compared to other contemporary Columbia releases such as the $3.5 million *Song Without End* (1960), *Suddenly, Last Summer* (1959), *Anatomy of a Murder* (1959), and *A Raisin in the Sun* (1961), Fuller's pictures do not appear to be the blockbusters the studio was trumpeting in the trades.[64] Instead, Fuller's two releases seem again to fall into the "in-betweener" category, designed to headline on a budget. Written to revitalize their given genres through the incorporation of sensational subject matter, *The Crimson Kimono* and *Underworld, U.S.A.* find Fuller more consistently utilizing constructive editing and indirect representation to vividly present hard-hitting action and violence.

Fuller began production on his first film financed by Columbia, *The Crimson Kimono*, in early 1959. Shot in black-and-white with a cast of unknowns, the film wrapped after approximately a month of production at the studio and on location in Los Angeles's Little Tokyo.[65] *The Crimson Kimono* is the story of two L.A. police detectives who fall in love with the same woman while investigating the death of a stripper. Fuller stamped the otherwise standard detective story with his own signature by setting the tale within L.A.'s Nisei (second generation Japanese-American) community and creating an interracial romantic triangle. The film is narratively and stylistically organized to heighten contrasts in tone and style, juxtaposing the detectives' initially peaceful home life with their action-packed professional world. When one partner falls for the object of the other's affection, violence seeps into their personal relationship, revealing a surprising case of reverse racism. While some critics consider it a minor work, *The Crimson Kimono* is notable both for how Fuller revitalizes a generic formula through an examination of race and relationships and for how the narrative is harnessed to Fuller's dominant staging strategies during this period: master-shot long takes with camera movement contrasted with action scenes reliant on constructive editing. The net result is a pacy little number with a trailblazing story and some hard-thumping action sequences.

*The Crimson Kimono* opens with a wild jazz score and night shots of the streets of Los Angeles. A burlesque dancer named Sugar Torch (Gloria Pall) discovers a stranger with a gun in her dressing room, runs screaming down the street, and is shot dead. The detectives on the case are Charlie Bancroft (Glenn Corbett), a Caucasian, and Joe Kojaku (James Shigeta), a Nisei Japanese-American, partners and housemates since meeting in a foxhole during the Korean War. At the scene of the crime is a painting of Sugar Torch in a crimson kimono, a lead each man pursues through his own angle: Charlie hunts down Mac (Anna Lee), a delightfully inebriated bohemian artist, while Joe talks up his sources in the local Nisei community. Mac leads Charlie to the painting's artist,

Christine Downes (Victoria Shaw), who sketches the man that commissioned the painting, now a suspect in the murder. After the sketch is shown on television, someone takes a shot at Christine; pretending she is dead, the detectives move her to their apartment and ask Mac to act as mother hen. While Charlie is wooing Christine, Joe manages to track down Shinto (George Okamura, also the film's stunt coordinator), another possible witness, and the mountain of a man gives the two detectives a rough time in a pool hall. Joe also finds himself attracted to Christine, although he resists his feelings in deference to Charlie. Christine finds Joe more to her liking, though, and conflict with Charlie seems inevitable. Joe's frustration boils over in an exhibition kendo match with Charlie, as he nearly beats his best friend senseless. Projecting onto Charlie his own fears of racial prejudice, Joe accuses his partner of not wanting him to date Christine because he is Japanese and she is Caucasian, but Charlie insists he is only feeling "normal, healthy, jealous hate." After Christine and Mac broker a truce between the men, the foursome track down Roma (Jaclynne Greene), the killer of Sugar Torch, at the Nisei Festival in Little Tokyo. A chase ends in gunfire, and the dying Roma reveals to Joe she wrongly believed her lover to be involved with Sugar Torch. Joe sees a parallel in his own lack of trust in Charlie, and he reconciles with his partner. Joe and Christine kiss as the boisterous Nisei Week Grand Parade surrounds them, but Joe and Charlie's partnership is no more.

In *The Crimson Kimono*, Fuller's familiar themes of identity, trust, and betrayal emerge from a race-inflected narrative that traces the dissolution of one couple and the formation of another. At the outset, Charlie and Joe's relationship is a lot like the layout of their apartment: just as their flat features two distinct bedroom wings that open onto a central living area, both men have different characteristics yet are united by a shared history and professional purpose. Fuller highlights the visual metaphor during the first scene in their apartment, when a long take with camera movement tracks Charlie from his bedroom into Joe's, and the two end up in the living room together, sharing the frame. Charlie is revealed to be a rough-edged ladies' man, Joe more arty and professionally minded. While they follow individual leads in their work, they reunite to support each other, as thrillingly illustrated in their tag-team attack on Shinto in the pool hall. Christine is the force that divides the two men and causes them to question their loyalties, but she poses a different problem for each: she makes Charlie jealous, but Joe fearful: is the displeasure he sees on Charlie's face the sign of suppressed racism? Joe's fear is understandable, but unsupported; the film's Caucasian characters—Charlie, Christine, Mac, Sugar Torch, Roma—are all immersed in Japanese culture and never view Joe as a man set apart. Even Christine's attraction for Joe has nothing to do with "difference"; rather, she considers him to share her artistic, intellectual side. This is the twist to the story: not only is the romantic triangle solved with the Nisei getting the Caucasian girl, but in the end, no one bats an eye. Fuller's refusal to play the "a colored man is dating my daughter!" card is incredibly bold for 1959 and refreshing even today. In contrast with *House of Bamboo*—with its anachronistic kimonos, geishas, and tea ceremony–turned–jitterbugging contest—*The Crimson Kimono* does not exoticize Japanese culture as much as present it as an ordinary facet of life in Los Angeles.

While much attention has been paid to the role of race in *The Crimson Kimono*, critics tend to overlook its crafty visual style. At times the film bears the scars of its fast-and-cheap origins, particularly in its occasionally unmotivated lighting, spotty continuity, and improvised optical shots. Yet the cinematography by Sam Leavitt can also be quite nuanced, and Jerome Thoms's editing adds a percussive force to many of the action scenes. *The Crimson Kimono*'s average shot length of 9.5 seconds reflects a less consistent use of the long-take master shot than in earlier Fuller pictures. While the number of shots per scene can be high, the number of camera setups is typically quite low, as often several angles are intercut in an efficient alternative to complete coverage. This strategy enables Fuller to create patterns of repeated camera setups that heighten kineticism and graphic conflict within a scene. As it places in stark contrast scenes organized around long-take master shots and those designed for maximum visceral effect, *The Crimson Kimono* is exceptionally illustrative of Fuller's stylistic work. The discontinuity in the film's visual style reflects its dual romantic and professional plotlines; one minute the narration lulls you into the laid-back rhythm of home life, the next minute an action sequence grabs you by the collar and shakes you.

The opening scenes establish several dominant stylistic tendencies that run throughout the film: long-take scenes are followed by highly edited scenes, resulting in sudden shifts in tone and action, and series of shots contain opposing movements within the frame, creating graphic contrasts and heightening kinetic effects. A comparison of two domestic scenes in Joe and Charlie's apartment and the subsequent action scenes in the poolroom and the kendo match illustrates how tonal shifts and changes in the visual style amplify developments within the narrative. While camera movement and mise-en-scene emphasize the altering dynamics of the main characters' relationships during long-take domestic scenes, rapid editing and graphic contrasts punctuate the action, as Charlie and Joe first work as a team, then turn on each other.

The first pair of scenes visually contrast Charlie wooing Chris in his apartment and the poolroom battle with Shinto, emphasizing conflict within and between shots, as well as between entire segments. The initial three-and-a-half-minute sequence shot of Chris and Charlie talking utilizes camera movement and blocking as an alternative to analytical editing, suggesting the formation of a romantic couple in a manner completely in keeping with classical norms. The subsequent forty-five-second poolroom scene of Charlie and Joe subduing Shinto dramatically alters the tempo in its rapid editing, emphasis on movement, and clashing screen directions. The effect of the difference in visual style is jarring, jolting the viewer away from the serene enjoyment of Chris and Charlie's budding affection.

As in all of the film's scenes shot in Charlie and Joe's apartment, the first half of this sequence exists primarily to develop the characters' backstories and to advance the romantic subplots and impending domestic conflict. The primary narrative actions include Chris flipping through a book of mug shots, Charlie answering the door and getting more mug shots, and Charlie calming Chris down and subsequently making a pass at her. Camera movement delineates shifts in the narrative, creating six distinct compositions in two different rooms within the one shot. While classical scene dissection is not strictly followed, the camera movement does function in a similar fashion, directing the viewer's gaze and emphasizing significant narrative development.

In contrast to the heavy editing in their previous scenes together, the sequence shot unites Charlie and Chris within the same frame and visually identifies them as a couple. When Chris flips through the mug shots, for instance, she sits in the midground of a medium shot on the right side of the frame, while Charlie sits on the other side of the table in the foreground left. Although the two are having a conversation they are both facing the camera on different planes, enabling the viewer to follow the characters' dialogue and reactions simultaneously. The composition thus functions in the same manner as a shot–reverse shot editing pattern but unifies the couple in the shared frame and maintains the production efficiency of the sequence shot. Camera movement and blocking jointly function to bring the couple together in the climax of the scene. After Charlie joins Chris in the bedroom, the camera arcs into a two-shot medium-close-up of him sitting next to her on the bed with his arm around her shoulder. Charlie asks if he can date her after the case is over and, as the two kiss, the swelling of the score punctuates their union. While a sequence shot is an unusual choice, in this scene it both fulfills the goals of classical analytical editing and emphasizes the formation of the romantic couple. In addition, the sequence shot lays the foundation for the subsequent shift in mood and style.

As is true throughout the film, the tenderness of the domestic scene is quickly interrupted by and visually contrasted with the bone-crunching action of the partners' professional lives. The phone rings at the end of the sequence shot, halting the score; a quick track out to a medium shot and Charlie's barking voice further mark the shift in the emotional tenor of the scene. As Charlie reaches out to hang up the phone, the scene abruptly cuts to Shinto in the poolroom smashing a pool cue across a table in front of Joe. The cut between Charlie's arm moving to the left and Shinto's hand slamming down on the right creates the first of many graphic conflicts produced through opposing motions in the scene. In sharp contrast to the prior three-minute, thirty-four-second long take, the poolroom scene contains twenty-three shots in less than a minute, with two-thirds of the shots lasting a second or less. Over half the shots are unique camera setups, although repeating pairs of shots play an important role in demonstrating the coordinated teamwork of Charlie and Joe and in producing visceral effects. On the score, strings, horns, and timpani accompany the action, often directly responding to a character's blow in a cartoonish fashion.

The initial shots within the poolroom establish the primary stylistic strategies of the scene and the partners' fighting style. As Shinto throws a series of chairs through the rear window and Joe ducks out of the way, repeated figure movement and sound produce a propulsion/duck/crash pattern. Charlie's arrival at the pool hall marks the beginning of four pairs of repeating shots joined by matches on action that are edited into an ABA/CDCD/EDEDE/FGFG pattern; each set involves movement within the frame in opposing directions that heightens the energy of the fight. From the establishing shot of the poolroom Fuller cuts to a medium shot from behind Shinto, revealing each partner facing the camera on either side of their opponent in the mid-ground, then ducking out of the way as he throws pool balls at them. This shot establishes the strategy of the partners—each will attack Shinto from a different side—that illustrates their teamwork and dictates the rhythm of the rest of the scene.

Whether the partners are joined within the same shot or pictured alone, the movement of one mirrors the other, producing patterns of repeated action in opposing directions. For example, Shinto gets kicked in the stomach (cymbal crash!), then doubles over. Joe and Charlie then simultaneously karate chop Shinto from opposite sides, first on his neck (crash!) and then in his side (crash!). Assigning a cymbal crash only to the blows of Charlie and Joe comically suggests their particular potency and creates the appearance of dominance, while the repetition of conflicting screen directions produced by each partner's blows results in a series of graphic conflicts. Fuller continues this strategy by cutting in to closer shot scales and placing the camera in the middle of the action with Shinto. The action-reaction editing pattern, graphic conflicts, and overt use of the soundtrack create a redundancy of stylistic cues that forcefully exaggerate the effects of combat.

1

2

Frame enlargements of the tag-team attack by Charlie (Glenn Corbett, left) and Joe (James Shigeta, right) on Shinto (George Okamura, dorsal in both frames) during the pool hall scene of *The Crimson Kimono*. Fuller maximizes the intensity of the sequence by juxtaposing the direction of movement from shot to shot: Charlie strikes from the left and Joe strikes from the right.

Graphic conflict produced from shot to shot further intensifies the climax of the fight. The last segment begins with a close-up of Charlie in the mid-ground left facing the camera and Shinto in the foreground right facing Charlie. Charlie throws a punch that sails from left to right into Shinto's jaw; a reverse angle then depicts a close-up of Joe backhanding Shinto from right to left in the frame. The two shots repeat again at even shorter lengths. The alternating screen direction of the blows and accelerated cutting rate intensifies the attack on Shinto and endows it with a percussive power. This final repeating pair is followed by a shot that joins the separate attacks into the same frame: Shinto wobbles in profile in the mid-ground of a medium close-up, while Charlie delivers another right hook from the background and Joe's arms appear from the extreme right foreground with a double karate chop to both sides of Shinto's head. Movement in depth combines with the established pattern of the partners' alternating mirror attacks to punctuate Shinto's collapse.

The Korean giant finally goes down, but the battle is not yet over; the final phase of the fight accelerates the pacing of the movement, graphic conflicts, and synchronized sound effects developed throughout the scene to create a final crescendo of kinetic action. As if the camera is shooting from the optical point of view of Shinto, a medium close-up of Joe planting his hands and beginning to kick cuts to a reverse angle of Charlie completing the action and stomping both feet directly at the camera. The continuation of the figure movement across the shot–reverse shot pattern emphasizes the unity of Joe and Charlie's physical effort, a strategy expressed in the editing throughout the scene, while also heightening the visceral nature of the attack aimed at the viewer. The soundtrack continues in a self-conscious manner, with a plucking harp accenting Joe's approach, while horns and a cymbal mark Charlie's final deliverance of the blow. With Shinto out of sight and the direction of the kicks aimed squarely at the camera, the viewer becomes the target of the detectives' combined blows and the recipient of a particularly shocking jolt. In the final shot of the scene, Shinto falls to the floor between the two detectives, releasing the tension accumulated from ever closer, louder, and faster stylistic cues. Repetition, patterns of action-reaction, rhythmic editing, music, contrasting screen direction, and attacks aimed at the camera all combine to produce a scene with unusual kinetic strength. Designed less for clarity than for maximum visceral impact, the poolroom sequence completely upends the flirtatious mood of the previous scene, inverts its deliberate pacing, and transforms the viewer from observer to victim in a jarring, unsettling fashion.

While the conflicts expressed through the visual style in this pair of scenes set the partners' domestic and professional lives in opposition and pit them as a team against an opponent, later scenes utilize similar stylistic techniques to illustrate domestic tensions and the dissolution of the partnership. This shift is most clearly seen in the sequence juxtaposing another apartment scene with the kendo battle. In the first part of the sequence, Charlie, Chris, and Mac converse in the apartment during another long take, dancing around the question of why Joe is so out of sorts, while a sketch of Joe by Chris literally stands between Charlie and Chris in the composition. The prop self-consciously enables the absent partner to be present in the scene, making physical Charlie and Joe's rivalry for Chris's affection. After Charlie heads off to the kendo match, still ignorant of Chris's feelings, Mac tells her: "Love is like a battle, Chris. Somebody has to get a bloody nose." This most Fullerian of observations cues the cut to the kendo match, where Mac's wisdom plays out in force.

As at the end of the pool hall sequence, Fuller constructs the kendo match so that the viewer is in the middle of the action, with each contestant aiming directly at the camera. In this instance, however, instead of working together to defeat a common enemy, Charlie and Joe seek to defeat each other. The emotional trauma that prompts the breakdown in their relationship is expressed visually through the chaos of the battle, as one combatant (finally revealed to be Joe) breaks the rules and strikes the other repeatedly over the head. In contrast to the clear alternation of punches coming from opposite screen directions that initially marks the pool hall close-ups, in the kendo battle the repeating pair of close-ups of Charlie and Joe suggests a flurry of attacks seemingly from all sides. Rather than clarifying the narrative action, the fast editing, tight framing, graphic matches, soundtrack, and screen direction primarily emphasize the motion and sound of the blows themselves, sacrificing narrative coherence for kinetic effects. The ambiguity surrounding who is striking and when also adds immensely to the suspense of the scene, as it initially prevents the viewer from recognizing which partner is the aggressor and which is the victim.

As the match progresses, the cinematography, editing, and score create confusion as to who is winning the fight; subsequent reaction shots then clarify Joe's rule violations and dangerous attack on Charlie. Seeing each man from the optical perspective of the other, the viewer is literally in the middle of the fight, both attacker and victim, and a participant in the kinetic intensity of the scene rather than merely a witness. The lengthy repetition of the blows, musical punctuation, close reaction shots, and strikes from opposing directions all heighten the violence of the attack and turn the viewer's sympathies away from Joe, previously the more appealing of the two partners. By utilizing in the kendo match the same stylistic strategies applied in the pool hall scene, Fuller encourages the viewer to consider the change in Joe and Charlie's relationship.

Whereas style is used in the pool hall scene to depict the partners' methodical teamwork, the addition of parallel movement within the frame, faster editing, and ambiguous costuming makes the space and narrative action in the kendo match much less clear than in the earlier scene, transforming the partners' teamwork into blind fury.

The visual style in *The Crimson Kimono* is much more self-conscious and discontinuous than that seen in Fuller's more subtle, carefully regulated Twentieth Century–Fox pictures. While his films from both periods feature dialogue scenes with long-take masters that utilize camera movement and blocking for the sort of narrative punctuation provided by classical scene dissection, *The Crimson Kimono* also goes a step further, using unmotivated tracking shots, props, and lighting in a highly suggestive fashion. In addition, cutting between long-take scenes and highly edited scenes, as well as crosscutting between the domestic and police storylines, create jarring shifts in tone and visual style. During action scenes, rapid editing, character movement, graphic conflicts, and sound effects add to the kineticism of the fights and amplify the release of characters' emotions. These scenes carefully choreograph sound and image to prompt a visceral response, even, as in the kendo battle, at the expense of creating a coherent sense of space and narrative.

An important benefit of utilizing these stylistic strategies is their production economy. While *The Crimson Kimono,* like *House of Bamboo,* features location shooting and a finale that takes place in the midst of a local event, its mise-en-scene, cinematography, and editing demonstrate that a little can go a long way. Sets are spare, lighting is makeshift, close-ups are favored, camera setups are repeated, and long takes with quick cut-ins or optical shots replace complete scene dissection. Although *The Crimson Kimono* lacks the polish of *House of Bamboo,* its action scenes nevertheless display a frenetic, breathless quality that elicits a more direct engagement than the distanced beauty of *House of Bamboo.* The mix of languid long-take conversations with kinetic action scenes; the abrupt shifts in tone, often for ironic or comic effect; and the exploitation of graphic conflict—all are indicative of Fuller's poststudio work in the late 1950s.

With a rather conventional detective story, no known stars, and lacking color or widescreen, *The Crimson Kimono*'s main selling point was its interracial romance, which Columbia highlighted extensively in print ads in a manner that irritated Fuller.[66] Perhaps in an attempt to capitalize on its portrayal of the Japanese immigrant community, *The Crimson Kimono* opened first in San Francisco at the 2,700-seat Paramount Theater. Headlining a double bill with *Juke Box Rhythm* (1959), the film did "fair" before moving in subsequent weeks to headlining spots in a few first-run theaters.[67] While some trade reviews found an exploitable angle in the interracial romance, and the *Motion Picture Herald* praised Fuller's direction as "exciting, unconventional, and geared for realism," other critics thought the different plot strands of the film did not weave together very effectively and objected to the insertion of "highfalutin dialogue" into a genre picture.[68] Without critical attention outside of the trades or a simultaneous first-run release to a number of major markets, *The Crimson Kimono* seems not to have benefited from a coordinated publicity campaign or from a well-orchestrated release schedule indicative of most A product. Instead, the film dropped to a supporting role after its first three bookings, playing on the bottom half of double bills with Columbia's *Battle of the Coral Sea* (1959) within five weeks of its initial release. Although no box office tally is available, *The Crimson Kimono* might have done well enough to make a profit if it was initially budgeted quite low and released first as a headliner only for a chance at additional returns beyond the flat fees it would generate when distributed on the bottom half of the bill. In any event, Columbia agreed to finance and distribute a second Fuller film with slightly greater star power and higher production values.

Fuller's follow-up for Columbia, the dark revenge saga *Underworld, U.S.A.*, returned him to the world of cops and criminals and saw him further develop his hard-hitting visual aesthetic. The title arrived courtesy of an article on modern-day organized crime written by Joseph Dineen and purchased by Columbia. Fuller drafted an original story to go with it, but production was delayed almost a year due to an actor's strike and script changes negotiated by the PCA. Finally, with a budget of approximately $1 million, the film shot on the Columbia lot for twenty-six days after a week of rehearsal.[69] Fuller brought in veteran cinematographer Hal Mohr to develop the film's high-contrast, black-and-white photography, while Jerome Thoms again edited the picture. Completed in August 1960 but still requiring PCA cuts as late as November, Columbia held up the film's release until the following February, then slowly distributed it over the next year.

As with *Pickup on South Street, Underworld, U.S.A.* attracted PCA criticism for its excessive brutality and sexual situations; the 1956 Code revisions further targeted the initial draft of the script for its failure to depict upstanding law enforcement. PCA negotiations on *Underworld, U.S.A.* were more prolonged and suggestions more thoroughly enforced than during the review of *Pickup on South Street,* however. Not only had Code revisions increased the regulation of violence and crime, but Fuller was also no longer supported by the pressure that a major studio could apply to the PCA. As a result, Fuller could not ignore PCA suggestions as easily and relied more on constructive editing to achieve his desired kinetic effects than on the spatially and temporally unified presentation of violence characteristic of *Pickup on South Street.*

*Underworld, U.S.A.* opens on New Year's Eve in the wrong side of town, as street kid Tolly Devlin (David Kent) celebrates by rolling a drunk and getting in a fight. After Tolly is patched up by bar owner and mother figure Sandy (Beatrice Kay), the two witness a shadowy beating in the adjacent alley that results in the death of Tolly's dad. Intent on his own brand of justice, Tolly refuses to cooperate with the police investigation and instead begins his journey from an orphanage to reform school to jail. While in prison, the grown Tolly (Cliff Robertson) has himself assigned to the hospital wing, where one of the four men who killed his father lays dying. Before the man expires, Tolly extracts the names of the other three killers: Smith (Allan Gruener), Gunther (Gerald Milton), and Gela (Paul Dubov), now all lieutenants of crime boss Connors (Robert Emhardt). On his release from jail, Tolly vows to hunt them down. He reconnects with Sandy, whose gin joint has been taken over by the syndicate, and breaks up the beating of Cuddles (Dolores Dorn), a prostitute targeted by Smith. Tolly has Cuddles provide evidence against Smith to Driscoll (Larry Gates), the head of the Federal Crime Committee, while the local police chief on the syndicate's payroll commits suicide under investigation. Tolly begins working for both sides, operating as a safecracker for the syndicate and breaking into Driscoll's safe, while planting documents in the safe that suggest Smith, Gunther, and Gela are cooperating with Driscoll. In order to protect his own interests, Connors arranges for Gus (Richard Rust), his sunglasses-wearing hit man, to kill off his lieutenants one by one. Enjoying it all tremendously, Tolly thinks himself satisfied and slowly thaws to the idea of starting a new life with Cuddles. Their chance for happiness is blown, however, when Connors orders Tolly and Gus to kill Cuddles. Tolly confronts Connors at his poolside office and drowns him, but is fatally injured himself. He finally staggers back into that same, fateful alley where his father died and takes his last breath in the arms of Cuddles and Sandy.

*Underworld, U.S.A.* is best viewed as Fuller's follow-up to *Pickup on South Street,* a companion piece inflected by the freedoms of independence. Both films feature an obsessive, antisocial protagonist; a battered, good-hearted woman of the streets; an older, wise female helpmate; a central criminal enterprise; and an (un)healthy dose of vicious violence. Both protagonists, cold and self-interested, initially resist the affections of the female lead, only to sacrifice themselves when she is threatened. Neither is fully redeemed, however; Skip walks out of *Pickup on South Street* with no indication of changing his ways, while Tolly dies with the same anger that propelled him through his whole life. While Skip is motivated by money, Tolly is more of a sociopath, characterized by the clenched, twisting fist he makes first in reform school, then as a safecracker, again when he is out of jail, and finally in death. No pretense of a happy ending is possible for such a character in Fuller's cinematic universe. *Underworld, U.S.A.* also features more digressive episodes and tonal shifts than seen in the tight, unified narratives produced by Fuller for Twentieth Century–Fox. The sequences dealing with the corruption of local officials—such as the police chief's suicide and Gus's threatening attack on a young girl—divert the plot from its central narrative thread, while sharp tonal shifts between scenes can also jolt the viewer out of immersion in the story. Both of these traits are markers of Fuller's work in the late 1950s and 1960s, as he organized his narratives for increasing sensationalism.

Fuller's goal for *Underworld, U.S.A.* was to differentiate the film through sex, violence, and a detailed presentation of criminal methods—much as he and Zanuck attempted with *Pickup on South Street*—but his status as an independent left him with few cards to play when negotiating with the PCA. When Fuller wrote the script for *Underworld, U.S.A.* in the late 1950s, the industry was operating under the revised Production Code that circumscribed the portrayal of law enforcement, criminals, and violence. The Code now specifically required that law enforcement officials retain the upper hand in scripts and banned the detailed presentation of criminal methods and protracted scenes of cruelty and brutality. By specifically designing the *Underworld, U.S.A.* script as an exposé of organized crime that fully integrated drug use, prostitution, venereal disease, and widespread violence into the story, Fuller immediately ran afoul of the revised Code. Although the Globe Enterprises distribution contracts with Columbia do not survive, it is likely that they required Globe to deliver a film with a PCA seal, much like Globe's contracts with Fox and in keeping with the standards of the major distributors. While the necessity of complying with the Code forced Fuller to eliminate many of the details in the script that illustrated the powerful growth of organized crime, it also encouraged him to develop further the crisp, elliptical editing style he had already begun to explore in *The Crimson Kimono.*

In interviews in preproduction publicity as well as promotional materials, Fuller described *Underworld, U.S.A.* as an "adult" gangster film, both sensational and "realistic." By suggesting that the film's presentation of sex and violence was an authentic depiction of organized crime, Fuller hoped to differentiate his picture from the flood of films about gangsters and the syndicate that hit American screens in the wake of the success of *Al Capone* (1959). Fuller trumpeted his plans for a different kind of gangster film in a *Variety* article entitled, "'Frankly, My Next Pic Is All Action, Sex 'n' Violence,'" written during the scriptwriting process. He suggested that *Underworld, U.S.A.* would be unique in the current production cycle because it was set in the contemporary world of organized crime, rather than in the 1920s, and "there will not be a single policeman, FBI man, or undercover agent in the picture. Nor will there be any scenes in a nightclub, bar, or saloon." Fuller also stated that the film would contain lots of action and sex, not for their own sake, but because, "If you have a story about gangs, you must show how they live and operate and how they use violence to terrify people." His aim, he says, is "not to resolve anything," but merely to awaken people to the insidious presence of gangsterism among seemingly legitimate businesses.[70]

Fuller's intention of producing an "adult" film about organized crime quickly encountered strenuous objections from the PCA. Script revisions on *Underworld, U.S.A.* took over a year, with four different drafts submitted to the PCA, as well as nine sets of revised pages; after the film was completed, Fuller screened it for PCA officials and agreed to additional cuts. The PCA rejected Fuller's November 1959 first draft out of hand due to seven large-scale violations of the Code that were so integral to the story they could not be removed without undermining the plot itself. The violations included: overwhelming brutality and eighteen personalized killings, "a sheer bloodbath" that utilized "shocking and sickening" methods; the general absence of law enforcement and its corruption or impotence when depicted; the presentation of prostitutes, prostitution, and a brothel; extensive treatment of drug use and the profits derived from drug trafficking; the dramatization of venereal disease; unrepentant sex outside of marriage; and unrepentant adultery.[71] The amount and nature of the violence in the draft script of *Underworld, U.S.A.*, as well as the weak presentation of law enforcement, made it especially vulnerable under the 1956 revision of the Production Code, which strengthened the regulatory measures controlling the depiction of crime. Venereal disease also remained a banned topic, and while the PCA's enforcement of restrictions against prostitution and drug use was not as vigilant as a decade before, detailed references to the profits available in each caused a great deal of concern. In order to produce *Underworld, U.S.A.*, Fuller needed to reconceive how to present the "reality" behind gangster life and business without violating the protective measures of the Production Code. In doing so, he agreed to eliminate some of the differentiating elements he originally promoted in the October 1959 *Variety* article.

The second draft of *Underworld, U.S.A.* that Fuller submitted to the PCA contained significant story changes, including the increased presence of law enforcement and new backgrounds for the female characters. The revision features the subplot of District Attorney Driscoll's partnership with Tolly in order to heighten the presence and power of law enforcement. In addition, Sandy, Tolly's mother figure, is no longer explicitly identified as an ex-prostitute, the madam of a brothel, or a victim of VD; instead, she runs a coffee joint that used to be a bar. Tolly's relationship with Mary, now renamed Cuddles, is no longer explicitly consummated, nor is Cuddles any longer engaged in an affair with Connors, the head boss; instead, Cuddles is merely a call girl that desperately yearns for a normal life and works under the prostitute boss, Smith. These revisions addressed the majority of violations targeted by the PCA, with the notable exception of excessive brutality and the script's emphasis on the drug trade. As a result, the PCA deemed the story of the second draft acceptable. In the PCA's response to the revised script, Geoffrey Shurlock commended the complete story overhaul: "We wish to express our appreciation for this fine job of rewriting, particularly that aspect of the story in which law enforcement is given some stature."[72] Nevertheless, Shurlock indicated the script still contained too much brutality and too many references to organized prostitution and drug trade profits. More significantly for Columbia, the film's distributor, the script was over 130 pages long, a length that would result in a two-hour-plus movie. Another revision was needed to address PCA concerns and shorten the script length.

In the third draft, dated May 1960, Fuller streamlined the script to under 120 pages and reintroduced the sort of excessively brutal acts that had generated criticism of *Pickup on South Street*. Shurlock drew attention to scenes that included the use of a broken whiskey bottle as a weapon, stomping on hands, kicking of prone victims, punching of women, a revolver-in-the-mouth suicide, a forced drowning, clubbing with a gun, multiple punching of the same victim, multiple gunshot wounds to the same victim, and an overly long fight to the death.[73] Only three of the problematic scenes were flagged in the prior script, suggesting that Fuller incorporated additional violence in the third draft as a means of counterbalancing the heightened presence of law enforcement and maintaining the raw, sensational vision of gangster life that he hoped would differentiate the film. Shurlock also requested changes in scenes that imply Tolly and Cuddles are having a sexual relationship, specifically those with suggestive dialogue or staging that places both characters on the same bed. Dialogue concerning the prostitution racket, including references to a prostitute's union, a "stand-up strike," and chaining prostitutes "to the houses" raised additional concern.[74] Without the weight of a production head like Zanuck or a major studio behind him, Fuller either had to acquiesce to PCA demands or to discover a way around them. Based on the subsequent PCA reviews of the final draft of the script and various revised pages, Fuller quickly eliminated or changed problematic dialogue but remained committed to incorporating sexually suggestive situations and violence into the script. In his notes on the final draft, Shurlock encourages the film "to establish by indirection" and advises moving offensive actions out of frame, a strategy Fuller adopts through the use of constructive editing.[75] Sequences involving the death of the police chief and the murder of Gunther illustrate how PCA directives participated in transforming not only the content but also the visual style of *Underworld, U.S.A.*, encouraging Fuller to create his desired effects through elliptical editing.

As the Production Code strongly restricted the depiction of suicide, Fuller had to find a visual solution that would enable him to suggest the manner of the chief of police's death. The PCA first draws attention to the suicide of the chief in the third draft of the *Underworld, U.S.A.* script, noting, "The action of the Chief of Police jamming the revolver muzzle into his mouth and pulling the trigger is sickeningly gruesome. We ask that you substitute some other less gruesome business."[76] PCA comments on subsequent drafts and revised pages do not again raise the issue, suggesting that Fuller rewrote the scene in an acceptable fashion. Though he may have changed the script itself, it seems Fuller actually shot the suicide as originally written. During the November 16, 1960 meeting to review the finished film, the PCA notes additional cuts agreed to by Fuller, including one in reel six: "The business of the Chief of Police putting his pistol barrel in his mouth to commit suicide will be eliminated. The suicide will take place out of scene, and the audience will not know the method of self-destruction."[77] The presentation of the suicide in the release print carefully negotiates the PCA's directive to keep it "out of scene" as well as Fuller's desire to suggest as much as possible.

Rather than simply eliminating the entire sequence of the suicide, the film retains much of the original action and inserts a visual replacement for the muzzle shot. In the same medium-long shot that serves as the foundation of the entire scene, the police chief turns to the rear of the set and removes a gun from a cabinet, then walks to the center-left background, with Driscoll in the center-right foreground. The shot scale and staging make it difficult to precisely identify what is in the chief's hand, but his dialogue suggests that he is unwilling to risk the lives of his family by testifying against the syndicate. Facing the camera, the chief begins to lift the gun; in a cut to an extreme close-up he says, "God forgive me." Rather than holding on the medium-long shot for the entire sequence, the cut to the extreme close-up further obscures the chief's physical action while at the same time confirming that he is about to commit an unforgivable act. A quick return to the medium-long shot shows the chief with the gun moving upward by his chest and Driscoll leaping at him, yelling "No!" The final shot of the scene is an extreme close-up of a photo collection of all the police officers in the unit. A bullet pierces the glass and hits the chief's photo in the center. A dissolve reveals the head-line of the *Graphic:* "Police Chief Kills Self to Escape Investigation." By cutting before the gun reaches the chief's mouth, the scene addresses the PCA's primary concern of not illustrating the method of suicide. The bul-let shattering the glass and piercing the chief's photo visually stands in for the moment of impact, suggesting by substitution that the chief is dead. To a more sophisticated viewer, the location of the photo on the wall and the trajectory of the bullet might also suggest that the chief has shot up and through himself. By dissolving to the newspaper headline, the narration further clarifies the action and underlines the chief's moti-vation, providing a moral undertone to an otherwise reprehensible ac-tion. While the intervention of the PCA made the scene less graphic, the narrative action is no less clear.

In addition to using a visual substitute for what could not be explic-itly shown, *Underworld, U.S.A.* also relies heavily on constructive edit-ing to "establish by indirection," as illustrated by the sequence depicting Gunther's murder. The scenes surrounding the murder of Gunther went through several different revisions in the script, with the method of death becoming increasingly vicious in the third and fourth drafts and subsequent revised pages. As noted in the objections to the script pro-vided by the PCA, the second draft featured Gunther being killed by three bullets, while the third draft had Gela hitting Gunther on the head with a gun and subsequently punching him multiple times, although the PCA does not in this instance indicate the exact method of Gunther's death.[78] By the fourth draft, Fuller added a new bit of business: not only does Gela still swipe at Gunther multiple times, but Connors also throws a pot of hot coffee in Gunther's face. In keeping with its strategy of encouraging that brutality be shifted offscreen, the PCA asks that Gela's initial hit be performed out of frame, and that subsequent hits and the thrown coffee be eliminated.[79] The revised pages seemingly con-tinue to ramp up the violence, as the PCA now objects to the addition of Gunther having kerosene poured over him and being set alight as "too sadistically brutal." Shurlock suggests omitting this sequence, arguing, "It will be sufficient to establish, as you do . . . that his 'charred body' was found in his car."[80] Again Shurlock proposes implying violence rather than actually depicting it, but it seems Fuller again ignored the suggestion when shooting the film. As with the suicide of the police chief, Fuller acquiesces to the PCA only after the screening of the com-pleted picture. PCA notes cite their compromise: "The entire footage of the gangster sloshing gasoline on the victim in the back seat of the car will be cut. The victim's frightened face will be shown in a flash shot, then the gangster will throw a match into the car and walk away."[81] While Fuller lost the gasoline shot(s), he escaped with the rest of the sequence intact and a significantly more explicit murder than if he had originally followed Shurlock's suggestion and never filmed the immolation. As an examination of the sequence illustrates, the absence of the gasoline shot does not rob the sequence of its brutal intensity—if anything, it may even heighten it.

The assassination of Gunther is a model of constructive editing, involving the viewer directly in the murder through the need to imagine that which is not explicitly presented. In a series of discrete close-ups and medium shots, Gus lights the match; Gunther awaits the fire; Gus throws the match; the car explodes in flames; and Gus removes his sunglasses. Collectively, the shots suggest Gunther's execution without actually depicting it. Viewers must piece together the action in the scene, imagining for themselves the moments when the match hits the car, the fuel tank catches fire, and Gunther burns to death in the backseat, writhing in agony. While the explicit presence of gasoline has been cut from the scene, the viewer may identify the liquid covering Gunther's face in the extreme close-up as an accelerant; however, even if the viewer assumes the liquid is merely fear-induced sweat, the method of execution remains clear. The scene ends with Connors leaning over to Gela, glancing toward the flames that fry Gunther in the background, and wryly adding, "Gimme a light." We laugh at the pun, but it's a guilty laugh, for we recognize that the callousness of the gangsters has become for us a source of entertainment.

In less than one minute of screen time, Tolly's false information has turned Gunther from a trusted gang leader into a pile of ashes. Because the viewer knows about Tolly's tip before Gunther does, the fast-paced cuts between Gunther and his executioners function less to reveal that he is about to die—the viewer already anticipates this—but to reveal precisely *how* he will die. The suspense lies in the method, in that which the PCA most wanted to conceal, and the use of constructive editing involves the viewer in discovering the method more intensely than if the gun blow and gas sloshing were actually shown. Because viewers must mentally piece together the content of each shot in order to understand the entirety of the action, they perform an active role in the scene's presentation of a painful death. The use of constructive editing thereby fulfills not only the PCA's recommendation to "establish by indirection," but also Fuller's desire to "awaken the public as to what is going on in the rackets" by providing them with the sensation of participating in an execution.[82]

While PCA guidelines encouraged the use of constructive editing in this scene, the same editing technique is found in other scenes that were never marked as problematic by the PCA—perhaps because they were written as shot, already "indirect." Constructive editing that leads to a marked tonal shift also occurs earlier in the film when Gus the hit man runs over a young girl on a bicycle (see figs. on p. 22). The full effect of the murder is

1                                    2

Fuller uses constructive editing in *Under-world, U.S.A.* to bypass Production Code Administration complaints about the fiery execution of Gunther (Gerald Milton) by Gus (Richard Rust). As seen in these frame enlargements, Fuller elides Gunther's ac-tual death, relying on viewers to infer his immolation.

3

felt once the final shot of the girl sprawled on the pavement cuts to a scene that begins with Tolly proudly (and stupidly) pulling two giant, plucked chickens out of a bag in Sandy's kitchen—one for each of his women! The kinetic intensity of the rapidly edited chase is contrasted with the long take conversation in the kitchen, while the tragedy of the girl's death is quickly undercut by the comically inappropriate presentation of dinner. These editing strategies efficiently and inexpensively enable Fuller to con-trast scenes visually and punctuate tonal shifts, mixing horror and humor in a startling way. While Fuller occasionally utilized constructive editing in the early years of his career—such as in the openings of *I Shot Jesse James* and *Pickup on South Street*—he incorporated the technique into films more frequently as an independent producer, suggesting that PCA oversight may have pushed his visual style further in that direction.

Never at a loss for creative ideas, Fuller produced a rather unusual trailer for *Underworld, U.S.A.* to promote its realism, combining some scenes from the production with him addressing the audience and ex-plaining his reasons for writing the story and how he researched the facts.[83] No national promotion accompanied the film's release, however, and few critics outside of the trades reviewed the film. Those who did re-view *Underworld, U.S.A.*, however, responded positively, allowing that the story was formulaic but applauding Fuller's taut direction, particularly the consistent use of close-ups. Britain's *Monthly Film Bulletin* even went so far as to compare the film to earlier works by Robert Wise and Fritz Lang, describing *Underworld, U.S.A.* in a back-handed manner as "distinguished precisely by those virtues which Fuller's previous melodramas have so notoriously lacked—modesty of concept, an incisive narrative flow, in fact, sheer craftsmanship."[84] *Variety* found the film ideal for saturation booking, but if it did play widely, it was only for undocumented secondary runs.[85] Although *Underworld, U.S.A.* shared the hard-boiled attitude of *Pickup on South Street,* it enjoyed little of the earlier film's success. In May 1961, *Underworld, U.S.A.* popped up at neighborhood theaters in New York with the thriller *Mad Dog Coll* (1961), followed by a handful of bookings in first-run situations at both the top and the bottom of the bill.[86] Even more expensive than *The Crimson Kimono* but effectively receiving the same type of release, *Underworld, U.S.A.* likely never turned a profit.

Fuller's aesthetic impulses changed little during the 1950s—he continued to craft his films for direct emotional impact—but the manner in which his impulses were expressed and the market into which he released his pictures changed dramatically. Fuller's status as the writer, director, and producer of his Globe pictures freed him to complete projects that broke more distinctly from classical and generic norms. The tight, efficient narratives and stylistic refinement of his Fox years were replaced by brash exuberance, as outsized characters, overstuffed plots, startling tonal shifts, and a more emphatic visual style become increasingly dominant. Globe was in the right place at the right time, but it produced idiosyncratic films for a market that was ever-more difficult for "in-betweener" pictures to exploit. By the late 1950s, most in the industry recognized that the era of the old-fashioned programmer was over. Big pictures with multiple stars, color, widescreen, and location shooting dominated box office, while those low-budget films that did make money exploited topical gimmicks and were increasingly aimed at youth. The move to Globe from Fox enabled Fuller to make the kind of movies he wanted while still enjoying financing and distribution from major studios. The catch was that the films needed to maintain profitability in order for Globe to hold onto future financing and distribution. After a series of disappointing box-office returns, Fuller no longer enjoyed the luxury of multiple-picture deals with several studios. Making little in profit participation from his own films and devoid of any savings due to a recent divorce, he was also unable to finance productions on his own, as he had for *Park Row.* By the early 1960s, Fuller thus had to pick up jobs where he could, doing freelance work while trying to put together the next financing and distribution deal. His experiment with his own production company was over.

# CHAPTER FOUR

# The Freelance Years, 1961–1964

fter the collapse of Globe Enterprises, Fuller continued the rest of his career as a writer/director for hire. Rather than making a new financing and distribution deal himself or a slate of films as an independent producer, Fuller now primarily relied on other producers to come to him with an offer for financing. Given the spotty box-office returns of his last few films for Globe, such an offer could be perceived by a producer as a risk, unless the project particularly suited Fuller's talents or was developed so inexpensively that little risk was involved. At the same time, Fuller was selective about joining projects already in development, while he had little ability to pick and choose producers for his own original scripts. Combined with the continued decline of the programmer, the net result for Fuller was a production slow-down.

Although *Merrill's Marauders*, Fuller's first gig as a freelance director, returned him to the world of big-budget action films he experienced at Twentieth Century–Fox, for the rest of the decade he scraped together work in television and in very low-budget filmmaking. After finishing *Merrill's Marauders* in 1962, he wrote and directed an episode of the popular television western *The Virginian* and directed an hour-long story about a troubleshooter for the Department of Health, Education, and Welfare that aired on *The Dick Powell Show*. The following year he made a deal with Fromkess & Firks Productions, Inc. to write, direct, and produce two pictures to be distributed by Allied Artists, negotiating an advance plus a third of the net profits of each film.[1] Leon Fromkess, a former vice president of Samuel Goldwyn Productions, included the two films as part of a five-picture contract he and Sam Firks signed in November 1962 with Allied.[2] Founded in 1946 as a subsidiary of Monogram to handle the production and distribution of higher-budget films, by the early 1960s Allied Artists relied largely on independent producers for its often inexpensive product. The Fromkess-Firks deal threw Fuller back into the sort of low-budget filmmaking that he initiated his career with at Lippert, but now Fuller began producing a slightly different kind of movie, one grounded less in genre and more in sensation and controversy. While neither *Shock Corridor* nor *The Naked Kiss* attempt in any way to reach out to the youth market, they fall closer to the exploitation category than any other films in Fuller's career, pushing topical buttons and playing with taboos in a fashion that bordered on tasteless—and sometimes crossed the line. Blunt gut punches with heavy social overtones, they remain among Fuller's most audacious and unsettling films.

### *Return to War:* Merrill's Marauders

While Fuller was editing *Underworld, U.S.A.*, he accepted an offer from independent producer Milton Sperling to direct *Merrill's Marauders,* the true story of the deadly march made by Brigadier General Frank Merrill and his men behind enemy lines in Burma during World War II. Fuller initially resisted Sperling's call to direct, intent as he was on completing for Warner Bros. his own World War II story, *The Big Red One,* but Jack Warner encouraged Fuller to view Merrill's story as a "dry run" for his own film.[3] Sperling had been working on the Merrill project since 1959, when he purchased the screen rights to *The Marauders,* an autobiography written by one of Merrill's lieutenants, Charlton Ogburn, Jr.[4] Two screenwriters had already taken a shot at the adaptation by the time Fuller and Sperling began scouting locations in the Philippines at the end of November 1960; Fuller himself completed a draft upon their return, and the final writing credit was shared by him and Sperling.[5] Cooperation from the Department of Defense and the U.S. Army Special Forces enabled the production to be based at Clark Air Base in the Philippines and to enjoy housing, vehicles, equipment, and communications at no cost, while the Philippine Army provided twelve hundred soldiers for four days of work doubling as Japanese. Sperling crowed to studio chief Jack Warner that the production budget of only slightly over $1 million was a fraction of what the Technicolor and CinemaScope feature would have cost without military assistance.[6] Production commenced in March 1961 for a planned forty-one day shoot around Clark, the jungles of Luzon, and the Pampagna mountains; within a week rain began to slow the picture, forcing Fuller to improvise material when locations could not be reached and eventually to cut scenes entirely. Though the production ended six days over schedule, both Sperling and Warner praised Fuller's effort. In a letter to Warner, Sperling described Fuller as "a tough, knowledgeable man with a no-nonsense attitude about picture making," to which the studio head replied, "Sam Fuller is a gutty guy and that's why he is where he is. We can use more guys with blood, sweat, guts, tits, and sand!"[7]

*Merrill's Marauders* depicts the legendary efforts of the American 5307th Composite Unit (Provisional) in Burma in 1942. Led by Brigadier General Frank Merrill (Jeff Chandler), the footsoldiers—all volunteers with two years' experience in jungle warfare—are ordered behind enemy lines to prevent the unification of German and Japanese forces in India. The film picks up the unit on its way to Walawbum to destroy the main Japanese supply base. Already exhausted, the men look forward to relief by the British. After capturing Walawbum, however, Merrill receives orders to take out the railhead at Shaduzup and then cross the mountains to assist the British at Myitkyina, the Japanese gatehead to India. Knowing his men are already hungry, tired, and ravaged by disease, Merrill accepts they must do the impossible—survive a five-hundred-mile journey and still have the strength to defeat the enemy. Lieutenant Lee Stockton (Ty Hardin), the head of Merrill's point platoon and his surrogate son, reluctantly supports the decision, though Merrill only reveals to him the initial goal: Shaduzup. The men slog through swamps and rivers to the railhead, where the battle disintegrates into chaos and confusion. With the living now as inert as the dead, the unit's doctor declares them unfit to continue, suffering as they are from an "accumulation of everything." Merrill ignores him and decides to continue to Myitkyina, announcing: "When you're at the end of your rope, all you've got to do is make one foot move in front of the other." Upon hearing the orders, Stockton resists sending his men into certain death and requests permission to be released from command. Merrill denies his request, and the unit heads out into the mountains, ground down by exhaustion. After defending the initial attack by the Japanese outside of Myitkyina, Merrill realizes they must advance into Myitkyina itself. Exhorting his spent unit to stand and fight, Merrill suffers a heart attack, and Stockton rallies to take his place. Against all odds, the men march out; narration reveals their success at Myitkyina and the eventual toll: of the three thousand soldiers who began the journey, only one hundred remained in action.

The military support that Sperling wrangled for the picture brings new levels of authenticity to Fuller's depiction of war. Unlike *The Steel Helmet, Fixed Bayonets,* and *China Gate, Merrill's Marauders* was shot entirely on location in areas that could actually pass for central Asia (i.e., not in a studio, Griffith Park, or Columbia's ranch). For the first time we track with the soldiers through actual swamps and across a real mountainside, making their physical experience that much more palpable. Additionally, the cooperation of the American and Philippine armies enabled Fuller to work with extras that not only had military training but also could reasonably replicate the thousands of soldiers involved in Merrill's engagements. No longer did twenty extras have to stand in for two hundred, and Fuller's extreme wide shots during the battles allow the viewer to register the different waves of enemy attack and the overwhelming odds facing the Marauders. Access to military ordinance further heightens the intensity of the battles, freeing Fuller from relying on stock footage to suggest an artillery barrage; explosive devices in *Merrill's Marauders* fall loud, fast, and frequently, increasing the nerve-wracking impact of the combat scenes.

With its emphasis on narrative clarity and cohesion, the script for *Merrill's Marauders* also reflects the influence of Sperling on Fuller's storytelling and recalls the tight plots of his Twentieth Century–Fox years. From the opening narration, which uses stock footage and maps to carefully contextualize the struggle for Burma and purpose of Merrill's mission, to the constant discussion amongst the officers of where they are and what shape the men are in, to the animated maps that illustrate each stage in the journey, each element within the narrative works in a redundant fashion to clarify the action. The digressive episodes that allowed for didactic conversation and colorfully individuated characterization in *China Gate*, *The Steel Helmet*, and even to an extent in *Fixed Bayonets* are largely absent in *Merrill's Marauders*. Politics plays no role in the soldiers' motives or actions, and only Merrill and Stockton receive any kind of back-story. The intimacy of the platoons that formed the basis of Fuller's previous war pictures is here replaced by the broader strokes necessitated by following large-scale troop movement, and dialogue overall is kept to a minimum.

Though *Merrill's Marauders* is more streamlined than Fuller's previous combat pictures, it maintains his investment in depicting the absurd ironies, tangled emotions, and mind-numbing exhaustion experienced by soldiers during war. Once again, a delightfully dedicated mule driver is part of the unit, poignantly dying as he carries the load his animal was too exhausted to support. And harkening back to the influence of Short Round on Zack in *The Steel Helmet*, Merrill's men find themselves touched by simple human kindness in the midst of the horror of war. After the battle at Shaduzup, local villagers bring the drained soldiers bowls of rice and water, an act of wordless generosity that reduces a tough sergeant to tears. As ever, Fuller's footsoldiers remain obsessed with sleep, food, and personal health, but the overall physical toll of warfare achieves new emphasis in *Merrill's Marauders*. The tedium and strain of marching are broken only by brief rest and the chaos of battle. Over and over, the soldiers discuss their overwhelming desire to see the conclusion of their mission, but the mission just keeps being extended—at the end of the movie, we leave the men still marching. Though the narrator triumphantly announces the unit's eventual success at Myitkyina, what we take away is our memory of what we have seen—not a successful mission accomplished, but a mission that never ends.

Fuller (lower left, in white shirt and baseball cap, with cigar) and his crew get wet during the production of *Merrill's Marauders*. Shot in CinemaScope on location in the Philippines, the film exploits the widescreen frame to show long lines of weary men marching through the jungle. *Courtesy of the Academy of Motion Picture Arts and Sciences*

The fight at the Shaduzup railhead most fully embodies Fuller's vision of the nightmare of warfare. The sequence begins with a series of static shots of the tracks, trains, and oil tanks of the depot, all devoid of men. No clear visual connection links the shots together, making ambiguous the arrangement of space. Suddenly, the Americans and Japanese converge, and Stockton's platoon hunkers down among a maze of hulking concrete blocks. The blocks create a confusing series of alleys and blind spots, and a rapid montage depicts American and Japanese soldiers running and shooting in every direction. First an American soldier will enter a corridor and be shot; then a Japanese soldier will enter the same corridor in the same area and also be shot. The editing follows no clear action-reaction pattern, and the opposing forces hold no delineated geographic position; as a result, the viewer is often unsure of the national identity of the soldiers, who their targets are, and who is shooting at them—all that is clear is that some soldiers are shooting, and others are falling to the ground. The lack of consistent screen direction and spatial continuity leaves the viewer, like the soldiers, grasping for an understanding of what is going on. We think we see an American shooting another American. Is that what we saw? The action develops so quickly we can't be sure. Finally, a high-angle shot provides an overview of the battle, revealing circles of the blocks arranged like the petals of a daisy, one after the other, shielding men firing at all angles. The impression is of men cornered, unclear of their position and shooting wildly at anything that moves. This is the lesson Fuller tries to impart: war is chaotic, and desperate men do what is necessary to survive. At battle's end, a crane follows Stockton, traversing 180 degrees, as he steps from block to block high in the air, surveying the scene. His is the only movement within the frame, around him only anonymous bodies. The full weight of what it means to be an officer, to order men into battle, falls on his shoulders. Fuller closes the scene as he opens it, with high-angle static shots of the railyard, now carpeted with the dead—an unsettling vision of war's toll, a vision that complicates what it means to "win."

The contradictory nature of leadership in war—a theme Fuller first explored in *Fixed Bayonets*—is at the heart of *Merrill's Marauders* and is vividly expressed through the characters of Stockton and Merrill. Exposition early in the narrative characterizes the relationship between the two as that of adopted son and father, one a designated successor to the other. Merrill oversaw Stockton's unit during the previous Burma incursion in 1940, and when the young soldier was wounded but had no family to notify, Merrill wrote about him to his own wife, including a photo of his protégé. Merrill's confidence in Stockton is summed up in his exclamation to his friend, Doc: "Some day that boy's gonna be a general!" But Stockton finds it difficult to distance himself from the soldiers he leads—soldiers he once fought beside as an equal. He suffers every time he receives a dead soldier's dog tags and struggles to write the necessary letter to the deceased's family. A telling shot at Walawbum encapsulates Stockton's predicament: Merrill has just told Stockton of the mission to Shaduzup ("Think you can stand losing more of your friends?"), and now Stockton must tell his platoon. Over the shoulders of Merrill and Doc in the foreground left, we see Stockton in the far right distance relaying the news; wordlessly, the men swarm past Stockton until he is alone in the field, and Merrill turns grimly away. Command has isolated Stockton from his platoon, and Merrill knows it is he who has brought this to bear. The distance between the two within the frame suggests the difference in their years—Merrill, at the end of his career as a leader, Stockton at the beginning—but Merrill's keen attention to his lieutenant's struggle reminds us that he shares it, too. Stockton may be sending a platoon out to die, but Merrill is sending all three thousand men.

As he later reminds Stockton, "When you lead, you have to hurt people—the enemy and sometimes your own." The ugly paradox of command—that ordering an attack on the enemy means ordering the death of your own men—is highlighted in a poignant shot after the battle at Shaduzup, once Merrill has told Doc that he will force the unit on to Myitkyina regardless of their lack of fitness. The composition frames Doc in the far left distance, Merrill in the far right distance, and in the foreground center is the medic, attending to a stream of dying and wounded men. Our eyes are drawn to the injured soldiers, the moral burden that Merrill carries, the weight that divides him from even Doc, his closest friend. This is the weight that Denno so feared to carry in *Fixed Bayonets*.

At the end of the film, when Merrill goes from one collapsed soldier to the next, kicking their boots and exhorting them to follow him and continue to fight, one cannot help but think back to Fuller's story of his own experience on D-day. Pinned down on Omaha Beach with an exit just blown open, Fuller saw his own commander, Colonel George A. Taylor, stand up amidst the German barrage and yell, "There are two kinds of men out here! The dead! And those about to die! So let's get the hell off this beach and at least die inland!" Then Taylor kicked and swore at his understandably cowering men until they got their asses off the ground and ran behind him, through the bullets and to the breach.[8] Fuller later memorialized this moment in *The Big Red One*, but the ending of *Merrill's Marauders* was, as Jack Warner predicted, a dry run—an opportunity to acknowledge the experience of the infantry shared between soldiers. When Stockton takes Merrill's place and prods his men to rise and fight, he is no hero, but a man with a job: to do the impossible, to survive, and to try to live with himself afterwards.

Released by Warner Bros. in Los Angeles over Memorial Day weekend and throughout the country in a large-scale rollout from June through August 1962, *Merrill's Marauders* garnered Fuller glowing reviews in national publications as well as in the trades.[9] *Boxoffice* notes that the film's ninety-eight-minute running time allows it to be shown easily as either a first or second feature, but it headlined or ran solo in downtown and neighborhood theaters both during its initial outing and re-release the following year.[10] *Variety* reported the film's rentals—the amount of money collected by the distributor after theaters receive their share of the box-office gross—to be $1.5 million, ranking the picture fifty-first for the year and likely to break even or be profitable.[11] *Merrill's Marauders* once again demonstrated Fuller's ability to make unique yet crowd-pleasing big pictures when provided with the resources. After production on the film was complete, Fuller expected to return to Columbia to make the third film of his deal—reportedly either *Powder Keg, Cain and Abel,* or *Pearl Harbor*—but Columbia financed and distributed no additional pictures from Globe.[12] Fuller's career as a freelance filmmaker would continue.

### Adult Exploitation: Shock Corridor *and* The Naked Kiss

*Shock Corridor,* the first of Fuller's two pictures for Fromkess-Firks, is an astonishing provocation. Inspired by the story of Nellie Bly, a journalist who in 1887 posed as a patient in order to write an exposé of the Black-well's Island mental hospital, *Shock Corridor* concerns Johnny Barrett, an ambitious reporter who angles to be admitted to a psychiatric institution in order to solve the murder of an inmate named Sloan and win the Pulitzer Prize. The first film Fuller made with Stanley Cortez, the much-lauded director of photography on *The Magnificent Ambersons* (1942) and *The Night of the Hunter* (1955), *Shock Corridor* was shot in two weeks during February 1963 on several barren interior sets for a cost of $222,000.[13] Fuller enjoyed complete production control, as well as final cut. *Shock Corridor* features some of the most extreme characters and situations in all of Fuller's work. His interest in the clash of opposing elements reaches its apotheosis in this film, as the narrative contrasts real identities with assumed identities, sanity with insanity, and restraint with hysteria. The setting of the film and the nature of Johnny's interviews provide Fuller with a broad platform to address America's failings, and his impulse to provoke rather than to be tasteful leads to an abundance of truly alarming sequences. The sensationalism of *Shock Corridor* thus lies not just in its exposé of contemporary social ills and near-parodic depiction of mental illness, but also in its ability to elicit visceral responses from the viewer, to literally produce shocking sensations through the presentation of narrative and stylistic conflict.

 *Shock Corridor* opens with a portentous quote from Euripides: "Whom God wishes to destroy he first makes mad." Assisted by Swanee (William Zuckert), his editor, and Dr. Fong (Philip Ahn), a psychiatrist, reporter Johnny (Peter Breck) "trains" to appear mentally ill, but encounters resistance from his girlfriend, Cathy (Constance Towers). After Johnny withdraws his love, Cathy relents and appears before the police, claiming to be Johnny's sister and the victim of his sexual advances. Johnny succeeds in being committed, bunks with an overweight, gum-smacking opera fanatic, Pagliacci (Larry Tucker), and falls prey to a group of crazed nymphomaniacs. His goal is to interview the three patients who witnessed the murder of Sloan during their brief moments of lucidity: Stuart (James Best), a Korean War veteran who hides behind the identity of a Confederate general to block his guilt over siding with the North Korean Communists; Trent (Hari Rhodes), an African-American who crumbled under the stress of integrating a university and now adopts the identity of a KKK member; and Boden (Gene Evans), a nuclear scientist who regressed to childhood rather than accept responsibility for his deadly creations. While Johnny collects information, he dodges a food fight, a race riot, and Cathy's growing concerns. The plot gradually suggests the erasure of the division between Johnny's actual sanity and pretend insanity until his faked symptoms are his real problems and his experience of mental illness matches that of the men he interrogates. After undergoing electroshock therapy, Johnny discovers the name of the killer. He then loses his memory and eventually his mind, freeing the name of the killer—an attendant named Wilkes—whom Johnny subsequently attacks. An epilogue reveals that Johnny regained sanity long enough to write his article, but is now back in the institution. "What a tragedy," his doctor says. "An insane mute will win the Pulitzer Prize."

Fuller draws heavily from conventions found in detective stories and social problem pictures in *Shock Corridor,* but these elements are merely window dressing. The murder mystery appears to be the means to achieve Johnny's ultimate goal—the Pulitzer Prize—and its overarching structure provides the skeleton of the plot. Yet Johnny's Clue-like search for who killed Sloan in the kitchen with the butcher knife is actually the film's MacGuffin. The bulk of the narrative concerns itself not with uncovering a murderer, but with revealing the thin line between sanity and insanity, between what is real and what is imagined. Likewise, the trappings of the psychiatric exposé primarily function as springboards for sensationalism, as generic motivation for antic, extreme behavior, unpredictable action, and gross tastelessness. Setting his story in a "loony bin" freed Fuller to cut loose from logic, causality, and coherence. And cut loose he did. The narrative of *Shock Corridor* is fraught with implausibility and excessive emotion to an even greater degree than is usual for a Fuller picture, producing a viewing experience that ranges from laughter to disbelief to horror.

Fuller's goal in *Shock Corridor* was to use the psychiatric setting to immerse the viewer in a world of conflict and contradiction where opposing forces consistently collide—often within the same person. The ambiguity surrounding role-playing and the difference between sanity and insanity are reflected in the narrative and visual construction of the film. While many of Fuller's narratives contrast scenes with differing tones, *Shock Corridor* incorporates opposing elements *within* individual scenes and characters to blur distinctions, heighten conflict, and throw the viewer off guard. This strategy is first illustrated in the scene following the opening credits, in which Dr. Fong interrogates Johnny. Johnny appears to have sexual feelings for his sister, but when he expresses too much knowledge of fetishism, Dr. Fong cuts him off and throws open the curtains. The viewer is surprised to discover that Johnny is a reporter training to seem like a sex offender, while Dr. Fong is merely his tutor. The status of the relationship between Johnny's role-play and his core identity supplies the underlying tension of the film, as he must appear unbalanced enough to be believable and trustworthy in the hospital, but must think clearly enough to find the witnesses, ask the right questions, and learn the identity of the killer. Johnny's obsession with winning the Pulitzer Prize prompts him to remain in the hospital, even as he suffers headaches and hallucinations; yet remaining in the hospital only exposes him to further mental and emotional pressure and the threat of insanity. Johnny's paradoxical dilemma is mirrored by Cathy's inner conflict: "I want you, Johnny, but you, you want the Pulitzer Prize." Like Johnny, Cathy is also a strangely "split" character. A proper, well-dressed woman who references Shakespeare, Dickens, Twain, and Freud (though on wildly inappropriate occasions), Cathy strips for a living, a job whose risks Johnny equates with his role-play: "Those hookers didn't knock down your guard and the lunatics won't damage mine!" As part of Johnny's investigation, Cathy, too, must take on a role, as Johnny's sister rather than his sweetheart. While the distinction between the two states remains troublingly clear to Cathy, Johnny's eventual confusion over her identity provides yet another indication of his slide toward madness.

Fuller employs a number of different stylistic techniques to cue viewers to Johnny's inner thoughts and feelings, thereby allowing us to both objectively recognize and subjectively share his mental decline. Johnny's voice-over provides background information on the people he encounters, his "plan," and his experiences. The first time they appear on screen, characters are subject to a brief voice-over biography, complete with hobbies ("Witness number one: Stuart. Farm boy from the Bible Belt."). As Johnny deceives the doctors and other patients, the voice-over alerts the viewer to the real motives behind his actions and what steps he will take next ("The next question's got to be about fetishism, according to Dr. Fong's script."). When Johnny begins to fall apart, the voice-over also registers his confusion and frustration with what is happening to him ("I've got to get my voice back! Don't panic!"). The voice-over thus acts as narrational shorthand, simultaneously providing exposition and access to Johnny's conscious thoughts, enabling us to distinguish between when Johnny is pretending to be insane and when he actually is.

Johnny's superimposed dreams of Cathy early in his hospital stay similarly function to illustrate the divide between his consciousness and unconscious. A Tinker Bell–sized Cathy in strip gear is superimposed on close-up shots of Johnny fidgeting in his sleep. Eerie music provides an aural cue that Johnny is dreaming. The diminutive Cathy tickles Johnny with her boa, speaks in a sexy voice, and taunts him with threats of infidelity: "I don't like being alone, Johnny, but you made me be alone, Johnny. I have the right to find another Johnny." These images of Cathy exist in striking contrast to the "real" Cathy in the rest of the film, alerting us to their existence as Johnny's unconscious fears. Tinker Bell Cathy moves in a different manner, speaks with a different voice, and expresses different concerns than the practical, worried, but supportive real-world Cathy. Johnny talks back to her in his sleep, further revealing his desires: "I miss you, Cathy. My yen for you goes up and down like a fever chart." Voice-overs and dream sequences are not subtle devices—they explicitly tell the viewer what characters know and how they feel—and Fuller employs them here (as well as his florid dialogue) in a highly suggestive fashion, drawing us in to the already feverish mindset of Johnny.

The dueling roles played by both Johnny and Cathy mirror the divided minds of the psychiatric patients, and Fuller taps this inner conflict to create tension and release repressed emotion. One of the characteristics of the patients is how quickly and easily they shift between restraint and hysteria, sanity and insanity. Johnny adopts this trait as a sign of his own assumed illness when he initially explodes in Dr. Menkin's office in an effort to be committed. During Johnny's first meal at the hospital, this behavior is also demonstrated by his fellow patients when a food fight erupts over a disagreement about medication. As no consistent factor sparks these outbursts, they initially take the viewer by surprise; their unexpected appearance in the middle of a scene leaves the viewer in suspense, warily looking for what will set off the next eruption. Dance class, a hallway, a door—inside any space lurks the potential for unleashed emotions and violence. The effect is quite like that produced by the narrative structure of *The Steel Helmet*: viewers feel that danger may be around any corner, and like the child slowly cranking the jack-in-the-box, anxiously await the next time they'll get thwacked.

Johnny's accidental entry into the nymphomaniac ward is a prime example of how Fuller orchestrates the build-up and explosion of emotion for maximum visceral effect. Recalling Johnny's nightmares of Cathy looking elsewhere for love in his absence, the sequence violently illustrates the effect of thwarted desire, drawing the viewer in as witness and participant. As the segment opens, Johnny's voice-over of discovery ("Nymphos!"), the extreme close-up of his hand struggling to turn the locked doorknob, and point-of-view editing patterns all highlight his entrapment, binding the viewer to Johnny's growing fear. Once it becomes clear that Johnny cannot make it out of the room, the formal construction of the scene alters to emphasize the hunger and hysteria of the women's attack. A high-angle long shot depicts the women encircling Johnny and suddenly throwing him to the floor; the camera cranes down to watch as the women hunch over him like a pack of lions feeding on a baby deer, their heads bobbing to get another bite out of him. The angles, camera movement, and compositions formally position Johnny as a helpless victim and the viewer as one of the manic women. The frenzied emotion expressed in the attackers' physical actions is intensified by what is going on around them: One woman slowly circles the group singing "My Bonnie Lies Over the Ocean," while another scribbles furiously on the wall, chanting "I like coffee, I like tea," as Johnny begins to cry out in pain. The attack startlingly reduces the confident, smart reporter to quivering sexual bait. By constructing the scene to first visually align us with Johnny and then insert us within the hysterical violence, Fuller encourages us to respond to both the victim's fear and the attacker's exhilaration. The thrill of the sequence is decidedly unnerving, leaving the viewer, like Johnny, a bit agog. "Where did *that* come from?" we wonder.

Fuller provides us with additional clues regarding the experience of mental illness during sequences in which individual patients slip into and out of psychotic episodes. Frequently, subjective sound signals a patient's initial psychic break, as with the opera music that accompanies Pagliacci's pantomime of murder, the bugle horns and distorted strings that cue Stuart to dance a frenzied "Dixie," or the voices inside Bodon's head. This strategy suggests for the viewer what it is like to be insane—to be unable to distinguish between fantasy and reality—by subjectively presenting the patients' conflation of what is real and what is imagined. Conversely, a novel narrative and stylistic pattern involving subjective visions punctuates the arrival of clear thought for Stuart, Trent, and Johnny (after he has forgotten the name of the killer). As each character talks, a hallucination sparks his memories and prompts him to recall the past. The visions of Stuart, Trent, and Johnny are marked by a change in film stock, as the movie's 35mm black-and-white switches to color, 16mm and 35mm unsqueezed anamorphic images of Tokyo, a South American aboriginal tribe, and a waterfall, respectively. The sudden appearance of the subjective images dramatically changes the look of the film, and along with the musical score draws attention to the characters' resulting moments of lucidity. Here again Fuller exploits the clash of dueling forces—sanity and insanity, reality and fantasy, sound and image—to startle viewers and shake us into an awareness of the patients' subjective experiences.

Fuller caps the dissolution of the line between Johnny's real sanity and fake psychosis with two explosive sequences stylistically designed to literally assault the viewer's senses. First, Johnny's shock treatment functions as a visual and aural summary of the emotional traumas wrecked by his institutionalization, a barrage of his intermingled fears (insanity) and desires (Cathy). In a silent medium-close-up, Johnny is strapped down on a table with a rag in his mouth and electrodes on his head. When the switch is pulled, he heaves violently. Dialogue and images from previous scenes, including Cathy stripping, Stuart violently dancing to "Dixie," the nymphos, and the race riot instigated by Trent are superimposed on top of him. The cutting rate of the superimpositions increases rapidly, emphasized by the sound of Johnny screaming above a descending piano scale. Dialogue, image, and score unite in a fevered crescendo that overwhelms the viewer with an excess of stimuli and produces a buildup and release of tension akin to that experienced by Johnny. Both in its cataloguing of traumas and in its visceral effect, the shock treatment presages Johnny's final hallucination and his complete submersion in insanity.

Johnny's mental tipping point is the most outrageously "weird" sequence of Fuller's directorial career, a self-conscious expression of Johnny's inner torment that astounds, confounds, and exhausts the viewer. The sequence begins with a close-up of Johnny, head in hands, wracking his brain in voice-over to remember the name of the killer. A sound of thunder rumbles, and Johnny looks up. He sticks his hand out; a drop of rain hits his palm, accompanied by a "plink" sound effect. "Did you feel that? It's beginning to rain," he tells Pagliacci. Here Fuller stylistically conflates the real and imagined worlds of Johnny. It literally seems to be raining inside, yet logic tells us that it does not rain indoors, and therefore that Johnny must be imagining the rain. Johnny looks down the corridor to his left, prompting the camera to slowly pan left. The camera follows Johnny's shadow, thrown long and dark across the wall. The hard, low-key side light creates "two" of Johnny, visually illustrating the split in his psyche between light and dark, sanity and insanity. The pan comes to rest on a long shot of the corridor filled with patients. This wide-angle shot, which began on Johnny (objective) and was prompted by his look, now appears to be what he is looking at, i.e., his optical point of view (subjective). The sound of thunder and music continues on the soundtrack, increasing the tension and confusion. The sound track offers the viewer access to what Johnny is thinking, but the visual track confirms that what Johnny thinks is false. The sequence thus mixes objective and subjective stylistic cues rather than clearly delineating a switch to Johnny's subjectivity. Following another thunderclap, the swelling score accompanies a second cut in to Johnny looking at his hand. The music, as well a shot that repeats the earlier pan but reveals the corridor to be empty, complete the transition into Johnny's subjectivity. The exact repetition of the pan visually contrasts the real and the imagined: in reality, patients line the corridor, but in Johnny's mind, he is alone. This sudden change confirms for the viewer that both sound and image are no longer in the realm of reality.

In order to achieve maximum impact, Fuller saves the most formally extreme illustration of hysteria for the moment in which Johnny fully breaches the divide and crosses into insanity. With the transition from objectivity to Johnny's subjectivity complete, the rest of the sequence abandons any pretense toward maintaining a unified presentation of time, space, and action. The camera reverses its pan down the corridor and moves to the right, across Johnny's shadow; just as his face enters frame right, the scene cuts to a series of disorienting shots united by fast, disjunctive editing, and accompanied by a crescendo of music, sound effects, and general screeching. Johnny has gone over the edge, and the viewer is subjectively swept along for the ride. Spatial and temporal continuity are no longer maintained: the close-up of Johnny looking left is followed by a long shot of the corridor, flooded with rain, and a drenched Johnny writhing at the far end; the edit suggests that Johnny is looking at himself further down the corridor. This shot is followed by a discontinuous high angle of Johnny sitting on the bench (where we first found him), barely wet. A long shot of Johnny in the corridor, pounding on doors in the rain, cuts to an extreme low angle of his jaw and screeching mouth, protruding from the top of the frame. The highly unusual angle of this shot presents an unnatural view of Johnny, shocking and disorienting the viewer. The effect is multiplied when the shot is used at the end of the sequence, with frame direction reversed. Sound effects of thunder and lightening heighten the subjectivity, while an optical lightening strike cues a series of low-angle color shots of overflowing waterfalls. As with the hallucination sequences of Stuart and Trent, the color shots express what Johnny is seeing; a parallel is created between the visions (and therefore the insanity) of Stuart, Trent, and Johnny. Yet Johnny's hallucination is even more complex than the others, as it removes all objective mediating devices and completely plunges the viewer into Johnny's subjectivity. The conflation of objectivity and subjectivity, as well as the use of disjunctive editing, unnatural camera angles, and different film stocks fly in the face of classical rules concerning continuity and clarity, thereby providing the utmost shock to the viewer's system. When the sequence is complete, the viewer is as drained as Johnny.

Rather than resolving the conflict in a false fashion—as in *Forty Guns*—or destroying the protagonist—as in *The Steel Helmet*—the nar-

Frame enlargements from Johnny Barrett's (Peter Breck's) "weird" mental breakdown in *Shock Corridor*. Fuller fragments the presentation of space and time from shot to shot and floods the hallway with rain to subjectively depict Johnny's descent into madness.

rative of *Shock Corridor* accomplishes both: following Johnny's revelation of the killer to Dr. Cristo, exposition reveals Johnny is released, writes his story, wins his Pulitzer, and embraces his girlfriend—all offscreen—while onscreen he immediately ends up a catatonic mute. This resolution, coupled with the Euripides quote that opens and closes the film, provides *Shock Corridor* with the appearance of a morality play. The didactic interludes that function as the three witnesses' backstories also appear to bolster some critics' contentions that the film posits America as insane. Each of the three witnesses to Sloan's murder contains in his personal story an indictment of a contemporary American attitude: Stuart suggests Americans are sitting ducks for Communist propaganda if they are not taught to take pride in their country's history, Trent is a disturbing embodiment of the evils of racism, and Boden warns against Cold War paranoia and nuclear aggression. As with the more didactic passages of *Run of the Arrow* and *China Gate*, the personal confessions of the three witnesses feature minimal stylization. The characters are photographed alone in the frame in tight shots, focusing the viewer's attention on their faces and words. In his moment of lucidity, each man offers a progressive parable, an irrational lesson à la Fuller. The film's form suggests that widespread social problems—ignorance of history, prejudice, and paranoia—are what made these men insane.

The characterization of Trent and the presentation of the race riot are perhaps the most jaw-dropping examples of how Fuller presents the viewer of *Shock Corridor* with a diseased America in a melodramatic manner designed to provoke. The viewer first glimpses Trent walking down the hallway after he lowers a sign he is carrying that reads: "Integration and Democracy Don't Mix, Go Home Nigger." The moment is startlingly contradictory on multiple levels. Rhetorically, the sign opposes two ideas, integration and democracy, that are in fact closely aligned, as both are associated with the equal treatment of individuals. The illogical opposition reveals the absurdity of the sentiment, and provokes the viewer to recognize just how *un*democratic segregation is. When Trent lowers the sign to reveal that he is African-American, an additional shock is produced, as the person he is telling to go home is himself. Much more so than the schizophrenic identities of Stuart (Confederate general) and Boden (six-year-old child), Trent's assumed role as a white Klan leader has a powerfully discordant effect. The color of his skin clearly identifies him not only as the opposite of whom he thinks he is, but also as the victim of the very same rabid sentiments he spews.

As the ugliness continues, Trent attempts to attack another black patient, discusses with Johnny the founding of the KKK, and delivers a hate-filled speech about returning America to Americans. On the narrative level, the episodes function both to provide necessary exposition about Trent's character and as a tool to bring him and Johnny together in solitary confinement so Johnny can witness Trent's moment of lucidity. At the same time, their timely invocation of civil rights strife, Trent's role as the riot's ringleader, and their formal construction all contribute to the sequences' inflammatory effect. Both rhetorically and physically, the scenes reference the domestic battles that made daily headlines in early-1960s America: lunchroom sit-ins, the integration of schools, the resurgence of the KKK, the strong-arm tactics of the White Citizens' Council, attacks on Freedom Riders, and lynchings. With the bombing of the 16th Street Baptist Church in Birmingham, Alabama, that killed four African-American girls occurring just days after the release of *Shock Corridor* in 1963, the cries of "black bombs for black foreigners" and "America for Americans" reverberating through Trent's speech gain an alarming authenticity. That the man delivering the sermon and leading the riot is black increases the unsettling effect of the scene just as it highlights the absurdity of the racist rhetoric. During Trent's speech, increasingly rapid

A mockup of a lobby card for *Shock Corridor* illustrates how advertising positioned it as adult exploitation, emphasizing the film's revelatory nature and its presentation of sex, violence, and controversial material. *Courtesy of the Wisconsin Center for Film and Theatre Research*

editing, graphic conflict between shots, and extreme changes in shot scale punctuate the gospel of hate, visually and sonically expressing the growing wave of hysteria that is finally broken by Trent's exhortation, "Let's get that black boy before he marries my daughter!" that sets off the full scale riot.

Fuller's creation of such a loud, confident, proud racist was exceedingly bold, and his decision to make the character African-American simply flew in the face of propriety. In 1963, at the height of tension over civil rights, the representation of racist characters in motion pictures was still very circumspect so as not to offend white moviegoers, particularly in the South. Creating an African-American character who hates blacks is something that just was *not done*—which is precisely why the idea was so perversely appealing for Fuller. Many of Fuller's films illustrate a willingness—if not an eagerness—to ignore polite conventions of good taste in order to shock the viewer. Of these instances, the character of Trent is perhaps the most disturbing. Trent is a slap in the face—a series of slaps, a barrage—designed to rouse the viewer into an awareness of the hypocrisy of racism. Yet within the context of the murder mystery,

Cathy's stripping, the nymphomaniacs, Stuart's manic "Dixie" dance, and the assorted chases and fistfights, the viewer understands Trent and the race riot not as a mere polemic, but as an extreme provocation, an attempt to really gut punch the audience. Fuller wants to wake up viewers to truth, but he does this by appealing to us physically and emotionally through conflict and contradiction rather than through reasoned discourse. He still wants to *entertain.*

With strong exploitation value, major promotion, and organized first-run distribution, *Shock Corridor* appeared to have more going for it than many of the low-budget films Fuller released through Globe. As the film lacked stars and sported minimal production values, its primary selling point was its sensational material, highlighted in a national promotional campaign that featured publicity in major newspapers and gossip columns as well as print, radio, and television ads emphasizing the sex, violence, and "adults only" content.[14] *Shock Corridor* premiered first-run in September 1963 in New York to "okay" box office at the Palace and the Trans Lux art cinema; the following week the film also bowed in Chicago at the Roosevelt, a theater that catered to fans of action, where returns were "hot."[15] Opening wider in its third week, the film headlined or played at the top of a double bill in medium to small houses and drive-ins in four major cities, ranking seventh in weekly grosses. *Shock Corridor* garnered widely varying reviews, with some praise in the trades and frequent condemnation in the general press, typified by *Film Quarterly's* description of it as "one of the most preposterous and tasteless films of all time."[16] Trade predictions concerning the film's potential earnings were similarly split; *Boxoffice* considered it a "strong boxoffice entry" while *Variety* found the story "so grotesque, so grueling, so shallow and so shoddily sensationalistic that [Fuller's] message is devastated. . . . [I]t is difficult to see where [it] can have any really appreciable boxoffice impact."[17] *Variety's* prediction largely played out, as exhibitors reported consistently below-average takes during the majority of *Shock Corridor's* subsequent first-run dates. Despite *Shock Corridor's* top play dates and intensive exploitation campaign, it only returned $128,000 to Allied Artists from the box-office gross, or a little above half of its production costs.[18] The film's extreme didacticism and often crass presentation of mental illness clearly were not well received when it was distributed as the headlining feature in downtown theaters. Although the film would enjoy an extended release in France and eventual cult status in the United States, in 1963 there was little room in the domestic market for such an oddity.

Fuller's second film for Fromkess-Firks, *The Naked Kiss,* is also a picture that proves the adage, "One person's trash is another person's treasure." While at the time of its release the guardians of good taste at

*Cosmopolitan* declared it the worst film of the year, many Fuller fans name it as one of his greatest achievements. As was true of *Verboten!*, *The Naked Kiss* had few pretensions to even programmer status. Produced for less than $200,000, it was distributed by Allied Artists as a solid B picture. *The Naked Kiss* reteamed Fuller with cinematographer Stanley Cortez, editor Jerome Thoms, and actress Constance Towers, but still provided him with little in the way of stars, budget, or production value; instead, Fuller amped up the sex and sensationalism. A woman's picture made for the adult exploitation market, the film concerns a reformed prostitute who falls in love with the leading citizen in a small town, only to discover he is a pedophile. The contrast between truth and appearance, reality and dreams is again a major theme, revealed through visual weirdness and the viewer's increasing subjective alignment with the protagonist.

*The Naked Kiss* traces the rise, fall, and eventual redemption of Kelly (Constance Towers), a call girl with a knack for helping children. We first see Kelly angrily beating a man before we know anything about her. The plot then takes her to Grantville, where she arrives fronting as a saleswoman for Angel Foam Champagne and adroitly picks up a police officer named Griff (Anthony Eisley). After she shares her wares with him, Griff tells her Grantville is clean—and subsequently sends her to be a "bon-bon" in a brothel over the river. Rather than take his recommendation, Kelly decides to stay in Grantville and change her life. Tough-talking yet warm-hearted, fiercely independent yet desiring marriage and children, Kelly embodies the contradictory impulses of so many of Fuller's female characters. She rooms with the town spinster, Miss Josephine (Betty Bronson), and becomes a nurse at an orthopedic hospital for disabled children. Griff, however, questions her motivations, but she insists on her sincerity. Kelly is invited to a party at the house of Grant (Michael Dante), the town's wealthy benefactor and Griff's best friend, and makes a visible impression. During a later visit, Grant and Kelly listen to "Moonlight Sonata" and discuss Goethe and Byron; he shows her home movies from Venice and says if she pretends hard enough, she'll hear the voice of a gondolier. She does, imagining herself in Venice with Grant, and the two kiss. Though the kiss initially repulses her, she brushes away her doubts and returns his affections. Grant and Kelly eventually plan to marry, and when Griff threatens to reveal her past, she tells him Grant already knows. Despite her sordid history, Kelly appears to have found bliss. Then, arriving at Grant's house one day with her wedding dress, Kelly discovers him molesting a young girl. Grant tells Kelly they are perfect for each other because "We're both abnormal," and she promptly whacks him over the head with the phone. Grant's death turns Griff against Kelly, who is jailed for murder and abandoned by her friends. No one believes Kelly's discovery about Grant, though it confirms what she first suspected when they initially kissed. Finally Kelly remembers the identity of the child she saw Grant molest, and the attitude of the whole town changes, turning Kelly into a hero. But she has had enough of "polite society." Through with Grant-ville, Kelly heads for the next bus out of town.

In this tale of small-town, middle-class hypocrisy, Fuller continues to explore themes of deception and the contradictory nature of truth, carefully manipulating the range and depth of narration to shape the viewer's perception of Kelly. Fuller introduces the "things are not what they seem" motif right upfront, beginning, as usual, by throwing us for a loop. *The Naked Kiss* opens with an unstable medium close-up of Kelly's angry face, her arm moving forward with a purse as if to assault the camera (and the viewer). The second shot, also hand-held and approximating Kelly's optical point of view, is a medium close-up of a man reeling backward from the blow. A frenzied jazz score accompanies the attack. Whoa! Arriving in the middle of a fight between two unknown people photographed in shaky and violent shots takes the viewer by surprise, focusing attention on the visceral nature of the attack rather than on the reasons behind it. The juxtaposition of action and reaction shots emphasizes graphic conflict and movement from shot to shot, while the score punctuates the explosive nature of the blows. The scene continues, alternating the two medium close-up action-reaction shots and intercutting an occasional low-angle long shot as the two struggle and stumble past a wall of women's photos. Kelly's wig comes off; the beautiful blonde is bald! The man finally falls down, and in a medium close-up high angle Kelly squirts him with seltzer and says, "I'm not rolling you, you wretch, I'm only taking what's coming to me." Cutting back to the establishing shot, she then counts out $75, kicks him, and goes to put on her wig.

Even more so than the kendo battle in *The Crimson Kimono*, the visual style of the first scene in *The Naked Kiss* encourages a visceral response to an ambiguous event. By beginning mid-fight, denying an establishing shot or explanatory dialogue, alternating frontal point-of-view shots, and using a seemingly hand-held camera and a loud, expressive score, the narration overtly undermines any expectation the viewer may have of a conventional, clear introduction to the film's characters and situations. Instead, the viewer is visually and aurally assaulted, left with an impression of the physical sensation of the event rather than an understanding of the story. As after the wordless opening sequence of *Pickup on South Street*, the viewer is left to wonder, "What just happened here?" Additionally, as the narration highlights those features of Kelly most likely to elicit shock and disgust, it initially suppresses the potential

1

2

3

A production still from *The Naked Kiss* (1) illustrates how the camera operator recorded the kinetic, handheld shots at the beginning of the film. Actress Constance Towers (Kelly) lunges at the camera, while the frame enlargements below (2, 3) reveal Samuel Fuller reaching up to pull off her wig. Fuller moves so quickly his image is captured in only a handful of frames, making his presence invisible to the average viewer and preserving the shocking illusion that the wig merely falls off Towers's head.

*Top image courtesy of the Academy of Motion Picture Arts and Sciences* for a sympathetic emotional response to her character. The cinematography and music accentuate the kinetic force of Kelly's blows, and the sudden loss of her wig marks her as somewhat of a freak. We are left with a first impression of Kelly as strong, furious, crazed, and rather scary, and we are curious to learn her identity and motivation.

When Kelly arrives in Grantville, Fuller slowly provides information to fill in the gaps, increasing our access to her subjectivity and presenting her as a woman with a dream. At first, the motivations for Kelly's decision to settle in Grantville and work at the orthopedic hospital are unclear, and given the impact of the opening scene, viewers may suspect, like Griff, that Kelly is a con artist fronting as a "good woman." Limited access to her subjectivity increases the ambiguity, as little insight into her thoughts and feelings is provided other than what she says and does. Even use of Kelly's optical point of view is rare. The exceptions to this pattern are telling, however, as they involve interactions concerning children, marriage, and Kelly's attempt to alter her life: Kelly feeding a bottle to a baby on the street, Miss Josephine's story of her doomed engagement to the dead Charlie, a disabled child looking to Kelly for approval after walking, and most dramatically, Kelly stating her desire to change and asking Griff to help her. Once we see Kelly working at the hospital, the range and depth of narration dramatically increases, helping the viewer to fill in narrative gaps and clarify Kelly's traits and desires.

Two parallel dream sequences are key to this process. In the first, Kelly sits with her young patients in the hospital ward and tells them a story about a white swan that pretends hard and is turned into a boy. "And an old man told me if I pretend hard enough, I can play games with the little boy." The shot then cuts to a subjective vision of Kelly and the kids running and playing in the park. (One child shouts, "I have legs! I have legs!" Again, whoa, but in a weird way.) Within the vision, not only do the children show no signs of physical disability, but Kelly is dressed as a mother, not as a nurse. The framing story of the swan's wish and the content of the vision suggest that it illustrates Kelly's dream—for the kids to be healthy and for her to be a mother. Following Kelly's dramatic declaration to Griff of her desire to leave her life as a prostitute behind and the previous clues regarding her attraction to marriage and motherhood, viewers now suspect that her actions are genuine, and largely disregard initial negative impressions of her.

Several scenes later, a parallel dream sequence takes place with Grant and Kelly, and while only slightly less saccharine than the first, it is substantially more weird. The "Moonlight Sonata" sequence utilizes continuity editing techniques and classical scene construction to unify disparate times and spaces, joining footage from unalike sources into a seamless whole and "normalizing" an explicitly artificial visual presentation. The scene is divided into four segments, each increasing in subjectivity until the kiss in the final segment forces Kelly to question what is a dream and what is real. In the first segment, Grant and Kelly sit on his sofa and pretentiously discuss Venice and Lord Byron, while "Moonlight Sonata" plays on a tape recorder in the background. The segment consists of a frontal shot of them both and two medium-close-up shots of each alone; it establishes the space, cuts into a shot–reverse shot sequence, and reestablishes the space according to classical conventions. Nothing provides an inkling of the weirdness to come—like Kelly, we think everything is normal.

The second segment begins when Grant offers to take Kelly to the place of her dreams—Venice. Much as in the shots preceding Johnny's breakdown in *Shock Corridor*, subjective sound effects transition the scene from an objective to a subjective visual presentation. A shot of a flickering film projector is followed by Fuller's home-movie footage of Venice taken from inside a gondola going down a river. The sound of the flickering projector replaces the "Moonlight Sonata" music and signals a shift toward increasing illusion. The segment continues, cutting between footage of Venice and medium shots of Kelly and Grant on the sofa, with Grant offering a running commentary of the footage. Although no shot actually depicts both the couple and the projected image, their eyelines and commentary lead the viewer to infer that the Venice footage is their optical point of view—i.e., what they are watching on the screen. After a return to a medium shot, Grant asks Kelly if she hears the gondolier singing. A man singing Italian opera rises on the soundtrack, the first indication of the subsequent blending of real and fantasy worlds. A cut to the reverse angle tracks slowly toward Grant as he suggests that if Kelly pretends hard enough, she can hear the gondolier's voice. The camera then tracks in from the shot of Grant and Kelly together to isolate her in the frame. Kelly tilts her head, looks offscreen, and smiles dreamily. The music and camera movement cue the introduction of a subjective sequence, and as Kelly closes her eyes, the segment cuts to a graphic match of Kelly smiling with her eyes closed, lying on several pillows and listening to the singing. The musical overlap, direct cut, and graphic match elide the spatial discontinuity of the two shots. Set up by the point-of-view editing patterns and the music, the cut seamlessly transforms Kelly from a woman watching a gondola on a movie screen to a woman *in* a gondola—the gondola of her dreams. Fuller uses the tools of cinema to transform Kelly's reality into an illusion.

The third segment depicts Kelly's subjective vision of love with Grant, and its distance from anything resembling reality begs the viewer to question the truth behind the dream. The sequence uses continuity editing techniques to combine the home-movie footage taken from the

Venetian gondola with shots of a gondola in which Kelly and Grant lie, surrounded by pillows, in front of a gondolier on a darkened stage, as if the two sets of shots occupy the same time and space. As the stage gondolier begins to plant his pole, the segment cuts to home-movie footage depicting an actual gondolier continuing the same action; as Kelly opens her eyes on stage in a high-angle shot, the segment cuts back to a home-movie low-angle point-of-view shot of a bridge, as if the bridge is Kelly's optical perspective. Fuller intercuts the two types of footage to suggest that the shots of Venice are now Kelly's literal point of view—i.e., she is now in a gondola in Venice. Kelly's gondola, however, is strikingly artificial—it sits immobile, surrounded by darkness, its gondolier seen only from the waist down dipping his pole into thin air. Even the falling leaves look fake. While the continuity editing suggests an integration of the real and imagined Venice, the mise-en-scene self-consciously announces a discrepancy, highlighting the incoherence of the space presented onscreen. The pattern of alternation between the two types of footage continues, and with each return to the shot of Kelly and Grant in the stage gondola, the camera cranes in further, until the couple is actually kissing. Graphic matches, eyeline matches, point-of-view editing patterns, cutting on action, and alternation—all techniques of continuity editing—used in this segment to create the illusion of continuous space and time from shots that clearly are not part of the film's fictional world. The narrative emphasis on "pretending," the reflexive foregrounding of the flickering movie projector, and the use of home-movie and theatrically staged footage all work redundantly to suggest that Kelly's ultimate happiness with the man she loves is a dream that is not rooted in any semblance of reality.

The disorientation evoked by the scene comes to an end with a graphic match between Kelly and Grant kissing in the gondola and them kissing on the sofa, returning the narrative once again to the "real" world. The Italian opera has ceased, replaced only by a silence that punctuates a shift in tone and visual presentation. But something is not quite right: the kiss cuts to Kelly's optical point of view of Grant, her hands around his neck as she pushes him away. Her disgusted rejection visually suggests what is narratively confirmed only in the last act of the film—that Grant is a sexual predator. Grant's close-up alternates with the reverse of Kelly, returning the narration to a less self-conscious style but continuing to bind the viewer to her point of view. The camera then slowly tracks in to a close-up of Kelly, who pauses, blinks, smiles, and pulls Grant back toward her, seemingly shaking off any doubts about him. Darkness envelops their faces, and the camera pans down their legs and back to the flickering film projector, a reminder of the power of illusion.

In contrast to Kelly's attack on the (then) unknown man in the first scene, the visual style in these four segments does not aim to jolt the viewer in a visceral fashion; instead, it hews largely to classical conventions, utilizing analytical editing and alternating shots. What makes the scene "weird" is *how* these conventions are used. Kelly's subjective desire to visit Venice with Grant motivates a highly self-conscious sequence that calls attention to the ability of continuity editing to suggest a unified space and time when no such unity actually exists. The net effect is to emphasize the *discontinuity* of the fictional and fantasy worlds and the false construct of Kelly's dream. The stylistic presentation of this vision stands in sharp contrast to Kelly's vision of the children running and playing; the earlier dream world is presented as visually akin to the fictional world, with only a change in characters' appearances and abilities, while Kelly's dream with Grant stands apart from the rest of the film, stylistically implicated as an illusion. The visual difference suggests a narrative distinction as well: some dreams are worth chasing (motherhood, health), while others are merely a delusion (Venice, romance with Grant).

The narrative subsequently avoids any further hint of Grant's undesirability, however, and little information is provided to prepare viewers for the revelation of his crime. As a result, viewers share Kelly's surprise and horror when she discovers the true sickness at the heart of Grantville. As with the opening, the murder of Grant stands out for its startling content and style, but now style visually aligns us with Kelly rather than depicting her as unhinged and frightening. The scene begins with Kelly happily entering Grant's darkened house and hearing an unsettling song about mommy and a bluebird, aurally recalling an earlier scene in which Kelly sang with the children at the hospital. A medium shot of Kelly in the living room searching for Grant, wedding gown in hand, cuts to an extreme close-up of her face looking front, at first smiling, then slowly turning to stone. As she glances down and to the right, there is a cut to her optical point of view: a young girl named Bunny looks up, also in a frontal extreme close-up, her face half-darkened by shadow. A long shot follows Bunny's feet left across the darkened living room as she skips out the door. As during the death of Gunther in *Underworld, U.S.A.*, the constructive editing forces the viewer to piece together the scene's overall action and the meaning behind it based on what little information is provided in each shot. Because the narration has suppressed the source of the shadow and the spatial relationship between Kelly and Bunny, the action in the segment is initially unclear. Kelly, in extreme close-up as before, glances from left to center, prompting a cut to an extreme frontal close-up of Grant, looking up to meet her eyes. A shot–reverse shot pattern between Kelly and Grant begins, as the lyrics to the song plead,

"Mommy, tell me why there are tears in your eyes." The organization of the sequence around Kelly's glances sharply restricts the range of narrative information to what she literally sees. The viewer mentally assembles the visual information through her point of view, suspecting as Kelly does that her fiancé has molested Bunny. The high-contrast lighting, dramatic changes in shot scale, eerie song, and unclear spatial relations all emphasize Kelly's shock at both her discovery and Grant's subsequent explanation of his actions. Kelly's disgust, as well as the unsettling close-up of Bunny and the cultural taboo against child molestation, make us squirm in our seats.

In comparison to the opening scene, the visual presentation of Kelly's assault on Grant downplays the violence of her actions in only five short shots: Kelly switches the wedding-gown box into her left hand; her right hand picks up the receiver of the phone in close-up; in medium shot, she throws her arm forward; the dress and veil fall in front of the camera low to the ground; and the veil settles over the face of a prone Grant as Kelly kneels to collect the gown at the top of the frame. Fuller provides only enough information to suggest the basic action, as viewers never learn exactly what Grant was doing with Bunny or see the details of his murder. In addition, unlike Kelly's previous assault scenes or those in most Fuller movies, the attack only includes one blow, and the point of contact is elided. The visual style thus presents Kelly's action as instinctive rather than highlighting the violence of the strike. Fuller is not trying to provoke thrills here so much as recognition of Kelly's sadness.

As the scene closes, Fuller's stylistic choices highlight Kelly's state of shock and contrast her present situation with the promise of the recent past. The scene intercuts frontal medium shots of Kelly blankly staring ahead and folding her wedding gown with high-angle close-ups of the gown box. Sounds of Grant's projector overlay the shots of the box, aurally recalling Kelly's subjective visions of love from the "Moonlight Sonata" scene, now dashed. A series of six very short shots of empty spaces in Grant's house not directly motivated by the action further punctuate the contrast between Kelly's dreams and how they turned out. The first two shots in the series depict important motifs in Kelly and Grant's relationship: the tape recorder and the sculpture of Beethoven's bust; the next three duplicate the camera positions and framing of previous shots when Kelly and Grant were together; the last mirrors Kelly's point-of-view shot of Bunny running out the front door. Rather than imparting information in and of themselves, the formal union of these disparate shots brings Grant and Kelly's relationship full circle, illustrating both what brought them together and what tore them apart. The scene ends with an extreme long shot staged in depth of Kelly sitting with her dress box and Grant dead at her feet. Despite the high level of ambiguity in the scene, Fuller's use of constructive editing underscores the false nature of Grant's respectability and the complete destruction of Kelly's dream. Kelly is now broken and alone, eliciting sympathy for her situation and heightening suspense regarding her final fate.

The narrative and visual style throughout *The Naked Kiss* manipulate the viewer's understanding of appearances in order to illustrate most effectively the reversal of the moral hierarchy at the heart of the film. By the end, viewers recognize that the seemingly violent prostitute introduced in the opening was an upstanding individual all along; her personal integrity remains strong, regardless of her social standing, while events unmask other more "respectable" citizens for the hypocrites they are. Fuller carefully parcels out the amount and depth of narrative information in order to shape the viewer's response, using subjectivity and stylistic weirdness in a fashion as daring as in *Shock Corridor*. Although both films feature many examples of straightforward classical scene construction like the first "Moonlight Sonata" segment, they also demonstrate a distinct willingness to throw the conventional rulebook out the window in order to engage the viewer emotionally with the film. Based on the opening scene alone, or the restrained hysteria of some of the performances, *The Naked Kiss* might at first appear raw, unbridled, and even "primitive," but analysis demonstrates just how calculated and intricate its use of visual style is. Fuller takes us on a carefully crafted journey, encouraging us to look beyond appearances and labels, to sift the difference between what is an illusion and what is real.

As with *Shock Corridor*, *The Naked Kiss*'s combination of sex and violence is its primary selling point, but it received neither the promotional backing lavished on the earlier film nor the same pattern of intensive first-run distribution. Instead, the film quietly premiered in April 1964 in Constance Towers's hometown of Whitefish, Montana, before returning in May to headline in Boston and play on the bottom half of a double bill with Allied's *The Strangler* (1964) in Chicago.[19] *The Naked Kiss* continued to trickle around the country for assorted supporting dates, finally opening in New York City in late October below Allied's James Jones World War II–adaptation, *The Thin Red Line* (1964). While *Variety* correctly noted that *The Naked Kiss* "seemed destined for lower-case market in adult situations," trade notices were routinely positive, and the *New York Times* declared that the film had "style to burn," describing Fuller as "one of the liveliest, most visual-minded and cinematographically knowledgeable filmmakers now working in the low-budget Hollywood grist mill."[20] Despite largely enthusiastic critical response to the film, its scattered distribution in flat-fee situations limited box-office potential; given the low returns on *Shock Corridor, The Naked Kiss* most likely took in even less.

### Fuller Goes to Vietnam: The Rifle

While it is impossible to say whether or not the trend in Fuller's work toward excessive sensationalism would have continued beyond *The Naked Kiss* if his projects had been produced, an examination of one unproduced script from the mid-1960s suggests that, if anything, his taste for tastelessness was increasing. *The Rifle,* a Vietnam War picture, both continues the central conflict explored in *The Steel Helmet* and takes the didacticism and subjectivity of *Shock Corridor* to a new extreme. Recycling characters, situations, and plot points from earlier Fuller films, the script also features an array of oppositional elements and a melodramatic narrative structure designed to maximize conflict.[21] The title refers to an old M1 rifle that is carried by a young Vietnamese boy in the film's opening shot. A voice-over intones, "This rifle is dedicated to the living who die, the dead who live, the wounded who weep, and to the insane who fake sanity," recalling familiar themes and highlighting Fuller's obsession with contradiction. The overarching story concerns Colonel Zack, a Korean War veteran who has adopted a fourteen-year-old Vietnamese boy he discovered during an ambush. Zack promises the boy, Quan, that he will take him back to the United States when his tour of duty completes in a month, but unbeknownst to Zack, Quan is actually a Vietcong soldier who has been ordered to assassinate an American VIP. At the end of the film, Quan mortally wounds the VIP with the M1 rifle given to him by Zack, who must then pursue Quan as the enemy. This plotline lifts the two protagonists from *The Steel Helmet* and reconfigures their relationship in a more grim and unsentimental fashion, requiring the grizzled father figure to kill the son who betrayed him. The script exploits the conflict between the two by revealing Quan's allegiance from the beginning, thereby putting the viewer in suspense as to when Zack will discover Quan's betrayal.

While *The Rifle*'s central conflict is quite straightforward, it is surrounded by even more sensationalism than in *Shock Corridor*. Much of the action takes place during an extended patrol of a cast of characters that tests believability, even for a Fuller picture: Zack and Quan, a sergeant, a short timer, a medic, a wounded man, a black soldier named Griff, a draft card burner, a French reporter, a female doctor, a mute disabled boy named Patches, and a nun carrying a baby! Over the course of the patrol, the script reveals the conscientious objector to be both racist and elitist and suggests he uses his opposition to the war as a cover for his cowardice. Zack calls him "punknik" and tells him, "Your education was paid for by a lot of war casualties over the years . . . . [Draft] dodges are as old as war . . . and as phony as your principles." Clearly Fuller was not targeting the youth market with this one. In typical fashion, however, the opposing side fares little better. The French reporter paints a grim picture of the South Vietnamese officers who are America's allies, suggesting they are "sick with cowardice" and steal food from their own men, who in turn steal from the peasants. The weirdness that Fuller began exploring in *Shock Corridor* and *The Naked Kiss* also reappears in an even more jarring fashion during black-and-white scenes of Ho Chi Minh and Mao Tse-tung arguing over Quan's soul that are intercut with battle sequences. The disregard for social norms and propriety demonstrated in *Shock Corridor* is here multiplied exponentially, while subjectivity is used overtly for allegorical purposes. There is nothing subtle about this story.

Although the central conflict in *The Rifle* between Zack and Quan could easily form a sequel to *The Steel Helmet*, the surrounding narrative is so excessive and so contradictory that it seems unimaginable that the script could ever be made. Here the sensational realism that complemented genre conventions in *The Steel Helmet*, exploded in *Forty Guns*, and shifted more heavily toward sensationalism than realism in *Shock Corridor* has almost completely lost touch with verisimilitude, clarity, and coherence. Fuller's hard-hitting form of truthtelling stretches didacticism to an extreme and buries yet another surrogate father-son relationship under the weight of so many contradictory impulses the entire project veers toward camp. *The Rifle* is 1960s Fuller to the nth degree— provocative, excessive, and oblivious to the demands of the market.

*The Naked Kiss* marked an end to the primary phase of Samuel Fuller's work as a film director. By the completion of the film's run, Allied Artists executives reported that the company was seeking producers and creative talent who could supply "all or most of their own financing," with Allied acting only as distributor.[22] For the next two years the company remained mired in debt and unable to finance production or even provide advances to self-financing producers. The Fromkess-Firks deal was thus never completed, and Fuller lost another potential source of money for his films. With no profits to show for his last two releases, he had virtually no chance to form agreements with other distributors. In 1965, Fuller was invited to Paris to write and direct a modern adaptation of Aristophanes's *Lysistrata*, but financing fell through. After returning to Los Angeles, Fuller directed five episodes of the television western *Iron Horse*, two of which he also wrote. It would be fifteen years before his next Hollywood film played in theaters. In the late 1950s and early 1960s, Fuller's films rarely found an audience either as programmers or as low-budget exploitation films, as they operated in a market that reduced the former's chances for box-office success and primarily rewarded the latter only if targeted at youth. While Fuller continued to seek work as a director and remained an incredibly productive screenwriter, the increasing reliance on profits dictated by independent production effectively ended the initial phase of his domestic filmmaking career.

# CHAPTER FIVE

# The Final Battles, 1965–1997

**T**he last thirty-plus years of Fuller's career saw his passionate, gutsy filmmaking embraced by critics and younger directors even as his chances to complete projects were few and far between. After *The Naked Kiss*, Fuller directed only a handful of compromised and/or poorly distributed works, with his most personal achievement, *The Big Red One*, not even approximating his original vision until its reconstruction following his death. Though Fuller maintained an optimistic attitude and produced a steady stream of scenarios, screenplays, and novels, he was never again able to achieve the consistency of production he enjoyed during the 1950s and early 1960s.

Fuller's filmmaking during this period was defined by opportunity and marked by eclecticism. Only one of his projects, *The Big Red One*, originated solely with him; the rest were already in development when Fuller was approached to direct. As a result, an unusually large percentage of his work as a director during this period was on adaptations or screenplays already written by others. In addition, the majority of his final pictures were shot abroad with international casts and crews, distinguishing them in performance and style from his earlier movies. Finally, while Fuller supervised the initial editing of each picture and deposited a cut he approved with the producers, half of his late-period films were recut without his involvement. These factors result in a series of pictures that bear the least consistent relationship to each other and to Fuller's overall aesthetic compared to any other period in his career. Only *The Big Red One*—especially in its reconstructed form—and *White Dog* fully embody the spirit of his vision.

## Critical Recognition, Professional Frustration

The initial decades after the dissolution of the studio system were tumultuous for Hollywood, as studio executives struggled to define profitable production strategies, revise content regulation, and target their most loyal customers. Continuing a trend that began a decade earlier, the major studios in the 1960s released family-oriented blockbusters such as *Doctor Zhivago* (1965) and *The Sound of Music* (1965) to anchor their distribution slates, utilizing international locations and talent to add production value and increase foreign sales. A string of failed blockbusters from 1966 to 1968 and the reduction of revenues from selling broadcasting rights to television initiated an industry-wide recession in 1969, however, prompting a period of readjustment. At the same time, changing social mores and the increasing irrelevance of the Production Code forced a Code revision in 1966 and its replacement by a ratings system in 1968. A classification system that rated films according to their appropriateness for various age groups freed filmmakers from having to create pictures that appeared acceptable for all and enabled them to include more explicit material designed to appeal to mature audiences. With the box-office success of *Blow-Up* (1966), *The Graduate* (1967), and *Bonnie and Clyde* (1967), a younger generation of studio executives began to shape a new production strategy, one centered around comparatively lower-cost films that challenged classical conventions, embraced sex and violence, and were targeted at the most frequent moviegoers: youth between the ages of sixteen and twenty-four. From the late 1960s through the mid-1970s, Hollywood released more character-driven stories that featured looser plots, overt stylization, a mix of tones, and explicit sex and violence. Never before had the American film industry seemed so primed for the provocative pictures of Samuel Fuller.

Indeed, critical recognition of Fuller's work was on the rise around the globe, and he was considered one of the hippest contemporary filmmakers by the younger generation. Champions of auteurism—an approach that elevated directors who consistently placed a distinctive stylistic stamp on their work—had long been fans of Fuller, beginning with Luc Moullet and Jean Domarchi in France, who first wrote about him for *Cahiers du Cinéma* in 1956; continuing with the English critic V. F. Perkins, who introduced him to readers of *Movie* in 1962; and finally extending to America's Andrew Sarris, who wrote of Fuller in 1968 for *The American Cinema:* "It is the artistic force with which his ideas are expressed that makes his career so fascinating to critics."[1] In 1969 the Edinburgh Film Festival featured a retrospective of Fuller's work, publishing the first critical anthology on his films, and monographs by Phil Hardy and Nicholas Garnham followed in 1970 and 1971, respectively. Beginning with Jean-Luc Godard, admiring directors also approached Fuller to appear in their films. Dennis Hopper cast Fuller as a gun-toting film director in *The Last Movie* (1971), while Wim Wenders slotted him into a series of films beginning with *The American Friend* (1977) and concluding with his final screen appearance in *The End of Violence*

Writer/director François Truffaut (left) and Samuel Fuller (right), personal friends and lovers of cinema. Truffaut's generation of French film
critics was the first to identify Fuller as a significant American auteur.
*Chrisam Films, Inc.*

(1997). Even Steven Spielberg got into the game, placing Fuller in a bit
part in *1941* (1979) as a thank-you for *Hell and High Water,* one of his
favorite pictures. As his fourth decade in the film business dawned, Fuller
seemed to be everywhere—everywhere except behind the camera.

　Despite the seemingly receptive industrial and critical climate, Fuller
had very little success getting films produced and distributed from the late
1960s through the 1980s. A series of feature projects he wrote either col-

lapsed before production or ended up being directed by others: *The Flow-ers of Evil, The Eccentrics, Riata* (released as *The Deadly Trackers,* 1973), *The Klansman* (1974), *The Charge at San Juan Hill, Let's Get Harry* (1986), and *The Chair vs. Ruth Snyder.* Only *Shark!, Dead Pigeon on Beethoven Street, The Big Red One, White Dog, Thieves After Dark,* and *Street of No Return* bore Fuller's credit as writer-director in his later years, and he lost control of the editing of three of them. In between film projects, Fuller wrote adaptations and novels, including *The Naked Kiss* (1964), *Crown of India* (1966), *144 Piccadilly* (1971), *Dead Pigeon on Beethoven Street* (1974), *The Big Red One* (1980), *Quint's World* (1988), and the children's book *Pecos Bill and the Soho Kid* (1986). Traveling around the world; hanging out with the likes of Godard, Wenders, François Truffaut, Luis Buñuel, Roman Polanski, and Peter Bogdanovich; marrying Christa Lang in 1967 and welcoming daughter Samantha in 1975; and constantly writing, writing, writing—the man was not idle. But the nature of independent filmmaking was risky, financing and distri-bution were never certain, and Fuller's personal interests were not always in step with the direction of the film industry.

Among Fuller's multiple unproduced script projects from the late 1960s and early 1970s, several illustrate not only a continuation of the shift toward increasing subjectivity and sensationalism initiated in *Shock Corridor,* but also tentative attempts to meld his interest in topical themes with youth-friendly content. Three projects, *The Flowers of Evil, The Eccentrics,* and *Sound of Murder,* drop much of the didacticism of *The Rifle* in favor of a more playful approach to sex and violence that is integrated with stories drawn from popular culture. A lack of sentimen-tality and an embrace of irony run through all three projects, linking them to much of Fuller's earlier work. However, the material available on the latter two stories highlights the generational and cultural division be-tween Fuller and the industry's favored youth audience that undermined the market value of his yarns.

The first project, *The Flowers of Evil,* originated in the mid-1960s as a treatment written by Noel Burch and Mark Goodman of a modern-day *Lysistrata,* Aristophanes's tale of Greek women who withhold sex in order to force their men to end the Peloponnesian War.[2] According to interviews, Fuller developed the idea into a bizarre "semi-science fiction thing" about a secret society called the Flowers of Evil that enlists beau-tiful young woman who use sex, violence, and an enervating vapor to eradicate warfare around the globe. The opening scene allegedly fea-tures a ballet dancer who is a member of the Flowers bounding off a stage to avoid a killer female motorcycle gang, while the script ends in an ambiguous fashion typical of Fuller as the protagonist spirals end-lessly into outer space. While two American producers in Paris agreed to make the picture and *Variety* reported the imminent start of production in 1966, the project fell through when financing failed to appear.[3] *The Flowers of Evil* reflects Fuller's delight in turning genre conventions on their ear, as it takes the James Bond international spy genre so popular in the 1960s and turns its sexy temptresses into peacenik protagonists. Although it is difficult to gauge the tone of the film without access to a scenario or script, the story appears to contain a parodic tone similar to that of Fuller's later German production, *Dead Pigeon on Beethoven Street*.

Also in the late 1960s Fuller wrote *The Eccentrics*, a psychedelic melodrama set in a coastal hippie encampment and featuring interlocking romantic triangles, jealousy, betrayal, and multiple murders.[4] *The Eccentrics* inched closer to being produced than *The Flowers of Evil*, with a Spanish distributor on board and the casting of Jennifer Jones as the lead. A month before shooting was scheduled to begin, however, Jones backed out due to personal problems and the producers encountered legal trouble, prompting Fuller to drop the project and leave the country.[5] The story concerns Sherry MacMasters, an untraditional, Nobel Prize–winning author who is working on a book entitled *Imagination Is the Mistress of Riot*. For inspiration, MacMasters surrounds herself with artistic, unwashed youth who view her as a creative guru. Much of the plot consists of MacMasters's visions and dream images, until by the end of the picture she is so fully ensconced in her imagination that she has difficulty distinguishing the real world from her dream world. Here Fuller's experiments with subjectivity take their most fully developed form, as MacMasters's unconscious becomes the dominant narrative force, ultimately indistinguishable in the script from "objective" scenes in real life. As with the bleak ending of *Shock Corridor*, *The Eccentrics* concludes with MacMasters trapped by the experiment she created and unable to control the forces she unleashed. While the sexy spies of *The Flowers of Evil* might have had some youth appeal, not since *Verboten!* equated Germany's teenage neo-Nazis with America's juvenile delinquents did a Fuller script incorporate young people into the plotline in such a major way. *The Eccentrics* particularly exploits the flowering of the psychedelic era and the hippie subculture in its characterizations and settings. Nevertheless, the protagonist remains an outsider looking in, and the tragic consequences of her naiveté, as well as the working title of the project—*The Kooks*—suggest that Fuller harbored real ambivalence about the hippie community the script attempts to represent.

Other than *The Flowers of Evil* and *The Eccentrics*, most of Fuller's unproduced scripts from the 1960s and early 1970s ignore Hollywood's emerging focus on the youth market and hew toward war, thriller, and biopic stories; the lone exception is an early-1970s project entitled

*Sound of Murder,* described in treatment form as "a story of horror, rock music, and ecology."[6] *Sound of Murder* combines campy horror with rock and roll and intergenerational conflict, qualifying it as perhaps the only Fuller story of this era to include the key elements of a classic teen picture. The story concerns Swooner, an ecology spokesperson and former singing star of the 1920s and 1930s who lives next door to a music club and dreams about eradicating rock and roll. The scenario indicates that "in a weird scene," Swooner hatches a plan to build a glass sound booth with a deadly secret: when a certain decibel level is reached inside, the person listening to the music will be electrocuted. Using the glass booth, Swooner lures several local musicians to their deaths, but his plan begins to unravel when he sets his sights on Freddy Fulton, the hottest singing star of the day. Members of the Freddy Fulton fan club eventually track Swooner down and corner him, aided by a tip from Frye, Swooner's houseboy. Although Frye has pretended that he is mute, he actually loves rock music, and has been waiting for an opportunity to eliminate Swooner in order to inherit his property. At the end of the film, the fan club kids lock Swooner in the glass booth and force him to listen to rock music until he learns to love it; upon hearing the dreaded music, Swooner screams in agony, increasing the decibel level enough to kill him.

While the loopy plot of *Sound of Murder* contains all the right elements to appeal to the teenage drive-in crowd, its perspective and its timing illustrate why Fuller never successfully exploited the youth market. In order to fulfill the expectations of a teen picture, the plot needs to be told from the point of view of the young rock fans. *Sound of Murder* is scripted from the perspective of a character who not only does not like young people, but who also actually wants to kill them. While grumpy old people who just do not get it are an important oppositional force in teen films, they are not the protagonists. In addition, by 1972, when the film is set, rock is no longer quite the same rebellious and threatening music that had middle-class parents in a panic in 1956. Instead, rock is in the mainstream, adults have embraced it, and anyone who hates rock is likely to be considered a fuddy-duddy by a forty-year-old as much as by a kid who is fifteen. The cycle of rebellious rock and roll teenpics had waned by the late 1950s; at the start of the 1970s, purveyors of teen exploitation films like American International Pictures had already passed through beach movies, biker movies, and drug movies. With the release of *American Graffiti* in 1973 the teen picture confidently grew into adulthood. *Sound of Murder* would have been a fabulous AIP picture in 1957 with a little bit of tweaking; by the 1970s, however, it was behind the times.

While Fuller was a master of low-budget filmmaking and aggressively incorporated sex, violence, and topical themes into his films, any similarity between the narratives of his pictures and those dominating the youth exploitation market end there. The kinds of stories he was interested in telling simply did not lend themselves to the conflicts and genres that filled the 1960s and 1970s drive-ins. As Fuller moved into the final phase of his career, his mushrooming interest in extreme sensationalism, as well as his generational distance from teens, only carried him further away from major market trends.

### *Loose Ends:* Shark! *and* Dead Pigeon on Beethoven Street

The first Fuller project to make it into production after *The Naked Kiss* was *Shark!,* a mish-mash of a movie that Fuller disavowed after losing control of the final cut. The film began as one of a series of coproductions planned by Skip Steloff and Marc Cooper's Heritage Productions and José Luis Calderón's Cinematográfica Calderón, in which each producing partner put up half the financing and split international distribution rights.[7] The script was initially written by Ken Hughes, based on the Victor Canning novel *His Bones Are Coral;* Fuller rewrote the script and titled it *Caine,* eventually sharing screenwriting credit with John Kingsbridge. In his first film role, Burt Reynolds stars as a gun runner eager to escape a Sudanese town who hooks up with a mysterious couple searching for sunken treasure; also in the cast are Barry Sullivan of *Forty Guns,* the delightful Arthur Kennedy, and Mexican star Silvia Pinal. Steloff and his producing partners had such confidence in their relationship with Fuller that before production even began they announced a four-picture deal with him and plans to immediately shoot a sequel to *Caine* written and directed by Fuller as soon as the original was complete.[8] Budgeted at $300,000, *Caine* shot for nine weeks in the summer of 1967 on location in Manzanillo, Mexico—standing in for the Sudan—with Fuller improvising his shots as he went along.[9] Disaster struck toward the end of shooting, when stuntman José Marco, in the water with a docile bull shark, was attacked and killed by a white shark that broke through protective netting. The attack was captured on film and spawned a photo spread in *Life* magazine, prompting the title change to *Shark!* to increase the picture's exploitation value. After production wrapped, Fuller retired to Mexico City and spent a month editing the film. His cut was subsequently re-edited by the producers without consultation or approval, prompting Fuller to request that his name be taken off the project. It wasn't, and Fuller disowned *Shark!.* Needless to say, no sequel was ever shot, and whatever producing deal Fuller had with Steloff and Cooper was scrapped.

*Shark!* opens with the first in a series of underwater scenes, as a local Sudanese diver explores a shipwreck and then is attacked and killed by a shark. His mother is paid off by his employers, marine scientist Professor Mallare (Sullivan) and his comely ward, Anna (Pinal), who are supposedly on an expedition to collect fish specimens. Meanwhile, an American gunrunner named Caine (Reynolds) is approached and chased by a Sudanese Army patrol on a mountain pass, narrowly escaping from joining his truck in a fiery dive off a cliff. Caine hitches a ride to the nearest gritty Red Sea burg, where he meets the happily inebriated Doc (Kennedy) and the local police inspector, Barok (Enrique Lucero). Attempting to trade his watch for a ride out of town, Caine instead attracts the attention of Runt (Carlos Berriochoa), a shirtless, cigar-smoking child who takes a shine to the American. Doc hooks up Caine with Mallare and Anna, who are looking for a new diver, and Caine and Anna hook up on their own. Caine gets wise to their nonacademic interest in the shipwreck, said to hold $2 million worth of gold bullion, and uses his fists to demand an equal stake. When hired thugs sent by Mallare to discourage Caine injure Runt instead, Doc sobers up to save the child's life. Mallare and Caine then take a dive to raise the bullion, but as they lift the gold up to Anna, she tosses bloody bait into the water and attracts the sharks. Mallare is killed, but Caine escapes back onboard and knocks Anna unconscious. Barok arrives in a police boat to grab the bullion for himself, opening the ballast valve on Mallare's yacht and causing the boat to take on water. Caine overpowers Barok and throws him to the sharks, but then finds a revived Anna pointing a gun at him. Anna forces Caine onto Barok's skip and sails off herself with the bullion, blissfully unaware that her boat is sinking.

Given the dispute regarding the final cut of the film, it is difficult to assess Fuller's contribution to *Shark!*. Certainly the narrative bears his imprint. Fuller said of the script: "I liked the idea of making a story where, for once, the hero is really the heavy, the heavy is the girl, and there's another heavy and you find out in the end they're all heavies."[10] As suggested in the opening scenes, this is a world defined by a mercenary culture in which people feed on each other and sharks feed on all of them. The theme of deception and betrayal that runs through much of Fuller's work is the cornerstone of the film, coming to the fore most forcefully during the final sequence, an extended series of deadly double crosses. In Caine there is more than a whiff of the crafty self-interest that propels *Pickup on South Street*'s Skip, though none of that film's sexual heat and tender commitment rubs off on Caine and Anna; instead, the primary romance is between Caine and young Runt—another of Fuller's ornery child mascots—as they share loving glances and fall into each others' arms after a long run. Fuller's creative touch is also

Samuel Fuller (with cowboy hat and cigar) and Burt Reynolds (right) on the water during the production of *Shark!* One of the film's stuntmen was killed during a shark attack, boding poorly for a picture Fuller eventually disowned. *Chrisam Films, Inc.*

seen in the development of the secondary characters—always a bright spot of his—particularly the sloshed lugubriousness of Doc, the elder helpmate who serves the same narrative function as Moe in *Pickup on South Street*, Mac in *The Crimson Kimono*, and Sandy in *Underworld, U.S.A.* and the oddball quality of the grossly rotund innkeeper, seen inexplicably in a red fez and an *H.M.S. Pinafore* t-shirt—a wonderful bit of characterization as rewarding as Lightening Louie's deft use of chopsticks in *Pickup on South Street*.

Though the narrative of *Shark!* exhibits continuity with Fuller's earlier work, stylistic connections are harder to analyze, as the film lacks overall visual coherence. While Fuller's films do exhibit a range of stylistic approaches—some are more classically constructed than others, some rely on master-shot long takes or constructive editing or a combination of the two—they nevertheless feature visual strategies that are internally consistent, that suggest a formal design or plan. No such plan is evident in *Shark!* What we tend to see instead are isolated shots and sometimes sequences that are recognizably Fullerian, embedded within visually banal, poorly constructed scenes. Fuller's interest in tightly framed close-ups and in organizing space through glances is evident on occasion, and the action sequences contain some visual energy. An additional highlight is the underwater photography, particularly the use of point-of-view hand-held shots in the opening scene. Nevertheless, *Shark!* lacks the careful compositions, the subjective experimentation, the weirdness, and the vigor that mark Fuller's earlier efforts in the 1960s.

The distribution and exhibition of *Shark!* was as convoluted as its creation, though it ultimately grabbed major box office in the wake of *Jaws* (1975). Producing the film without a distributor attached, Steloff initially hoped to offer it upon completion to the major studios for worldwide distribution, rather than selling the rights territory by territory.[11] Apparently none of the majors bit, and the film was put on the shelf for two years. Finally, in late 1969, Heritage Productions announced premieres of *Shark!* in Mexico, Japan, the Far East, and at theaters in the San Francisco Bay area.[12] Regional distribution exchanges released the film in a scattershot fashion across the United States over the next several years, rolling it into neighborhood theaters in New York City in the summer of 1970 on a double bill with the biker pic *Rebel Rousers* (1970) and booking it onto Los Angeles screens the following June.[13] Without a national promotional campaign and coordinated distribution strategy, *Shark!* received few reviews during its initial release, though the *New York Times* did applaud the film's "oddities" that recalled Fuller's earlier work. After the tremendous success of *Jaws*, Steloff re-released *Shark!* in true exploitation style, retitling it *Man-Eater* and raking in $2.5 million in box-office gross.[14] When the film screened again in Los Angeles, it was on the bottom half of a double bill with *Linda Lovelace for President* (1975), but by then Fuller had moved on.

After several years focused on writing, Fuller had his next opportunity to get behind the camera with *Dead Pigeon on Beethoven Street*. Producer Joachim von Mengershausen approached him to write and direct the picture for the German television detective series *Scene of the Crime;* Fuller retained the American distribution rights.[15] Working with a limited budget, he shot in English on location in Cologne, Munich, and Bonn with a German crew and cast, plus American actor Glenn Corbett from *The Crimson Kimono*. A spoof of the detective genre, the film concerns an American private eye who goes to Europe to investigate an extortion ring after his partner is killed. Christa Lang, Fuller's wife, costars as the femme fatale. Fuller hadn't been back to Germany since World War II but was excited to work on location with cinematographer Jerzy Lipman, who photographed *Kanal* (1956) and *Knife in the Water* (1962), and to shoot during Cologne's annual Carnival as well as in a number of famous landmarks—including Beethoven's childhood home. For a man who slept one night during the war under Beethoven's piano in Bonn, the experience was heavenly.[16]

*Dead Pigeon on Beethoven Street* opens with a murder: Charlie Umlaut (Eric P. Caspar), a gunman for an international extortion ring, kills an American private eye sent to investigate the blackmailing of a U.S. Senator. Police wound and capture Umlaut on Bonn's Beethovenstrasse, setting him up in a hospital. The dead PI's partner, Sandy (Corbett), arrives in town to take over the case, but is unable to question Umlaut after the gunman hides behind incubating babies, throws a man in a wheelchair down the stairs, and flees from the hospital. Sandy tracks down Christa (Lang), the woman who posed with the Senator in the incriminating photographs, and tails her into a cinema where a dubbed version of *Rio Bravo* is showing. Sandy drugs Christa and fakes a photo of her with an Italian diplomat in an attempt to worm his way into the extortion ring. Christa reports back to her boss, Mensur (Anton Diffring), a champion fencer, who assigns her to play along with Sandy and discover who he really is. Acting on orders from Mensur, Sandy and Christa drug, take compromising pictures of, and extort an African diplomat and a Chinese trade delegate, only to run into problems with a Soviet commissar who finds his suggestive photos flattering and refuses to pay up. Sandy and Christa develop an attraction while working together, and Sandy reveals to her that he is trying to break up the extortion ring. Christa tells him he must confront Mensur, and the two separate. Christa is enveloped by the throng celebrating the Carnival in Cologne, where she is targeted by an unhinged Umlaut dressed as a clown. Sandy strangles Umlaut and escapes with Christa on the train, but when he goes to pick her up in Bonn her flat is empty. Sandy confronts Mensur at the fencing academy, who tells him he had Christa killed; Mensur then goads Sandy into a sword fight, and Sandy literally throws the entirety of Mensur's pointy weapons collection at him, eventually cutting off his head. Finally retrieving the negative of the Senator's compromising photos, Sandy turns to find Christa with a gun pointed at him, demanding the negative so she can take Mensur's place and continue the extortion ring. Sandy, already wounded, throws her to the ground and escapes, but Christa follows him back to Beethovenstrasse, where she shoots him in the leg. She catches up to him as he crawls away from her, and, apologizing, raises her gun to finish him off. To her surprise, Sandy shoots her with a gun hidden in his pocket, and she becomes the next dead pigeon.

The tone of *Dead Pigeon on Beethoven Street* confounds many viewers, as the film fully enacts the conventions of the detective genre while not seeming to take them very seriously. Fuller described it as a "cartoon caper," considering it a lighthearted comedy. He tips his hand rather clearly in the opening credits, presenting the primary cast members whooping it up in Carnival regalia and himself dressed as a clown. Yet this is not a laugh-out-loud film; rather, it is playful in a knowing fashion, acknowledging its fictional existence with a wink and a nod. From the opening credits, to the character names (Charlie Umlaut, Dr. Bogdanovich), to the use of clips from *Rio Bravo* and *Alphaville* (1965), the references to *The Maltese Falcon* (1941) and *Kiss Me Deadly*, the broad caricatures and lack of psychological realism and crazed killer clown, Fuller emphasizes the film's nature as constructed entertainment. This is a film, after all, in which the femme fatale is a failed actress and the central conceit involves role-playing and faking reality. Some scenes perfectly balance the generic and comedic aspects of the narrative, such as Sandy's everything-but-the-kitchen-sink battle with Menseur, while others hew so close to narrative conventions that there is nothing humorous about them other than their offbeat execution. In the latter instances, such as Christa and Sandy's final double crosses, it is the stylistic presentation that distances viewers and reminds them they are watching a film.

The style of the picture incorporates many of Fuller's dominant visual strategies while suggesting the influence of the young European New Cinema directors who so admired his work; the contributions of Lipman and editor Liesgret Schmitt-Klink are likely central in this regard. The zooms, hand-held traveling shots through crowds, play with projected surfaces and reflections, jump cuts, rapid associational montage, and appearance of West German art rock group Can on the soundtrack all link the film with the European art cinema of the 1960s and 1970s, and the most stylistically interesting sequences are those in which these elements intermingle with techniques more central to Fuller. Christa's final attack on Sandy provides an intriguing case in point, as it is structured quite similarly to Griff's showdown walk in *Forty Guns*, but with an important twist. As in the earlier film, Fuller uses constructive editing to organize space, initially cutting between close-ups of Sandy's face or a wider shot of him crawling away and tight shots on Christa's legs as she follows him. Halfway through the sequence, a wide shot of Sandy lying on the ground cuts to an extreme close-up of Christa's eyes, initiating a new pair of repeating shots. The dramatic difference in framing between the two provides a jolt, while the focus on Christa's eyes emphasizes her grim determination; without any establishing shot, we are left in suspense as to when she will catch up with Sandy. Finally, the sequence cuts to a close-up of Sandy's worried face, and a shot over Christa's shoulder of her pointing the gun at him. Up until this point, the constructive editing pattern, isolation of specific body parts, and progression of the scene roughly mirrors that of the equivalent sequence in *Forty Guns* and achieves similar effects. After Sandy shoots Christa by surprise, however, her reaction shot optically zooms in and lit-

In this frame enlargement from the end of *Dead Pigeon on Beethoven Street*, Christa
(Christa Lang) literally cracks up thanks to an optical effect, a fitting conclusion to Fuller's
most playful film.

erally breaks apart, as if her image is reflected in a mirror that has shattered. The optical effect occurs first in close-up and is then rapidly repeated in extreme close-up, until the shards of Christa's face fall below
the frame in a third shot. This is Fullerian weirdness, popping up in a
fashion that lays bare the construction of the filmic surface. When you
make a movie that gleefully announces, "Hey guys, I'm making a movie,
and we're gonna have some fun," why not have the femme fatale's crack
up be just that—a crack up?

Although *Dead Pigeon on Beethoven Street* won enthusiastic support
in Europe and among Fuller's growing fan base, it continued the trend of
limited domestic release for his films. Emerson Film Enterprises booked
the picture into the Beverly Theatre in Los Angeles at the end of 1973
and allegedly at a handful of Midwestern drive-ins soon after; reviews in
the *Los Angeles Times* and *Boxoffice* were favorable and considered the
film within the aesthetic context of Fuller's previous output.[17] The release

was so scrawny, however, that Fuller saw no revenue from his ownership of the American distribution rights.[18] *Dead Pigeon on Beethoven Street* played more widely in Europe, where it premiered theatrically at the Edinburgh Film Festival and closed the London Film Festival, receiving rave reviews from the English press.[19] The assessment of the film in *Variety* after its London screening proved accurate, identifying it as candy for "European buffs" but noting "its facile dialog and predictable shenanigans limit it for first runs."[20] Given its brief American release and the buzz attached to it in Europe, *Dead Pigeon on Beethoven Street* began to attain holy grail status among Fuller cultists in North America, who saw in it an appealing form of anarchy. The awe-struck review in *Take One* summarizes the critical consensus regarding Fuller as a brilliant primitive: "This film is so relentlessly inventive and bizarre, breaking every rule of the known cinema, that the question must be asked: Is Fuller a madman or a genius. The answer is: both."[21]

### A Personal Journey: The Big Red One

Fuller's ultimate attempt at conveying a subjective experience of war was *The Big Red One*, the first film he made in the United States since *The Naked Kiss*. *The Big Red One* originated in Fuller's exploits as a footsoldier in the army's First Infantry Division during World War II. Fuller originally conceived of the project a decade after the end of the war while he was still under contract at Twentieth Century–Fox, announcing in *Hollywood Reporter* that he planned to do the picture as an independent production in color and CinemaScope after completing *House of Bamboo* and *Run of the Arrow*.[22] In October 1957, Warner Bros. purchased from Globe Enterprises the rights to Fuller's original unpublished story of *The Big Red One*, contracting to have him write a screenplay and, if accepted, produce and direct the film. The studio advanced Fuller $12,500 for the screenplay and agreed to cover the costs of a scouting trip to Europe; if the picture was produced, Globe would receive 20 percent of the net profits.[23]

Fuller returned from Europe and completed the first draft of his screenplay in early February 1958. Interoffice communications between Warner Bros. executives suggest Fuller had a difficult time cutting down his script to a length that appeared cost-effective to produce, and before attempting to budget the picture or contact army officials to secure possible cooperation, the studio requested three additional revisions.[24] Finally, in mid-March, with the script at 178 pages (one page approximating one minute of screen time), Warner Bros. executives sat down with Fuller to discuss the feasibility of the existing draft. Fuller and his military advisor, Major Raymond Harvey, had found three Army installations they believed could pass for the North African and European battlefields indicated in the script and that could contribute weapons and troops to defray production costs.[25] Yet the wide-ranging terrain, three beach landings, references to naval and air support, numerous tank and infantry battles, and large numbers of explosions among troops indicated in the script still caused tremendous concern, and ultimately Warner Bros. passed on the project.[26] While Fuller commonly cited the reason Warner Bros. declined to produce *The Big Red One* as his rejection of John Wayne as the lead—a role Fuller felt ill-suited him—it is more likely that Fuller could not produce a cut-down version of his script that the studio considered logistically and financially feasible.

Fuller's final 1958 script contains a basic story and narrative structure that remained unchanged through all of its later incarnations, a story of wartime survival told through the eyes of four young footsoldiers and their battle-hardened sergeant as they retrace the steps Fuller took with the First Division. Almost all the primary elements of Fuller's evolving vision originate here: the circular plot that begins with an accidental murder after the end of WWI and concludes with a parallel incident at the end of WWII, the invasion of North Africa and the surrender of the Vichy French, the tank battle at the Kasserine Pass, the escape of the Sergeant from a POW hospital, the invasion of Sicily, the landing at Omaha Beach on D-day, the invasions of Belgium and Germany, the battle in Hurtgen Forest, the invasion of Czechoslovakia, and the liberation of the Falkenau concentration camp. The story's key characters are also present, though in some cases in an embryonic form: a WWI-retread sergeant; Griff, an aspiring cartoonist who struggles with killing; Zab, a cynical cigar-smoker; Johnson, a fresh-faced country boy; and Vinci, an experienced replacement who becomes one of the team.

While the core of Fuller's story is consistent from the Warner Bros. scripts through to the 1980 theatrical release and the 2004 reconstruction, its presentation was initially much more traditional and accessible.[27] Fuller makes an obvious effort to at least acknowledge classical and generic conventions in his early script, making copious use of animated maps and discussions by upper echelon officers to clarify the geography and purposes of the various campaigns and to convey the "fighting spirit of the First Division." The unit's commanding lieutenant, captain, colonel, and general play prominent roles, and as the plot progresses, members of the unit are promoted until Griff is commanding his own squad. The narrative focus is thus not simply on the squad itself but also on how it is integrated into the Army's overall objectives. Each of the primary characters is also given an opportunity to sow some wild oats, a common narrative strategy thought to bring female viewers to the war genre: the sergeant discovers a tent full of French-Arab women in North Africa who are drinking and dancing and enjoys the company of one whose figure is "an arsenal of sex"; the lieutenant cuddles with an Italian girl who's always dreamed of a big, strong man like him; Vinci falls in love with and marries an English-woman who previously dated the captain; Griff snuggles with a French resistance fighter, "a symbol of sex even in her rough peasant coat and pants," saving her from being raped by a German soldier; Johnson sleeps with a Belgian girl who quotes Benjamin Franklin; Zab rolls around with a German countess in a castle; and the sergeant has a romantic interlude with a young concentration camp victim at Falkenau before she dies in his arms. Whether or not these escapades would have broadened the film's viewership is debatable, but they certainly constitute the script's most fantasy-fueled scenes. Additionally, extended sequences involving Vinci discovering his grandmother's house in Sicily, preparation for D-day in Liverpool, the French resistance, the Battle of Aachen, the Battle of the Bulge, and Griff waking up in Beethoven's house never made it into Fuller's later versions—understandable omissions, as they contribute little to the film's central themes or tensions. While the collapse of the Warner Bros. deal was a major disappointment to Fuller, robbing him of perhaps his only opportunity to shoot with the resources that could have supported the entirety of his original vision, it nevertheless allowed him to continue tinkering with the narrative of *The Big Red One* for nearly twenty more years, tinkering that would produce a more focused, distinctive approach to his story.

After years of hearing Fuller's yarns about his experiences in World War II and his desire to realize *The Big Red One*, Peter Bogdanovich agreed in late 1976 to produce his old friend's picture, taking the idea to Paramount studio chief Frank Yablans. Intrigued, Yablans advanced Fuller $5,000 in "cigar money" to begin writing a new script.[28] By the time the script was complete, Yablans had left Paramount and the new regime let the option expire. With the assistance of attorney Jack Schwartzman, Fuller's script reached the hands of Merv Adelson at Lorimar, a new independent production company. Adelson gave the go-ahead to begin preproduction with the understanding that the budget would remain tight, payment to principals would be deferred, and Fuller would receive a percentage of the profits.[29] Early in 1977 Fuller scouted locations in six to seven countries, resulting in an initial budget between $8 and 9 million; then logistics proved a nightmare, Lorimar slashed the budget, and preproduction stalled.[30] Gene Corman, an experienced producer of two war films in Europe, replaced Bogdanovich and suggested shooting in Israel, as its varied topography could stand in for North Africa, Sicily, and Normandy. Finally the project was back on track.

Shooting began early in 1978, although it would take two-and-a-half years for the film to hit screens. Lee Marvin, a WWII combat veteran who served in the Pacific, was cast as the grizzled sergeant; Fuller claimed he took to the material "like a hooker to a brothel." Fuller brought Marvin and a small production unit up to Big Bear in California to record snow scenes for a few days in January, but the bulk of the shoot took place over the summer, with nine weeks in Israel and one week in Ireland, all on schedule and on budget.[31] The young actors Bobby Carradine, Bobby Di Cicco, Kelly Ward, and a post–*Star Wars* (1977) Mark Hamill played the roles of Zab, Vinci, Johnson, and Griff, respectively, forming a tight unit on and off set. Marvin served as their role model and mentor, teaching them to shoot and offering guidance based on his own military experience. Fuller attacked production with his usual efficiency, rehearsing the staging with the actors, planning compositions and movement with cinematographer Adam Greenberg, and shooting master shots and close-ups with generally only one to two takes. During battle scenes Fuller directed with a pistol in each hand, shooting blanks at extras to cue them when to die ("You're dead! You're dead!"); an assistant stood behind him, constantly reloading the pistols and passing them over Fuller's shoulders, so the "killing" could continue uninterrupted. If you didn't die as directed, Fuller would shoot you again. When Greenberg completed a useable take, Fuller yelled, "Forget it!" and the unit moved on to the next camera setup.[32] Production completed in September 1978, with a negative cost of $4.5 million—by far Fuller's largest budget yet, but an extraordinarily small sum for a project of such tremendous scope. Fuller delivered his cut to Lorimar at what he later recalled as four-and-a-half hours; Lorimar brought in editor David Bretherton to reduce the length to under 120 minutes without the input of Fuller, and composer Dana Kaproff began work on a score. Once again, Fuller had lost control of a film in postproduction, but unlike with *Shark!*, his personal stake in *The Big Red One* prompted him to accede to Lorimar's requested cuts, however difficult it might have been. Once the re-editing was complete in 1979, the film's cost had risen to $6.5 million.

*The Big Red One* as originally released maintained the narrative structure and primary characters of Fuller's 1958 script but redirected its emphasis, resulting in an episodic, abstracted story of five footsoldiers in the European theater whose only interest is survival. The presence of commanding officers ranking above the sergeant largely disappears, and the soldiers' day-to-day life is isolated from the strategies of the higher-ups or any political purpose. The five protagonists emerge as an impenetrable circle, wary of admitting replacements who will only end up killed. While the sergeant remains as weary but wise as ever and Johnson is largely unchanged, Griff's moral struggle with killing comes to the

The core cast of *The Big Red One* formed a tight unit during production. Mark Hamill (front left), Bobby Carradine (rear left), Bobby Di Cicco (rear center), and Lee Marvin (right front) relax during a break from shooting the D-day landing. *Chrisam Films, Inc.*

fore, Zab appears as a writer closely based on Fuller, and Vinci is no longer a replacement but a wisecracking member of the core unit. Though the sex scenes are eliminated, new bits of weirdness are added, including a birthing sequence in a tank and a shootout in an insane asylum, events that emphasize the ironies of wartime.

Elements from Fuller's earlier combat pictures coalesce into a unified whole. As in *The Steel Helmet*, boredom is relieved only by sudden violence, action is abbreviated, and no one volunteers for anything unless he wants to die. From *Fixed Bayonets*, Fuller transfers to Griff Denno's hesitation to shoot and moves the claustrophobic cave conversations to transport ships. The children of *The Steel Helmet* and *China Gate* reemerge in scenes set in Italy and Falkenau, where they are drawn particularly to the sergeant in moments of extreme poignancy. And the bond between Merrill and Stockton in *Merrill's Marauders* carries over into the union between the sergeant and his four men, one defined by shared experience, trust, and admiration. Significantly, the didactic discussions of *The Steel Helmet* and *China Gate* are absent in the film, as is, with the exception of the Falkenau sequence, vilification of the enemy. Fuller builds in parallels between WWII and WWI and between the protagonists and the enemy, suggesting that all war is the same, all soldiers are the same. The soldier's job is to kill, and his goal is to survive. End of story.

Fuller's stylistic approach to the material matches that of the narrative, focusing intently on the actions and emotions of the five protagonists. Once again, Fuller wants us to *feel* what it is like to be a footsoldier, and so he makes liberal use of point-of-view editing and close-up reaction shots to provide us with access to the protagonists' subjectivity. Frequently he introduces the master shot and then cuts into a series of protagonists' close-ups, allowing us to gauge their responses as individuals and as a unit. These shots are essential, as there is little dialogue—especially during battle scenes—and only Zab's voice-over to guide our understanding of the characters' mindsets. Lacking the histrionic performances found in Fuller's more sensational films, *The Big Red One* relies significantly on small expressions and gestures to convey meaning. The visual construction of scenes encourages us to set aside the larger context of the battles and direct our attention to individual experience; as with the protagonists in the middle of the fight, we register only what happens in the immediate vicinity.

The staging of the D-day landing on Omaha Beach is a prime example of how Fuller telescopes enormously complex military maneuvers into the experience of just five men. In contrast to *The Longest Day* (1962), which took three hours to depict the D-Day invasion, *The Big Red One* summarizes the experience in eight and a half minutes. The scene begins with the five protagonists in the water, crawling to shore one by one. While Fuller's limited resources diminish the sense of realism—it looks like only fifty men are landing on Omaha Beach—Fuller turns this to his advantage by quickly cutting in to the main characters and highlighting their sense of isolation. The waves, reddened by the blood of the fallen, wash in close-up over a watch on a lifeless wrist: 6:30 A.M. Quick dialogue and a voice-over inform us that the men are pinned down, left without air, artillery, or bazooka support. The sergeant's unit must perform the bangalore relay, in which a fifty-foot-long dynamite tube has to be assembled by hand on the beach as the soldiers crawl toward the enemy bunkers. "I'd love to meet the asshole who invented it," Zab mockingly says in voice-over. Ever efficient, Fuller uses a limited number of camera setups to cover the sequence, relying primarily on a wide shot looking up the beach toward the Germans from the optical perspective of the pinned-down unit; a tighter reverse angle of the five protagonists behind a sandbar; and individual close-ups of each of the protagonists, reacting to the relay's progress. The sergeant calls out the numbers of seven men to attempt the relay. As each anonymous soldier goes forward, the camera stays with the five protagonists and we see what they see: every man dies. The reaction shots register their dread, as they know their own numbers will soon be called. Finally, the sergeant calls number eight: Griff, the character who has struggled with his own fear in combat. For the first time, the camera advances into the fire zone with a soldier, keeping us firmly in the subjectivity of Griff. Griff crawls onto the beach, but freezes; an extreme close-up registers his paralysis at the sight of a dead German. A cut to a close-up reaction shot of the sergeant communicates that he knows what is going on, but he won't let Griff shirk his job. The sergeant fires a round that hits next to Griff as a warning, and again close-ups register Griff's anger and the sergeant's insistence. Finally, Griff crawls forward and completes the relay. The unit now has a way off the beach. At the end of the sequence, the watch in the bloody water reads 9:15 A.M. This scene condenses the entire D-day invasion into the experience of one small squad, and ultimately the paralyzing fears of one soldier. Only fifty yards of the beach are seen, and no more than thirty men at a time. No sense of the larger battle is presented, and no sign exists of any Allies or even a discrete enemy. The grand scope of *The Longest Day* has been massively reduced in scale, allowing for an intimate vision of war that emphasizes what each man must do to survive.

Lorimar launched the worldwide promotional push of *The Big Red One* following its premiere at the Cannes Film Festival in May 1980, where response to the movie reflected the French adulation of Fuller.[33] United Artists distributed the film as part of its domestic pact with Lorimar, and $3 million was budgeted for advertising and promotion. UA scheduled a July 18 release in New York, Los Angeles, and Toronto, with the film opening wide two weeks later. Fuller made appearances at career retrospectives organized to accompany the debuts of *The Big Red One* in L.A. and New York, and he and Marvin traveled to promote the film's European release in the fall.[34] Reviews were almost uniformly strong. Many critics discussed the film as it reflected aspects of Fuller's past work and personal experiences; typical is Richard Schickel's review in *Time,* in which he suggests Fuller creates scenes and then leaves them "to work on his viewers' minds, as they imagine the memories must have, over the years, on his own."[35] *Variety*'s rave allows that WWII pictures had fallen out of favor but suggests "intelligent sell should allow film to reach both those who will respond to Fuller's artistry and mass audiences looking for strong action."[36] Unfortunately, *Variety*'s observation regarding the fading appeal of WWII pictures proved correct. *The Big Red One* opened ninth the weekend it went wide and earned only $2.3 million in rentals for the year, a huge disappointment for a film that cost $9.5 million to release.[37] Lorimar went bankrupt shortly after the film hit theaters. Fuller returned to writing. His fans began a long, twenty-four-year wait to see his original cut of *The Big Red One* reconstructed.

### *Inciting Controversy:* White Dog

Fuller's most controversial project and still one of his most rarely screened films is *White Dog*, the story of a young actress who hires an animal trainer to "cure" her stray canine, programmed from birth to attack blacks. The project originated with a story by Romain Gary that appeared in *Life* magazine and was brought to Robert Evans at Paramount, who commissioned a screenplay from Curtis Hanson and slated Roman Polanski to direct. The project stalled after Polanski's forced flight from the United States in 1977, only to be further developed with rewrites by Thomas Baum and Nick Kazan. In early 1981, faced with possible strikes by both the Writers Guild and the Directors Guild, Paramount fast-tracked *White Dog* as one of several films capable of wrapping before the work stoppages, bringing in producer Jon Davison, fresh off of *Airplane!* (1980).[38] Davison initially balked at the assignment, concerned that Paramount president Michael Eisner wanted a "*Jaws* on paws" exploitation film that would be a marketing nightmare.[39] Under contract with Paramount, Davison finally relented, now saddled with a project well into preproduction and scheduled for shooting in six weeks but lacking a workable script and a director. Davison contacted Hanson, a former colleague from Roger Corman's New World Productions, who recommended Fuller, a personal friend; both knew Fuller to be one of the few men in Hollywood who could prepare a script and direct on such short notice. Though already scheduled to fly to Japan and helm *Let's Get Harry*, Fuller signed on to *White Dog*, "excited as hell about doing Romain Gary's story," as the writer was an old friend.[40] Fuller and Hanson spent two weeks crafting a completely new script, with Hanson writing scenes and Fuller rewriting. At the same time, rising star Kristy McNichol was signed to headline, with supporting help from Jameson Parker, Burl Ives, and Paul Winfield. Operating with a budget of $7.1 million, Fuller shot for forty-four days—starting a month after the script was finished.[41]

Midway through production, Paramount brought in David Crippens, the vice-president and station manager of KCET, the local PBS station, and Willis Edwards, president of the Beverly Hills–Hollywood NAACP chapter, to act as consultants on the film's representation of race. Both read the script, met at various times with Jeffrey Katzenberg, head of

production at Paramount, Davison, and actor Paul Winfield, and provided notes. Both considered how African-American audiences might
respond to the film in the context of the ongoing serial slayings of black
children in Atlanta. Crippens indicated "I do not find the script racist"
but suggested clarifying the motivations of the black animal trainer who
deprograms the dog. Edwards anticipated unintended readings of the
film that "could cause a distribution problem if the Black population
were to collectively voice an objection to the subject matter." He recommended removing the racial content and producing a more conventional
horror/thriller film—an untenable option that seemed to completely
miss the point of the movie.[42] Katzenberg and Don Simpson, vice-
president of production, took the comments of Crippens and Edwards
extremely seriously, encouraging the consultants to provide both general recommendations to clarify the film's themes and comments on the
action and dialogue in specific scenes.[43] Though Davison did his best to
act as a buffer between Fuller and the notes coming from the consultants through Paramount executives, Fuller nevertheless resented the involvement of non-filmmakers, writing on one memo that summarized
the suggestions of Crippens and Edwards, "This is *why* the film was *not*
made for 6 years until *I came in with the non-racist approach*" (emphasis in original).[44] Katzenberg's recommended changes to the script based
on the consultants' notes also offended Fuller, who angrily called the
then thirty-year-old executive "Katzenjammer," a reference to the ill-
behaved children in the Katzenjammer Kids comic strip, and described
his ideas as "stupid, unimaginative, and insulting," reminiscent "of mes-
senger boys' memos."[45] Clearly Katzenberg was being cautious, trying to
protect the film and Paramount from controversy. To Fuller, however, the
young executive paled next to Darryl Zanuck, who protected Fuller's
choices even in the face of complaints from J. Edgar Hoover. The intru-
sion of outside consultants into production at the invitation of Paramount executives suggested to Fuller a profound lack of respect toward
him and a cowardly ambivalence toward the film's content.

The film as shot is set in Los Angeles, where struggling actress Julie
Sawyer (McNichol) accidentally hits a dog while driving home. After
bringing the white Alsatian to a vet, Julie is advised to drop it at the
pound. Instead, she takes the dog home and puts up "found" ads in the
neighborhood, growing increasingly attached to her new companion.
Julie's boyfriend, writer Roland Gray (Parker), is less enamored, as the
dog seems to find him threatening. The dog proves useful, however,
rousing itself from a TV viewing of *They Were Expendable* (1945) to
prevent Julie's assault by a would-be rapist. One day the dog chases a
rabbit and runs away, prompting Julie to search for him at the pound;
discovering the gas chambers, she determines to never turn him in. Julie

is thrilled when the dog returns, unaware that it has just viciously attacked and killed an African-American driving a street cleaner. The attacks continue when Julie brings the dog to a commercial she is shooting and he lunges after her black costar. Roland suspects the dog has been trained to attack and should be put down, but Julie decides to visit an animal trainer first. Carruthers (Ives), a robot hater who coaches animals for the movies, tells her the dog is too old to be reprogrammed, but his African-American partner, Keys (Winfield), expresses interest. Julie leaves the dog with Keys, who begins working diligently. One night, the dog stages a "prison break" from its large iron cage and gets loose, later chasing a well-dressed black man into a church and killing him. Keys recaptures the dog and rebuffs the renewed concerns of Carruthers and Julie, arguing for the importance of learning how to eradicate the dog's racist training. As Keys continues his work, the dog's prior owners respond to Julie's ad: an elderly man and his two granddaughters. Julie denounces the grandfather's racism and refuses to return the dog. At the animal compound, Keys believes he has made a breakthrough and stages a demonstration in the dog's cage for Carruthers and Julie. The dog no longer runs at Keys in fury, but does threaten Julie, only to respond warmly in the end. As the dog and Julie cuddle, the dog spots Carruthers, and races to attack him, prompting Keys to abandon his experiment and shoot to kill.

The narrative conceit of *White Dog* was a challenge from the start, as it suggested not simply "*Jaws* on paws" but *racist "Jaws* on paws." The previous draft of the script written before Fuller and Hanson's overhaul as well as Paramount's accompanying suggestions for revisions highlight the apparent difficulty studio executives had with initially recognizing the story's potential controversy. Paramount executives were looking for a "suspense thriller" that featured a "moving and emotional love story between a human and an animal."[46] The female protagonist's relationship with the dog was intended to provide her with the strength to overcome her victimization by men, resulting in the two becoming a team. At the same time, Paramount executives applauded the staging of an attack on a black pool man as "more shocking, more like a *Dog Jaws*," and embraced the script's "compelling" ending, in which Keys purposely retrains the dog to attack Caucasians, the dog attacks the protagonist, and then the dog commits suicide in despair.[47] While the Hanson/Kazan script Paramount was developing clearly identified itself as an exploitation picture—announcing after the title page: "This film should have a slight odor"—studio executives seemed to think the dog could be presented as a loving helpmate whose violence is redeemed by self-sacrifice.[48] That the dog's violence was targeted at a historically oppressed minority group, and that a member of this group then cynically adopts the tactics of those who most despise him, seems not to have troubled the executives, as love was shown to win the day.

Fuller and Hanson's rewrite openly grapples with what is implicit in the earlier script, transforming an exploitation story into an assault on the teaching of hate. The redrafting of Keys's character is central to this change. While Julie's character remains personally invested in the dog, it is Keys who is determined to save him, to demonstrate that hate is not innate but learned and can be overcome. Julie may be the audience stand-in, but it is Keys who is Fuller's moral voice. The overt discussion of racism within the film and the role model provided by Keys invests the dog's snarling attacks with a purpose glaringly lacking in the earlier drafts. Love is not enough to redeem violence—action is required. Though Keys fails, the suggestion is not that his efforts were naive, but that the dog simply snapped under psychological strain. Like the murder witnesses who Johnny Barrett questions in *Shock Corridor*'s psychiatric hospital, the dog has a moment of lucidity after his retraining and recognizes his affection for Julie but cannot remain in control for long. *White Dog* is Fuller's most complete expression of his belief in the power of education to change minds, an optimistic challenge to ignorance and bigotry. Unfortunately, the film soon became mired in delays and controversy, falsely charged with perpetuating the prejudice it so clearly challenged.

Postproduction on *White Dog* commenced in the fall of 1981, with rough cuts screened in October and November. Fuller was actively involved in the editing, responding to the notes provided by Paramount executives and agreeing to trim or cut many of the extreme-close-ups and long tracking shots that marked his work.[49] Thereafter, Paramount appeared uncertain of when and how to release the picture. According to *Variety*, the studio reported that the film's first preview screening in Seattle in early 1982 met with "average results," although its subsequent summer release in France by UIP netted "rave reviews and medium business."[50] Another preview screening ran in Denver in late summer, where 75 percent of the audience rated the picture good or excellent. Still Paramount held back the film. *Variety*'s June review suggests their fear: "Touchy theme will have Par treading carefully in eventual domestic distribution. . . . [A] tough sell is indicated."[51] Finally, on November 12, 1982, *White Dog* opened at five suburban and downtown Detroit theaters for a one-week test; though no official grosses were reported, Paramount described the reviews and box office as "not good."[52] The film went back on the shelf. Requests to screen it at the Edinburgh, London, New York, Los Angeles, and Telluride Film Festivals were all denied. In early February 1983, Paramount announced it would not play *White Dog* in theaters, claiming it did not justify the expense of release; instead,

Samuel Fuller and his lead actor on the set of *White Dog*. While promoting the film, Fuller interviewed the German shepherd for an article in *Framework* magazine. *Chrisam Films, Inc.*

the film would be made available for video and cable beginning in January 1984.

Influencing Paramount's hesitation behind the scenes was a media campaign to boycott the film organized by members of the Los Angeles chapter of the National Association for the Advancement of Colored People. "We're against the whole thrust of the film and what it says about racism," announced spokesperson Collette Wood.[53] Leading the charge was Willis Edwards, now working to create the same distribution problem he presciently anticipated when he initially signed on as one of Paramount's paid consultants. "The film has major overtones of racism," Edwards charged. "When you train a white dog to kill black folks, that gives the KKK and other white supremacist organizations ideas."[54] Edwards claimed he "repeatedly told Paramount that the film was racist"; while he may have done so verbally, no record exists within correspondence between him, Paramount executives, Davison, or Fuller that such a claim or anything like it was ever made.[55] Although Paul Winfield publicly countered that "The protective stance of the NAACP and other well-meaning groups is actually a disservice to black people," the NAACP campaign convinced NBC to drop plans to air the film two days after it paid $2.5 million for broadcast rights in January 1984.[56] Paramount freed the film to screen at the Edinburgh and London Film Festivals, and it opened to strong acclaim in London in April 1984. Not until 1991 did *White Dog* play again in the United States, however. "Holy shit," wrote Fuller in his autobiography, "if the chopping up of *The Big Red One* had put a few dents in my resolve to pursue moviemaking in Hollywood, then the lockup of *White Dog* had totally wrecked it! I was deeply hurt."[57] Saddened by the charges made by those ignorant of his work and angered by Paramount's lack of commitment to his film, Fuller and his family decamped to Paris, where they remained in self-imposed exile for thirteen years. Samuel Fuller's American filmmaking career was over.

### In Exile: Thieves After Dark *and* Street of No Return

Soon after Fuller arrived in Paris in 1982, he received an offer to cowrite and direct *Thieves After Dark*. The project was an adaptation of the novel *Le Chant des Enfants Morts* by Olivier Beer; Beer was a fan of Fuller's, and convinced French producer Jo Siritzky to finance the adaptation with Fuller attached to direct. Beer and Fuller agreed to write the screenplay together, although Fuller has suggested their working relationship was not very productive and he was mostly forced to go it alone.[58] Production got underway in Paris and the Alps at the end of 1982, with Bobby Di Cicco from *The Big Red One* and French actress Véronique Jannot starring. Fuller shot two versions, one in French and one in which the French actors spoke in English; the following May he supervised an American-accented dub of the English version, hoping to release it in theaters that would ordinarily not play a foreign film.[59]

*Thieves After Dark* is a contemporary love story set in Paris, chronicling the fateful romance of two unemployed youth. The film opens at the symphony, where French-American François (Di Cicco), an aspiring cellist, illegally watches the orchestra from backstage, only to be pulled away by a police officer who kindly lets him off the hook. Later, François bumps into Isabelle (Jannot), a wanna-be art historian, after they both experience frustrating interviews at an employment agency. In a pique of anger, Isabelle throws a chair through a glass wall at a manager, prompting François to maneuver her outside. They share a drink, and she shrugs off his advances; after a frenetic search he bumps into her again, splattering her with paint. Eager François cleans Isabelle up and follows her into bed, where they make love and discuss their lives under the watchful eyes of her cat. After a failed attempt at becoming street musicians, the couple brainstorm how to raise some money. A joke about being like Bonnie and Clyde turns into a plan to rob the three most annoying employment agency managers, thereby netting both cash and revenge. The first robbery proves gratifying, but the second is interrupted by the manager's young daughter, to whom they reveal their scheme. Keener on the couple than her father, the daughter gives them his expensive pocketwatch, which they fence with . . . Samuel Fuller. Now flush with cash, the couple decides to rob the third manager, nicknamed Tartuffe, just for kicks, but end up interrupting his voyeuristic perch on the balcony. The manager falls to his death, Isabelle screams, and a neighbor records their voices and sees them flee. Now pursued by the police, the couple borrow the car of the second manager's daughter and escape to the snowy Alps with cat in tow. François stows an injured Isabelle in the trunk of the car with the cat while he goes for medicine, but a local girl (played by Samantha Fuller) hears the cat and alerts the police. After a brief chase, Isabelle is shot and François returns fire, killing two officers. After returning to Paris, François heads back to the symphony, where he forcefully takes the place of one of the cellists, fulfilling his dream. Outside, the sympathetic officer learns that a witness reported Tartuffe's fall as an accident, and the pursuit of the couple was for naught; only now, Isabelle is dead, and François has two murders on his hands.

*Thieves After Dark* bears only a glancing resemblance to Fuller's other films, serving as a coherent, generic, *romantic* reminder of his ability to produce a wide range of work. Fuller's interest in oppositions and irony is present in the narrative, as the couple's role-play of Bonnie and Clyde evolves into reality in a wickedly unnecessary fashion. In the opening sequence, Fuller tricks the viewer into misidentifying François the same way the robbery victims later do, visually presenting him as a threatening stalker. The camera follows François in an extended Steadicam shot down a shadowy alley, as he conceals his face from a policeman and enters an unidentified interior. Once inside he hides in an alcove, and Fuller cuts from his glance to the lower half of a man carrying a cello case. The visual construction of the sequence and Ennio Morricone's anxious score prompt the viewer to anticipate that François wants something in the cello case and wants it in a vaguely threatening way. He does, of course, but what he wants is not what we expect. While the staging of the scene thus far cries "film noir," cueing the viewer to expect diamonds in the case and preparation for a crime, Fuller flips our expectations on their heads, revealing that François's desire is to *play* the cello, not steal what is inside it—and the cop outside who nabs him is actually his friend! It is a delightfully well-executed, purely Fullerian sequence. Unfortunately, no other sequences in the film resonate so strongly. (Though perhaps the cat, a favorite Fuller prop, also gives away the director's presence.)

Fuller's first film to be fully financed by a European company was also his first in quite some time to receive a cold shoulder from the continental press. When the film screened at the Berlin Film Festival in 1984, scattered boos were heard in the theater, and German critics found it lacking in credibility. In France, reviews were mixed, with some finding Fuller's sensibilities ill-suited to such a Gallic tale.[60] The *Variety* review found more to like, though it predicted "better results from foreign play dates than possible US distribution."[61] While the French version of the film was distributed in Europe by Parafrance, it never played theatrically in the United States, and Fuller's American version never saw the light of day.

After another fallow period in which Fuller kept busy writing, acting, and appearing in documentaries, he was approached in 1988 by producer Jacques Bral to write and direct an adaptation of pulp-fiction specialist David Goodis's 1954 novel, *Street of No Return*. Fuller jumped at the chance, as he and Goodis were friends in the late 1940s when both were churning out scripts for the studios and cheap paperbacks on the side.[62] Author of *Dark Passage* and *Down There*—later adapted for the screen as François Truffaut's *Shoot the Piano Player* (1960)—Goodis was a moody loner who wrote stories of violent passion, dark streets, and helpless despair. As with Fuller, Goodis was more widely revered in France than in America, and Bral considered pairing the two an inspired choice. Bral already had a script that Fuller set about reworking. The production shot for nine weeks in Sintra, Portugal, just outside of Lisbon, with Keith Carradine and Valentina Vargas as the story's thwarted lovers. In his autobiography, Fuller recalls the shoot ending on time and under budget; after supervising the editing he turned the film over to Bral, whom he alleges then recut it.[63]

The picture opens with a violent race riot on an anonymous urban street. Michael (Carradine), a homeless alcoholic, stumbles through the melee in search of liquor bottles. He bumps into a leather-coated, cigar-smoking woman whom he recognizes from his past and follows her back to a fenced-in mansion guarded by attack dogs; crouched behind giant milk cartons, he glimpses another woman, a beauty seemingly locked inside. Michael's discovery of the ethereal beauty prompts an extended flashback to an earlier time, when he was a successful singer-songwriter with a taste for gold ear clips and long, studded black coats (it's the 1980s). Scouting dancers for a music video, Michael enjoys the erotic twirls of Celia (Vargas), the stunning woman from the mansion. He picks her up and the two hit the sheets, though she tells him she is already attached. The two part ways, but Michael wants to see her again. They plan to run away together, but Celia must break it off with her boyfriend first. When Celia shows up for her escape with Michael, she is followed by her slimy boyfriend, his muscled enforcer, and the perpetually pissed-off cigar-smoking woman. It all ends poorly, with Michael's vocal cords slashed and the boyfriend threatening to kill him and Celia if they ever see each other again. The flashback ends, and Michael wanders back to the scene of the race riot, clearly a shell of his former self. Mistakenly arrested for the murder of a nearby dead cop, he winds up in jail and witnesses the police chief (Bill Duke) harassing and beating suspects from the riot. Michael stages a break with a handy water hose but ends up shanghaied by one of the riot suspects and taken to the cargo ship that serves as the black gang's headquarters. Another inventive escape ensues thanks to a hand grenade and the anchor rope, leaving Michael clinging to the undercarriage of the gang leader's jeep as it drives to the fenced-in mansion. Now inside, Michael overhears the gang leader plotting with Celia's slimy boyfriend to stage race riots and sell drugs as a means of deflating real estate values, enabling them to them buy low, rebuild, and sell high. The two toast to the glory of crack cocaine. Michael retreats and informs the police chief of the scheme behind the riots, then accompanies the police to a smoke-filled shootout at the mansion. The boyfriend's minions die colorful deaths, Celia is wounded, and the boyfriend is taken to jail. As thanks, the police chief allows Michael to shoot the boyfriend's testicles. In the final scene, Celia returns to rescue Michael from his life as a bum.

With its shirt-grabbing race riot, mercenary view of crime, and gritty urban milieu, Street of No Return appears at first glance to find Fuller on more comfortable generic ground than his previous picture. The trash-strewn, abandoned nighttime streets and raging gang warfare combine the architecture of Europe with the mise-en-scene of The Warriors (1979), creating a strangely anonymous Everycity abstracted from any reference to reality yet firmly rooted in film noir conventions. Cinematographer Pierre-William Glenn (Day for Night, 1973) attempts a brightly hazy, neon-inflected take on the high-contrast shadows that define the noir look, coming closest to capturing an equivalent during the climactic mansion shootout amidst billows of tear gas. Not only the world they move in but also the characters themselves recall noir tendencies, delivering hard-boiled dialogue and operating with a certain aggressive fatigue. Fuller inflects the material with his own absurd panache, ramping up the performances and emphasizing the cartoonish quality of the whole proceeding. The race riot opens in a particularly visceral fashion, with a close-up of a man getting whacked with a hammer in the head; subsequent shots move through the violence in extended Steadicam takes, enveloping the viewer in the mayhem. Perhaps the most intriguing sequence is the police assault on the mansion, as the use of tear gas in the many floors and hallways makes spatial relations ambiguous and increases confusion and surprise.

Despite the elements that link the movie to Fuller's earlier work and to
film noir—a narrative and visual style he is frequently associated with—
*Street of No Return* is his least coherent crime picture. The pairing of
Goodis and Fuller simply is not as simpatico as Bral first suspected.
Goodis wrote stories about characters whose worlds collapsed on top of
them, but Fuller told stories about characters who punched their world
in the nose. *Pickup on South Street* and *Underworld, U.S.A.* may share
the sharp shadows, urban underbelly, focus on crime, and hard-boiled
attitude that mark the film noir approach, but they pointedly do not
adopt the nonlinear narrative structure and passive protagonist so central to noir stories. Nonlinear narratives serve no purpose for Fuller, and
he never used them (except in this film); his protagonists are charging
forward, not looking back. While Fuller revised Goodis's story to create
more action and invest Michael with some agency, his character emerges
as an uneasy hybrid of the two writers' instincts. On the one hand,
Michael is largely passive, reliant on coincidence to rediscover Celia,
meet the police chief, enter the mansion and learn the plan, yet he is also
able to summon hidden strength and resourcefulness to escape from the
police station and the cargo ship. Primarily he just watches, his raspy,
high-pitched voice a reminder of his emasculation. The ending poses similar problems. Film noir conventions lead the viewer to suspect Celia will
either engineer a double cross to take control of her boyfriend's real estate empire or die in the end, robbing Michael of what he wants most.
Fuller himself seems more likely to have killed Michael. Yet the ending
portends bliss and roses for both, ringing false both to noir and Fullerian
tendencies. The pieces of *Street of No Return* simply do not form a complete picture; as viewers, we are left with a puzzle.

    *Street of No Return* debuted at Cannes in May 1989 and opened in
Paris in August, typically the slowest month for French box office. Reviews in France were mixed, with the mainstream press panning the film
and Fuller cultists lavishing praise.[64] *Variety* was similarly on the fence,
describing the picture as "disappointing as a chiller and especially as a
Fuller, though its large doses of action could interest B markets."[65] Absent an American distributor, the film finally premiered in the United
States as part of a retrospective of Fuller's work at Film Forum in New
York City in August 1991. Though judging it uneven, critics were
thrilled to see a Fuller film again. Fuller champion Georgia Brown said it
best: "[Fuller] at least never represents existence at the murky bottom—
life vulgar life—as *tasteful*. Lyrical yes; snug and respectable no" (emphasis in original).[66] *Street of No Return* was Fuller's twenty-third and
final feature film. He was seventy-seven at the time of its European release. After he completed two films for French television in 1990, Samuel
Fuller's career as a director was over.

As was true of so many of Hollywood's most seminal filmmakers, Fuller's later work was marred by frustration and inconsistency. Despite his growing cult status both at home and abroad, he lost control of three of his last six films and saw the limited release of four. For a man who came of age in Hollywood during an era when you could make a picture based on an impassioned pitch and a handshake deal, the long development process and anxious focus on the bottom line that marked modern moviemaking created an alienating environment. Only Fuller's relentless optimism and love of visual storytelling kept him in the game at all.

His films during this period did yield work of note. *Dead Pigeon on Beethoven Street* stands out as a reminder of Fuller's absurd sense of humor and affiliation with the young filmmakers of European New Cinema; beloved by them for so many years, he made a "fun Fuller" in their style. *White Dog* saw him return to the problem of racism and learned hate, one of the topics that obsessed him throughout his life; both the picture itself and the controversy surrounding it are a testament to his willingness to face head-on the paradox of America, a country that promises so much but often fails to deliver. *The Big Red One*, the most personal of his films, was his strongest thematic and aesthetic statement of the period, a narrative and stylistic summary of his work in the combat film genre and a personal exorcism of his fight for survival during World War II. In their own distinct ways, these three pictures successfully express Fuller's dominant aesthetic goal: to startle and arouse, inform and entertain.

Though Fuller never directed another feature film after *Street of No Return*, he remained busy writing and acting, particularly enjoying a trip with Jim Jarmusch back to Mato Grasso in 1993 to revisit the aboriginal tribe he first encountered while scouting locations for *Tigrero*, his final failed Twentieth Century–Fox project. The resulting documentary, *Tigrero: A Film That Was Never Made* (1994) depicts Fuller as vigorous and idealistic as ever, a role model not only for Jarmusch and director Mika Kaurismäki, but for young filmmakers and fans everywhere. At the end of his life, Fuller began writing and dictating *A Third Face: My Tale of Writing, Fighting, and Filmmaking,* a rollicking and inspirational autobiography that details his work as a journalist, a soldier, and a filmmaker. After suffering a debilitating stroke in 1994, Fuller died in 1997 in Los Angeles, surrounded by his family.

One of the brightest moments of Fuller's later career sadly occurred after his death, when *The Big Red One* was re-released in 2004 in a version reconstructed from his shooting script. Film critic and historian Richard Schickel, a long-time Fuller fan, initiated inquiries into the location of the movie's missing footage while working on a Charlie Chaplin project at Warner Bros. At first, only a few cans of outtakes turned up without accompanying sound, not nearly enough to extend the Lorimar version to Fuller's legendary four-and-a-half-hour director's cut. Schickel's pressure and persistence turned up additional footage, and careful matching to Fuller's shooting script revealed a significant number of missing scenes could be reinserted into the film. In the course of their detective work, Schickel and Bryan McKenzie, the editor of the reconstruction, discovered that Fuller's four-and-a-half-hour original cut was likely only a bit over three hours in length—there simply had not been enough footage shot during production to create a picture so long.[67] In total, McKenzie was able to return twenty-four lost sequences to the film and extend the length of an additional thirty-three, adding more than forty minutes to the running time. The new material returned some sex to the film; added ironic counterpoints and scenes of absurdity characteristic of Fuller; strengthened the parallel established between the Sergeant and his German counterpart, Schroeder; and included previously unseen cameos of Fuller as a war correspondent and Christa Lang as a double-crossing German countess. The film's characters are developed more deeply, while its themes emerge more clearly. In addition to reinserting cut footage, the reconstruction involved a digital restoration of all visual material, cleaning dirt and scratches from each frame, and a complete sound restoration, combining fresh effects and musical cues with the old to produce a deeper, denser, more resonant soundtrack. Finally, *The Big Red One* achieved a shape and sound that reflected Fuller's original vision, a fitting tribute to a filmmaker who struggled so hard in his later years to simply get his pictures up on the screen.

# Conclusion

●●●● amuel Fuller was an impassioned and emphatic man. He had
 ●●● the short stature and stocky build of a street fighter, and as he
●●●● aged his hair grew long and white like that of Beethoven, one of
his favorite artists. Years of cigars and whiskey brought a raspy, gravel-
like quality to his voice, and he spoke with the confidence and authority
of a man who had lived in the world, talking fast, with fury, repeating
words for emphasis, and pausing dramatically for punctuation. Inter-
viewers did not ask questions to be answered so much as provide a topic
for the next part of the performance. He demanded your attention. He
was a physical talker and would jab the air with his Camacho cigar to
underline an important point or jump from his seat and act out a scene
from a film or memory. He retained the energy of a newsboy who had to
hustle to make a sale and an optimism rare for one who had worked so
long in the film industry. He was an idea volcano, constantly erupting.
His forceful, colorful personality was "every boy's idea of what a director should be."[1]

Fuller aimed to make gut-punch movies, the kind you don't forget
when you walk out of the theater. His pictures are rarely subtle, but they
are sincere, and it is the depth of his belief that gives his films their
power. Fuller's aesthetic is distinguished by his desire to produce a direct
emotional impact on the viewer, to surprise, instruct, and entertain as a
means of revealing truth. His instinct was to challenge the classical,
generic, and cultural norms by which Hollywood put stories on the
screen, to upend audience expectations and to shock and unsettle the
viewer. Despite the seeming familiarity of their genre origins, Fuller's
original screenplays are truly his own, structured to reveal that life is
conflict, and truth is contradictory. His stylistic strategies seek to produce physical and emotional sensations through jarring juxtapositions
and kinetic effects. He wanted his audiences to go, "Whoa!" Throughout
his career, Fuller's artistic vision engages in an ongoing dialogue with ex-
ternal forces—including classical norms, production conditions, studio
oversight, censor regulations, and market trends—that dampen, empha-

size, or transform his inclinations. Fuller's films are thus marked by an uneven adherence to classical norms and cultural notions of good taste, ranging from the very conventional (*Hell and High Water*) to the very unconventional (*Shock Corridor*). Though the manner and means through which Fuller expressed his aesthetic interests changed over time, his artistic impulses and goals remained unwavering.

By the end of his career, some strategies adopted by Fuller had entered the mainstream, while others remained idiosyncratic. The self-conscious use of style, visceral staging of violence, and unsparing exploration of race, crime, and war that marked Fuller's films were increasingly integrated into commercial American releases from the New Hollywood period of the late 1960s on, an example of the flexibility of the classical system to absorb innovation. Fuller's deployment of irony, though, is unlike that seen in contemporary films, as it is intended not to distance us from the experience of emotion, but to push us toward it. At the same time, his overstuffed plots, abrupt tonal shifts, incongruent dialogue, and didactic interludes continue to set his work apart, linking it both with melodramatic narrative conventions and with camp. Contemporary studio executives would still likely pass on *Forty Guns* for the same reasons Darryl Zanuck did, while the volatile mix of melodramatic hysteria and social commentary in *Shock Corridor* will always raise a red flag with financeers seeking to make a safe buck. Though Fuller's work in the 1950s and early 1960s anticipated some developing narrative and stylistic trends within Hollywood, how and why he deployed his aesthetic strategies distinguished his work as unique.

Fuller's ability to produce the kinds of films he wanted to make was significantly affected by larger industrial trends. When he began directing in the late 1940s, the major studios were in the process of decreasing their annual output, especially in the low-budget range. Yet the sustained use of double features left exhibitors scrambling for films, opening a niche in the market for smaller producers like Lippert who continued to churn out B pictures. Lippert's need for talented directors and original product accounts for his willingness to grant Fuller his first directing job, as well as to offer Fuller increased production control, including profit participation, script approval, and eventually producer status. The undersupplied market for "in-betweeners" in the early 1950s thus helped Fuller to establish a reputation as a director able to produce low-budget action pictures with exploitation value, a reputation he could then parlay into a studio contract. Fuller lost significant aesthetic control when he signed with Twentieth Century–Fox, but he gained an opportunity to participate in the 1950s trend toward blockbuster filmmaking. Featuring Technicolor and CinemaScope, large casts with multiple stars, and exotic locations, Fuller's last two Fox pictures, *Hell and High Water* and *House of Bamboo,* are early examples of studios' efforts to differentiate their product from television by producing big-budget action films loaded with spectacle and international intrigue. These glossy, star-studded adventure films are precisely the kind of picture Fuller's independently produced programmers would have such a difficult time competing against a few years later.

Fuller's move into independent production in the late 1950s allowed him to indulge in a more emphatic visual style and less classical narratives, but it also saddled him with greater financial risk. Fuller's status as the writer, director, and producer of his Globe pictures freed him to complete projects that broke more distinctly from classical norms, such as *Run of the Arrow* and *Forty Guns,* two scripts Twentieth Century–Fox declined to develop. As his own producer, however, Fuller was increasingly reliant on ticket sales; he needed to demonstrate box-office success in order to acquire and maintain financing and distribution for his pictures. Fuller's best chances for high grosses were either in the big-budget, star-filled blockbusters he directed at the end of his career at Fox or in lower-budget, gimmick-filled pictures targeted at the emerging youth market. Fuller initially attempted the first route, producing *Run of the Arrow* as an A picture, but tepid returns relegated him to reduced budgets for subsequent features; only *Merrill's Marauders,* a freelance directing job, and *The Big Red One* and *White Dog* at the end of his career, returned him to the world of big-budget filmmaking. Fuller's involvement in the youth market was also limited; only *Verboten!* made direct appeals to youth, equating postwar gangs of German neo-Nazi teens with American juvenile delinquents. Although Fuller's independence provided him with greater creative control, his capacity to sustain his career was hampered by his inability to compete with the budgets, production values, and star power of major-release blockbusters and his indifference toward youth-oriented genres and humor. By the later half of his career, he was one among many directors in Hollywood operating on a freelance basis, reliant on others to develop projects and offer him work. The decline in his output and his control over his films was steep.

Fuller provides a fascinating case study of the challenges facing idiosyncratic directors after the cutbacks brought on by the disintegration of the studio system. The end of Fuller's contract with Twentieth Century–Fox both freed him to pursue more personal projects and placed him at the mercy of the market to an extent he had not previously experienced. His difficulties maintaining Globe Enterprises and the reduced output of his later years are an important illustration both of the risks inherent in independent production and of the support structure directors lost with the decline of the studio system. Other filmmakers known for their distinctive, low-budget work shared Fuller's struggle to find a niche in the new Hollywood: Jack Webb, Joseph H. Lewis, and Jacques Tourneur all ended up in television before retiring in the 1960s or early 1970s; Andre de Toth, Edgar Ulmer, and Joseph Losey returned to the more welcoming shores of Europe; while Budd Boetticher's determination to complete his dream project in Mexico effectively dried up his options in Hollywood. When comparing Fuller's career to those of his contemporaries, what is perhaps most striking is how his perseverance and commitment to his work enabled him to continue directing long after most of his peers.

Only by considering Fuller within the context of Hollywood's history and institutions can we appreciate the full range of his work and its varying relationships to formal, generic, and cultural norms. Such an approach provides us with a richer understanding of Fuller's films and career than can be offered through a model of auteurism reliant on biographical legend alone. Given the nature of Fuller's work and the frustrations of his career, it is easy to paint him as a willful outsider, a maverick bucking Hollywood conventions in favor of his own eccentric vision. Yet such a romantic picture does little justice either to Fuller or to Hollywood. Rather than describing Fuller as an outsider, it would be more accurate to call him an adaptive provocateur, a two-fisted filmmaker flexible enough to alter his techniques but ever faithful to his overall goal: revealing truth and arousing emotion.

# Notes

DV    *Daily Variety*

MHL    Margaret Herrick Library, Academy of Motion Picture Arts and Sciences, Beverly Hills, California

V    *Variety*

WB    Warner Bros. Archives, University of Southern California, Los Angeles, California

YRL    Young Research Library, Arts Library Special Collections, University of California–Los Angeles, Los Angeles, California

### Introduction (pages 1–23)

1. For a review of contemporary debates on film authorship, see John Caughie, ed., *Theories of Authorship: A Reader* (London: Routledge, 1981); David A. Gerstner and Janet Staiger, eds., *Authorship and Film* (New York: Routledge, 2003); Virginia Wright Wexman, ed., *Film and Authorship* (New Brunswick, N.J.: Rutgers University Press, 2003).

2. Studies concerning the impact of economic, industrial, and institutional forces on the authorship of directors include Paul Kerr, "My Name Is Joseph H. Lewis," *Screen* 24:4/5 (July/October 1983): 48–66; Justin Wyatt, "Economic Constraints/Economic Opportunities: Robert Altman as Auteur," *The Velvet Light Trap* 38 (Fall 1996): 51–67; and Lutz Bacher, *Max Ophuls in the Hollywood Studios* (New Brunswick, N.J.: Rutgers University Press, 1996).

3. For a discussion of the package-unit system, see David Bordwell, Janet Staiger, and Kristin Thompson, *The Classical Hollywood Cinema: Film Style and Mode of Production to 1960* (New York: Columbia University Press, 1985), 330–331.

4. For a discussion of authorship and biographical legends, see Boris Tomasevskij, "Literature and Biography," in *Readings in Russian Poetics: Formalist and Structuralist Views,* ed. Ladislav Matejka and Krystyna Pomorska (Ann Arbor: Michigan Slavic Publications, 1978), 47–55; David Bordwell, *The Films of Carl-Theodor Dreyer* (Berkeley: University of California Press, 1981), 4, 9–10.

5. See Ezra Goodman, "Low Budget Movies With POW!" *New York Times Magazine,* 28 February 1965, 43; Kevin Thomas, "Fuller: Recognition on a Low

Budget," *Los Angeles Times,* 26 May 1970, IV:1; J. Hoberman, "Sam Fuller: Gate Crasher at the Auteur Limits," *Village Voice,* 2 July 1980, 39; Eric Monder, "A Fuller View: An Interview with Sam Fuller," *Filmfax* 49 (March/April 1995): 73–76; Kenneth Turan, "A Role Model for Maverick Filmmakers," *Los Angeles Times,* 15 May 1995, F6–7; Robert Horton, "Sam's Place," *Film Comment* 32, no. 3 (May/June, 1996): 4–5; Adam Simon, "Sam Fuller: Perfect Pitch," *Sight and Sound* 8, no. 3 (March 1998): 20.

6. Colin Rhodes, *Primitivism and Modern Art* (London: Thames and Hudson, 1994).

7. Luc Moullet, "Sam Fuller—sur les brisées de Marlowe," *Cahiers du Cinéma* 93 (March 1959): 11–19.

8. Andrew Sarris, *The American Cinema: Directors and Directions 1929–1968* (Chicago: University of Chicago Press, 1968), 94; Manny Farber, "The Films of Sam Fuller and Don Siegel," *December* 12, no. 1/2 (1970): 171; Jean-Pierre Coursodon and Pierre Sauvage, *American Directors, Volume II* (New York: McGraw-Hill, 1983), 146–147.

9. J. Hoberman, "American Abstract Sensationalism," *Artforum* (January 1981): 43.

10. Quoted in Rhodes, *Primitivism and Modern Art,* 9.

11. Goodman, "Low Budget Movies," 42, 50.

12. See Kingsley Canham, "The World of Samuel Fuller," *Film* 55 (Summer 1969): 4–10; Mary Blume, "Samuel Fuller—'B' Director or Genius?" *Los Angeles Times,* 30 November 1974, II:5; Thomas, "Fuller," IV:1, IV:16.

13. Turan, "A Role Model," F8.

14. Interview with Fuller in Lee Server, *Sam Fuller: Film Is a Battleground* (Jefferson, N.C.: McFarland & Company, 1994), 55.

15. Samuel Fuller, "Film Fiction: More Factual than Facts," *Projections* 1 (1992): 132.

16. For comments from Fuller on his years in journalism, see Samuel Fuller, *A Third Face: My Tale of Writing, Fighting, and Filmmaking* (New York: Knopf, 2002); Server, *Sam Fuller.* For critical commentary, see V. F. Perkins, "Merrill's Marauders," *Movie* 2 (September 1962): 32; Hoberman, "American Abstract Sensationalism," 42–49; Phil Hardy, *Samuel Fuller* (New York: Praeger, 1970).

17. For Fuller's discussion of his time spent at the *Graphic,* see his interview in Server, *Sam Fuller,* 12–13; also Fuller, *A Third Face,* 39–63.

18. Samuel Fuller, "News That's Fit to Film," *American Film* 1, no. 1 (October 1975): 21–22.

19. Interview with Fuller in Steven Gaydos, "Going Hyphenate," *The Hollywood Reporter,* 18 March 1988, 18.

20. Interviews with Fuller in Samuel D. Berns, "Fuller Formula: Lots of Story and Promotion," *Motion Picture Herald,* 5 September 1959; "Slam Bam Sam," *Los Angeles Reader,* 2 December 1983, 13.

21. Samuel Fuller, "What Is a Film?" *Cinema* 2, no. 2 (July 1964): 22.

22. See Nicholas Garnham, *Samuel Fuller* (New York: Viking Press, 1971); Hardy, *Samuel Fuller.*

23. Tom Ryan, "Sam Fuller: Survivor," *Cinema Papers* 30 (December 1980/January 1981): 424.

24. Monder, "A Fuller View," 76.

25. For more on classical narrative norms, see Bordwell, Staiger, and Thompson, *Classical Hollywood Cinema*, 174–193.

26. Twelve of Fuller's seventeen pre-1970s films are identified as melodramas in trade publication reviews: *I Shot Jesse James, The Baron of Arizona, Park Row, Pickup on South Street, Hell and High Water, House of Bamboo, China Gate, Verboten!, The Crimson Kimono, Underworld, U.S.A., Merrill's Marauders,* and *Shock Corridor.* Steve Neale cites Fuller as an example of an action-oriented director whose films were frequently identified as melodramas in Steve Neale, "Melo Talk: On the Meaning and Use of the Term 'Melodrama' in the American Trade Press," *The Velvet Light Trap* 32 (Fall 1993): 70.

27. For an overview of melodrama definitions and key characteristics, see Ben Singer, *Melodrama and Modernity: Early Sensational Cinema and Its Contexts* (New York: Columbia University Press, 2001), 37–58.

28. The exceptions—*The Baron of Arizona, Park Row, Verboten!, The Naked Kiss, White Dog,* and *Street of No Return*—are all oddball melodramatic thrillers that contain aspects of multiple genres.

29. William R. Weaver, "Hollywood Scene," *Motion Picture Herald*, 23 August 1952, 32.

30. See Richard Thompson, "3X Sam: The Flavor of Ketchup," *Film Comment* 13, no. 1 (January/February 1997): 30–31; Stig Björkman and Mark Shivas, "Samuel Fuller: Two Interviews," *Movie* 17 (Winter 1969/1970): 25.

31. Björkman and Shivas, "Samuel Fuller: Two Interviews," 25. See also Server, *Sam Fuller*, 55.

32. Björkman and Shivas, "Samuel Fuller: Two Interviews," 25.

33. Vincent Price recalls Fuller using impromptu "visits to the set" as a way to arrange unpaid rehearsal time with actors on *The Baron of Arizona* (Interview in Server, *Sam Fuller*, 102). For more on rehearsals, see Server, *Sam Fuller*, 111, 117.

34. For more on the classical continuity system, see Bordwell, Staiger, and Thompson, *Classical Hollywood Cinema*, 194–213.

35. Interview with Fuller in Server, *Sam Fuller*, 56.

36. Interview with Biroc in Server, *Sam Fuller*, 117.

37. Interview with Fowler in Server, *Sam Fuller*, 120.

38. Ibid., 121.

39. *Park Row* has an average shot length (ASL) of thirty-five seconds, while *House of Bamboo*'s ASL is fourteen seconds. The ASL in Hollywood from 1947 to 1960 was eleven to twelve seconds according to Bordwell, Staiger, and Thompson, *Classical Hollywood Cinema*, 61. For the origin of the concept of average shot lengths, see Barry Salt, *Film Style and Technology: History and Analysis*, 2nd ed. (London: Starword, 1992), 144–147.

40. Moullet, "Sam Fuller," 14.

*Chapter One: The Lippert Years, 1948–1951 (pages 24–51)*

1. See Ted Okuda, *Grand National, Producers Releasing Corporation, and Screen Guild/Lippert: Complete Filmographies and Studio Histories* (Jefferson,

N.C.: McFarland & Company, 1989), 123–124; Frank Eng column, *Los Angeles Daily News,* 18 August 1949, 30–31; "Monogram, Lippert Co. May Merge; Negotiations Now in Progress," *V,* 26 July 1950, 7, 10.

2. He later claimed he offered to do the whole job for $1.50 if he could have final script and editorial approval, but union minimums resulted in a $5,000 paycheck. See Darr Smith column, *Los Angeles Daily News,* 21 July 1949, 25; David Wilson, "The Best Known War Movie Never Made," *Los Angeles Times Calendar,* 22 January 1978, 32.

3. Brian Taves, "The B Film: Hollywood's Other Half," in Tino Balio, *The Grand Design: Hollywood as a Modern Business Enterprise* (Berkeley: University of California Press, 1993), 313–314.

4. Lea Jacobs, "The B Film and the Problem of Cultural Distinction," *Screen* 33, no. 1 (Spring 1992): 5–7.

5. Taves, "The B Film," 317–318.

6. Tino Balio, ed., *The American Film Industry,* 2nd ed. (Madison: University of Wisconsin Press, 1985), 402–406; "U.S. 70% Dual, But B's Vanish," *V,* 24 February 1954, 3.

7. "U.S. 70% Dual," 3; "Duals Still Big in U.S.A." *V,* 12 January 1955, 5.

8. Anthony Downs, "Drive-Ins Have Arrived," *Journal of Property Management* 18, no. 3 (March 1953): 159.

9. Murray Schumach, "Hollywood Probe," *New York Times,* 14 May 1961, II:7.

10. William R. Weaver, "Fuller Makes Sleeper, But Can't Tell How," *Motion Picture Herald,* 4 June 1949, 33; Smith column, 25. Fuller claimed that profit participation came only with *The Steel Helmet;* see interview with Fuller in Lee Server, *Sam Fuller: Film Is a Battleground* (Jefferson, N.C.: McFarland & Company), 26.

11. Ezra Goodman column, *Los Angeles Daily News,* 5 January 1951, 22; Interview with Fuller in Server, *Sam Fuller,* 26. A biography of Fuller prepared by Twentieth Century–Fox for the press kit of *Fixed Bayonets* lists Fuller as receiving 20 percent of *The Steel Helmet* profits. See Samuel Fuller Clipping File, Core Collection, MHL.

12. Goodman column, 22.

13. See Eng column, 31; "Lippert Will Do 33 Pictures in New Year," *V,* 13 September 1949; "Extensive Foreign Plans By Lippert Include Fuller Film," *Hollywood Reporter,* 9 July 1951.

14. Samuel Fuller, *A Third Face: My Tale of Writing, Fighting, and Filmmaking* (New York: Knopf, 2002), 244–245.

15. Estimated budgets range from $105,000 to $138,000 in interviews, trade, and press articles, with $110,000 most often repeated. See "Screen Guild, Lippert Merge; Plan 14 Films During '48–'49," *Hollywood Reporter,* 22 February 1949; Eng column, 30–31; A. H. Weiler, "By Way of Report," *New York Times,* 30 January 1949, II:5.

16. Academy Oscar card, *I Shot Jesse James* Clipping File, MHL; "Picture Grosses," *V,* 23 February through 11 May 1949; Review of *I Shot Jesse James, New York Times,* 2 April 1949, 12; Fuller, *A Third Face,* 249.

17. Review of *I Shot Jesse James, V,* 2 February 1949.

18. Estimates of budgets and shooting days vary in interviews, trade, and press articles, ranging from $120,000 to $300,000 and eleven to twenty days, with fifteen shooting days mentioned most often. For production information, see "Lippert Will Do 33 Pictures in New Year"; Eng column, 31; Interview with Fuller in Server, *Sam Fuller*, 26; Fuller, *A Third Face*, 254.

19. Review of *The Baron of Arizona, Motion Picture Herald*, 18 February 1950, 198.

20. *The Baron of Arizona* revised final shooting script, James Wong Howe Collection, MHL.

21. Review of *The Baron of Arizona, New York Times*, 23 June 1950, 29; Review of *The Baron of Arizona, V*, 15 February 1950.

22. "Baron of Arizona Preem Mar. 1," *Film Daily*, 10 February 1950, 8; "Picture Grosses," *V*, 5 April through 19 July 1950.

23. Review of *The Baron of Arizona, Boxoffice*, 18 February 1950, 1117; Review of *The Baron of Arizona, V*, 15 February 1950.

24. "Monogram, Lippert Co. May Merge; Negotiations Now in Progress," *V*, 26 July 1950, 10.

25. Interviews, trade, and press articles indicate shooting schedules ranging from ten to twelve days, with ten most frequently mentioned, and budgets of $103,000 to $165,000, with $104,000 most frequently mentioned. See Review of *The Steel Helmet, Newsweek*, 29 January 1951, 91; Interview with Fuller in Server, *Sam Fuller*, 26; Arthur Marble, "Hollywood," *Sight and Sound* 20, no. 1 (May 1957): 9.

26. Fuller, *A Third Face*, 109–229.

27. "Sam Fuller in His Own Voice," *Scenario: The Magazine of Screenwriting Art* 4, no. 3 (Fall 1998): 94. Photographs of pages from the 1943 German Panzerarmee Afrika calendar that Fuller carried in North Africa and Italy are reproduced in *Scenario* on pages 90–96.

28. "Sam Fuller in His Own Voice," 93.

29. "Sam Fuller in His Own Voice," 90.

30. Jeanine Basinger, *The World War II Combat Film: Anatomy of a Genre* (New York: Columbia University Press, 1986), 176–177.

31. See the discussion of story causality and motivation in David Bordwell, Janet Staiger, and Kristin Thompson, *The Classical Hollywood Cinema: Film Style and Mode of Production to 1960* (New York: Columbia University Press, 1985), 19–23.

32. Quoted in Tony Crawley, "In War, as in Movies, There Are No Heroes. Only Survivors," *Films Illustrated* 9, no. 107 (August 1980): 434.

33. Review of *The Steel Helmet, V*, 3 January 1951; Review of *The Steel Helmet, Boxoffice* 58, no. 11 (13 January 1951): 1221. For discussion of the film's minimal production values, see Review of *The Steel Helmet, New York Times*, 25 January 1951, 21; Review of *The Steel Helmet, Monthly Film Bulletin* 18, no. 207 (April 1951): 253. For praise concerning realism, see Review of *The Steel Helmet, V*, 3 January 1951; Review of *The Steel Helmet, Motion Picture Herald*, 6 January 1951, 653; Review of *The Steel Helmet, Los Angeles Times*, 12 January 1951, III:6; Review of *The Steel Helmet, Los Angeles Evening Herald Express*, 12 January 1951, A14.

34. "Picture Grosses," *V,* 17 January through 21 February 1951.

35. David Wilson, "The Best War Movie Never Made," *Los Angeles Times* Calendar, 22 January 1978, 32; Letter from Sam Fuller to Hedda Hopper, 14 August 1954, Hedda Hopper Collection, MHL. For controversy, see Victor Riesel, "Plenty of Civil Liberties Here," *Hollywood Citizen-News,* 15 January 1951; · Victor Riesel column, *Los Angeles Daily News,* 17 January 1951, 30; *The Steel Helmet* PCA File, Production Code Administration Collection, MHL; Interview in Server, *Sam Fuller,* 27.

## Chapter Two: The Fox Years, 1951–1956 (pages 52–92)

1. Fox producer and screenwriter Philip Dunne also recalled a meeting in Zanuck's office that was interrupted by an explosion: "You could hear what sounded like a bomb going off and all the windows rattled. Darryl looked off into the distance and smiled and just said, 'That's Sammy Fuller blowing the ass out of Stage 16 . . .' Sammy had a violent streak and Darryl enjoyed it very much." For more on Fuller and Zanuck, see Lee Server, *Sam Fuller: Film Is a Battleground* (Jefferson, N.C.: McFarland & Company, 1994), 5–6; Interview with Richard Widmark in Server, *Sam Fuller,* 111; Interview with Robert Stack in Server, *Sam Fuller,* 115; Samuel Fuller, *A Third Face: My Tale of Writing, Fighting, and Filmmaking* (New York: Knopf, 2002), 264–331.

2. See Darryl Zanuck memo to Philip Dunne, 7 May 1953, Philip Dunne Collection, University of Southern California Cinema Library, excerpted in Aubrey Solomon, *Twentieth Century–Fox: A Corporate and Financial History* (Metuchen, N.J.: Scarecrow Press, 1988), 71–72.

3. See David Bordwell, Janet Staiger, and Kristin Thompson, *Classical Hollywood Cinema: Film Style and Mode of Production to 1960* (New York: Columbia University Press, 1985), 136; Lutz Bacher, *Max Ophuls in the Hollywood Studios* (New Brunswick, N.J.: Rutgers University Press, 1996), 9–13.

4. See Bordwell, Staiger, and Thompson, *Classical Hollywood Cinema,* 326; Douglas Gomery, *The Hollywood Studio System: A History* (London: British Film Institute, 2005), 119.

5. Twentieth Century–Fox Employment Contract for Samuel Fuller, 2 April 1951, Samuel Fuller Legal File, Twentieth Century–Fox Collection, YRL.

6. *Fixed Bayonets* press kit, *Fixed Bayonets* Clipping File, Core Collection, MHL; Solomon, *Twentieth Century–Fox,* 247.

7. Darryl Zanuck memo to Jules Buck and Samuel Fuller, 9 May 1951, and story conference notes on temporary script of "Old Soldiers Never Die," 25 June 1951, both in *Fixed Bayonets* Script File, Twentieth Century–Fox Collection, YRL.

8. Harry Brand, Twentieth Century–Fox Director of Publicity, "Vital Statistics Concerning *Fixed Bayonets!*" *Fixed Bayonets* press kit, MHL.

9. "Picture Grosses" column, *V,* 28 November 1951 through 30 January 1952; "National Boxoffice Survey," *V,* 12 December 1951, 3.

10. Review of *Fixed Bayonets, New York Times,* 21 November 1951, 20; Review of *Fixed Bayonets, V,* 21 November 1951; Review of *Fixed Bayonets, Boxoffice,* 1 December 1951, 1323.

11. "Top Grossers of 1951," *V*, 2 January 1952, 70; For international gross, see Darryl Zanuck memo to Philip Dunne, 1 August 1953, Philip Dunne Collection, University of Southern California, cited in Solomon, *Twentieth Century–Fox*, 78.

12. Fuller, *A Third Face*, 280.

13. "Exploitation Man's Dream Come True; Press to Go All Out for Fuller Film," *V*, 25 June 1952, 20.

14. Fuller, *A Third Face*, 280.

15. "Exploitation Man's Dream Come True," 7; Sheila Benson, "Fans Celebrate the Fullness of Fuller," *Los Angeles Times*, 16 July 1980, VI:1.

16. See "Picture Grosses" column, *V*, 10 September 1952 through 14 January 1953.

17. Robert Hatch, "The Movies This Month," *Theatre Arts* 36 (July 1952): 37.

18. Interview with Fuller in Server, *Sam Fuller*, 31–32; In 1954, a man named Walter Heller filed a "quiet title" suit in Los Angeles Superior Court to establish prior claim to *Park Row* "in an effort to realize some return on the boxoffice flop." See "Walter Heller in Move to Foreclose Park Row," *V*, 12 May 1954.

19. Darryl Zanuck notes during story conference for "Blaze of Glory" first draft continuity, 13 March 1952, *Pickup on South Street* Script File, Twentieth Century–Fox Collection, YRL.

20. Samuel Fuller, "Blaze of Glory" story outline, 25 June 1952, *Pickup on South Street* Script File, Twentieth Century–Fox Collection, YRL. The Baumes Law, on the books at the time in several states including New York, allowed for the automatic life imprisonment of any criminal convicted over three times, regardless of the crime or the age of the criminal.

21. Darryl Zanuck notes during story conference for "Blaze of Glory" story outline, 25 June 1952, *Pickup on South Street* Script File, Twentieth Century–Fox Collection, YRL.

22. Letter from Joseph Breen to Jason S. Joy, Twentieth Century–Fox Director of Public Relations, 29 August 1952, *Pickup on South Street* PCA File, Production Code Administration Collection, MHL.

23. Letter from Joseph Breen to Jason S. Joy, Twentieth Century–Fox Director of Public Relations, 16 September 1952, *Pickup on South Street* PCA File, Production Code Administration Collection, MHL.

24. See Nigel Andrews, "Fuller's Law of Filmmaking," *Los Angeles Free Times*, 8 August 1992, Weekend:13; Fuller, *A Third Face*, 304.

25. Interview with Fuller in Eric Sherman and Martin Rubin, *The Director's Event: Interviews with Five American Filmmakers* (New York: Atheneum, 1970), 148–149; Solomon, *Twentieth Century–Fox*, 248.

26. Letter from Joseph Breen to Jason S. Joy, Twentieth Century–Fox Director of Public Relations, 16 September 1952, *Pickup on South Street* PCA File, Production Code Administration Collection, MHL; See also letter from Joseph Breen to Jason S. Joy, Twentieth Century–Fox Director of Public Relations, 29 August 1952, *Pickup on South Street* PCA File, Production Code Administration Collection, MHL.

27. "National Boxoffice Survey," *V*, 24 June 1953, 3; "Picture Grosses" column, *V*, 3 June through 12 August 1953.

28. See Reviews of *Pickup on South Street* in *V*, 13 May 1953; *New York Times*, 18 June 1953, 38; *Time*, 29 June 1953, 92; *Film Daily*, 29 May 1953, 6; *Kinematograph Weekly*, 21 May 1953, 17; *Los Angeles Examiner*, 30 May 1953, I:8; *Los Angeles Times*, 30 May 1953, II:7; *Hollywood Citizen News*, 30 May 1953, 4; and *Theatre Arts* 37 (June 1953): 86.

29. "Top Grossers of 1953," *V*, 13 January 1954, 10.

30. Interview with Fuller in Server, *Sam Fuller*, 36; *Hell and High Water* press kit, *Hell and High Water* Clipping File, Core Collection, MHL; Solomon, *Twentieth Century–Fox*, 249; for on-set injuries, see "Actress Sixth Injury Victim on Jinx Sub Set," *Los Angeles Examiner*, 25 July 1953, I:10.

31. "Picture Grosses" column, *V*, 3 February through 31 March 1954; "National Boxoffice Survey," *V*, 24 February 1954, 3.

32. Review of *Hell and High Water*, *V*, 3 February 1954; see also Reviews of *Hell and High Water* in *Motion Picture Herald*, 6 February 1954, 2173; *Film Daily* 10, no. 22 (2 February 1954): 6; *Los Angeles Daily News*, 6 March 1954, 11; *Los Angeles Examiner*, 6 March 1954, 12.

33. "1954 Boxoffice Champs," *V*, 5 January 1955, 59.

34. See Memo from Lew Schreiber to Frank Ferguson, 26 August 1953, Samuel Fuller Legal File, Twentieth Century–Fox Collection, YRL; Memo from Lew Schreiber to Frank Ferguson, 2 April 1954, Samuel Fuller Legal File, Twentieth Century–Fox Collection, YRL.

35. Memo from Lew Schreiber to Frank Ferguson, 2 April 1954, Samuel Fuller Legal File, Twentieth Century–Fox Collection, YRL.

36. Memo from Lew Schreiber to Frank Ferguson, 28 July 1954, Samuel Fuller Legal File, Twentieth Century–Fox Collection, YRL.

37. *House of Bamboo* press kit, *House of Bamboo* Clipping File, Core Collection, MHL; Solomon, *Twentieth Century–Fox*, 249.

38. Memo from Darryl Zanuck to Buddy Adler, 7 October 1954, *House of Bamboo* Script File, Twentieth Century–Fox Collection, YRL.

39. See *House of Bamboo* final script screenplay by Harry Kleiner, 10 January 1955, and *House of Bamboo* dialogue and continuity taken from screen, 1 July 1955, in *House of Bamboo* Script File, Twentieth Century–Fox Collection, YRL.

40. Daily Production Reports in *House of Bamboo* Production File, Twentieth Century–Fox Collection, YRL.

41. "Picture Grosses" column, *V*, 6 July 1955, 8, 9, 16.

42. See Reviews of *House of Bamboo* in *V*, 6 July 1955; *New York Times*, 2 July 1955, 13; *Motion Picture Exhibitor*, 13 July 1955, 3994; *Motion Picture Herald*, 2 July 1955, 497; *Daily Film Renter and Moving Picture News*, 31 August 1955, 3; *Newsweek*, 18 July 1955, 83.

43. Vincent Canby, Review of *House of Bamboo*, *Motion Picture Herald*, 2 July 1955, 497.

44. "National Boxoffice Survey" column, *V*, 6 July through 27 July 1955; "Picture Grosses" column, *V*, 6 July through 7 October 1959.

45. Solomon, *Twentieth Century–Fox*, 226. For *Bamboo*'s reception in Japan, see "Nipponese Jeer Over Unrealistic 'Bamboo,'" *DV*, 31 September 1955.

46. Memo from Lew Schreiber to Frank Ferguson, 10 May 1955, Samuel Fuller Legal File, Twentieth Century–Fox Collection, YRL.

47. Letter from Frank Ferguson to Samuel Fuller, 1 September 1955, Samuel Fuller Legal File, Twentieth Century–Fox Collection, YRL.

48. Letter from Samuel Fuller to Frank Ferguson, 10 September 1955, Samuel Fuller Legal File, Twentieth Century–Fox Collection, YRL.

49. Letter from Frank Ferguson to Donald Henderson, 15 June 1956, Samuel Fuller Legal File, Twentieth Century–Fox Collection, YRL.

50. Memo from Lew Schreiber to Frank Ferguson, 9 August 1956, Samuel Fuller Legal File, Twentieth Century–Fox Collection, YRL.

51. Of all the majors, Fox resisted the shift to independent production the longest, maintaining the largest in-house producer roster of any of the major studios through 1958. "80 Indies Feeding Pix to Majors," *DV*, 19 December 1958, 1, 19. For a discussion of conditions at Fox following the departure of Darryl Zanuck, see Solomon, *Twentieth Century–Fox*, 119–131.

*Chapter Three: The Globe Years, 1956–1961 (pages 93–140)*

1. Philip K. Scheuer, "Fuller Sees Broadway as Film Story Testing Ground," *Los Angeles Times*, 3 February 1957, V:2; Ezra Goodman, "Low Budget Movies with POW!" *New York Times Magazine*, 28 February 1965, 42.

2. "Fuller Plans 6 Pix Yearly, Plus Video," *DV*, 16 May 1958, 1, 4.

3. For summaries of the postwar changes in the American film industry, see Thomas Schatz, *Boom and Bust: American Cinema in the 1940s* (Berkeley: University of California Press, 1997), 289–303; Tino Balio, ed., *The American Film Industry*, revised ed. (Madison: University of Wisconsin Press, 1985), 401–422; Peter Lev, *Transforming the Screen: 1950–1959* (Berkeley, University of California Press, 2003), 7–32, 197–216.

4. See Balio, *The American Film Industry*, 412; David Bordwell, Janet Staiger, and Kristin Thompson, *The Classical Hollywood Cinema: Film Style and Mode of Production to 1960* (New York: Columbia University Press, 1985), 317.

5. William R. Weaver, "Independents Supplied 219 Films During Past Production Year," *Motion Picture Herald*, 5 October 1957, 11–12; see also Schatz, *Boom and Bust*, 179.

6. See Balio, *The American Film Industry*, 416–419, 421–422; Matthew Bernstein, "Defiant Cooperation: Walter Wanger and Independent Production in Hollywood, 1934–1949," Ph.D. dissertation, University of Wisconsin–Madison, 1987, 27–43.

7. Balio, *The American Film Industry*, 416–422.

8. "In-Between Budgeters Fading," *V*, 16 January 1952, 7, 18.

9. See "3 Majors Thrive on 'B' Pix," *V*, 12 January 1955, 5; "Modesty (in Budgets) Returns," *V*, 27 June 1956, 3, 7; "B's Ride Again, Studios Busier," *V*, 16 January 1957, 17; "Blockbusters vs. Mainstreet," *V*, 6 February 1957, 5, 22.

10. Roger Corman with Jim Jerome, *How I Made a Hundred Movies in Hollywood and Never Lost a Dime* (New York: Da Capo Press, 1990), 36–37; Mark Thomas McGee, *Fast and Furious: The Story of American International*

*Pictures* (Jefferson, N.C.: McFarland & Company, 1984), 26–27; "AIP Head Slaps at Poor Imitation of Exploitation Films," *DV*, 24 March 1958, 11.

11. Hy Hollinger, "Teenage Biz vs. Repair Bills: Paradox in New 'Best Audience,'" *V*, 19 December 1956, 20.

12. Alain Silver and James Ursini, *What Ever Happened to Robert Aldrich? His Life and His Films* (New York: Limelight Editions, 1995), 14.

13. Tino Balio, *United Artists: The Company That Changed the Film Industry* (Madison: University of Wisconsin Press, 1985), 42.

14. Silver and Ursini, *What Ever Happened to Robert Aldrich?*, 15–19.

15. Quoted in Silver and Ursini, *What Ever Happened to Robert Aldrich?*, 26.

16. "'New' Film Biz; Old Dilemma: No Certain Formula," *V*, 9 April 1965, 4.

17. *Variety* speculated that teenagers resisted single features because they did not "meet their time-filling needs" when going out on a date: "Duals Still Big in U.S.A." *V*, 12 January 1955, 5. The shift in the content of profitable low-budget films is noted by *Variety* in its review of the top-grossing pictures of 1956. While the low-budget Ma and Pa Kettle films earned at least $2 million in previous years, the 1956 entry drew only $1.3 million. On the other hand, *Rock Around the Clock*, produced for under $300,000, earned $1.1 million domestically with expected international returns of $2.4 million: Gene Arneel, "109 Top Money Films of 1956," *V*, 2 January 1957, 1, 4.

18. Samuel Fuller, *A Third Face: My Tale of Writing, Fighting, and Filmmaking* (New York: Knopf, 2002), 332–334.

19. See *Run of the Arrow* payroll, *Run of the Arrow* File, RKO Pictures Collection, YRL; *Run of the Arrow* production notes, *Run of the Arrow* Clipping File, Core Collection, MHL.

20. *Run of the Arrow* production notes, MHL.

21. Letter from Geoffrey Shurlock to William Feeder, RKO Radio Pictures, 9 April 1956, *Run of the Arrow* PCA File, Production Code Administration Collection, MHL.

22. Review of *Run of the Arrow*, *V*, 29 May 1957. See also Reviews of *Run of the Arrow* in *Daily Film Renter and Moving Picture News*, 25 September 1957, 4; *New York Times*, 3 August 1957, 8; *Los Angeles Examiner*, 22 August 1957, I:23. The review in *Monthly Film Bulletin* 24, no. 282 (July 1957): 90 was most explicit: "Samuel Fuller's films have now achieved some notoriety for their use of excessive violence; in *Run of the Arrow*, killings, butcherings, beatings and arrow-pierced flesh are used as deliberate shock tactics, often quite gratuitous to the confused and rambling narrative."

23. Exhibitor advertisement for *Run of the Arrow*, *Motion Picture Herald*, 29 June 1957, 11–13.

24. "Picture Grosses" column, *V*, 31 July 1957, 8.

25. "Picture Grosses" column, *V*, 7 August through 6 November 1957; "National Boxoffice Survey," *V*, 28 August 1957, 3.

26. This assumes that the $1 million production cost cited is either correct or understated. See "Top Grossers of 1957," *V*, 8 January 1958, 30.

27. Notes of Twentieth Century–Fox Film Corporation Regular Meeting-

Executive Committee, 30 August 1956, Regal Films File, Twentieth Century–Fox Collection, YRL.

28. See Aubrey Solomon, *Twentieth Century–Fox: A Corporate and Financial History* (Metuchen, N.J.: Scarecrow Press, 1988), 132–133; "Skouras' 25 From Regal," *V,* 7 November 1956, 4; Notes of Twentieth Century–Fox Film Corporation Regular Meeting–Executive Committee, 9 January 1957 and Memo from Frank Ferguson to Lew Schreiber, David Brown, Arthur Kramer, Frank Mc-Carthy, 18 February 1957, both in Regal Films File, Twentieth Century–Fox Collection, YRL.

29. Production and Distribution Agreement between Regal Films, Inc. and Twentieth Century–Fox Film Corporation, 15 January 1957, Regal Films File, Twentieth Century–Fox Collection, YRL.

30. Memos from Frank Ferguson to Lew Schreiber, David Brown, Arthur Kramer, Frank McCarthy, 18 February 1957 and 15 August 1957, Regal Films File, Twentieth Century–Fox Collection, YRL.

31. Ibid.

32. *Woman With a Whip* Agreement between Globe Enterprises and Regal Films, Inc., 5 April 1957, Regal Films File, Twentieth Century–Fox Collection, YRL; Agenda for Twentieth Century–Fox Film Corporation Adjourned Regular Meeting—Board of Directors, 7 March 1957, Regal Films File, Twentieth Century–Fox Collection, YRL.

33. Notes on Twentieth Century–Fox Film Corporation Regular Meeting—Executive Committee, 9 January 1957, Regal Films File, Twentieth Century–Fox Collection, YRL.

34. Memo from Charles Einfeld to Ed J. Baumgarten, 21 May 1957, Regal Films File, Twentieth Century–Fox Collection, YRL; Memo from W. R. Fisher to Frank Ferguson, 4 June 1957, Regal Films File, Twentieth Century–Fox Collection, YRL.

35. "Picture Grosses" column, *V,* 15 May through 18 September 1957.

36. See Reviews of *China Gate* in *V,* 22 May 1957; *New York Times,* 23 May 1957, 40; *Motion Picture Herald,* 25 May 1957, 387; *Film Daily,* 10 May 1957, 6; *Daily Film Renter and Moving Picture News,* 6 June 1957, 6.

37. Fuller, *A Third Face,* 358.

38. Memos from Lew Schreiber to Frank Ferguson, 19 August 1953 and 26 August 1953, Samuel Fuller Legal File, Twentieth Century–Fox Collection, YRL.

39. Memo from Frank Ferguson, 13 May 1957, Regal Films File, Twentieth Century–Fox Collection, YRL; Untitled Memo 25 July 1957, Regal Films File, Twentieth Century–Fox Collection, YRL.

40. Memo from Darryl Zanuck to Philip Dunne, 7 May 1953, *Forty Guns* Script File, Twentieth Century–Fox Collection, YRL.

41. Ibid.

42. Ibid.

43. Server, *Sam Fuller,* 42; Fuller, *A Third Face,* 357–358.

44. See Reviews of *Forty Guns* in *Motion Picture Herald,* 28 September 1957, 545; *Daily Film Renter and Moving Picture News,* 15 October 1957, 5; *Monthly Film Bulletin,* December 1957, 151.

45. "Picture Grosses" column, *V*, 25 September through 6 November 1957.

46. *Forty Guns* was the first Fuller film identified by the trades as ideal for drive-ins. For references to the outdoor market, see Reviews of *Forty Guns* in *V*, 18 September 1957; *Film Daily*, 24 September 1957, 10; *Daily Film Renter and Moving Picture News*, 15 October 1957, 5.

47. "National Boxoffice Survey," *V*, 9 October 1957, 4.

48. Memo from Frank Ferguson to Lew Schreiber, David Brown, Arthur Kramer, and Frank McCarthy, 15 August 1957, Regal Films File, Twentieth Century–Fox Collection, YRL.

49. "Fuller Plans 6 Pix Yearly, Plus Video," 1.

50. See "RKO O'Seas Admin. Work to Rank Org.," *DV*, 26 March 1958, 1, 18; "O'Neill in Open-End Pix Financing," *DV*, 8 April 1958, 1, 4.

51. "Film Production Chart," *DV*, 9 May 1958, 15.

52. Quoted in Amy Taubin, "The Camera as Witness," *Village Voice*, 1 May 1990, 59.

53. See "Columbia Gets Release of Fuller's 'Verboten!,'" *Hollywood Reporter*, 1 April 1959; "'Verboten' Will Preem in Detroit, Milwaukee," *DV*, 27 February 1959, 2; "Rank Suspends U.S. Operation," *DV*, 17 March 1959, 1, 4.

54. "Picture Grosses" column, *V*, 18 March through 23 September 1959; Review of *Verboten!*, *New York Times*, 12 July 1960, 38.

55. Review of *Verboten!*, *New York Times*, 12 July 1960, 38.

56. "Fuller Plans 6 Pix Yearly, Plus Video," 1, 4.

57. Fuller originated two war pictures for Warner Bros.; his scenario became *The Tanks Are Coming* (1951), while his screenplay was rewritten as *The Command* (1954).

58. "Fuller Plans 6 Pix Yearly, Plus Video," 1, 4.

59. In May, 1959, *Variety* reported that of an estimated two hundred pilots produced that year, only twenty-five to thirty found a slot on the networks' schedules: "Exploit Pix Used as Pilots by WB," *V*, 12 May 1959, 8. For Globe's TV plans, see "Sam Fuller Launching Pilot for 'Dog Face,'" *DV*, 30 March 1959, 1; "Fuller Doing 2nd Series For CBS-TV," *DV*, 6 April 1959, 10.

60. Columbia Pictures Biography of Samuel Fuller, 2 September 1959, *The Crimson Kimono* Clipping File, Core Collection, MHL.

61. See "Col Into 'UA Policy' for Product," *DV*, 17 March 1958, 1, 4; "80 Indies Feeding Pix to Majors," *DV*, 19 December 1958, 1, 19.

62. "Col Prod'n Aim: $58–70 Mil Yrly.," *DV*, 6 January 1959, 1, 4.

63. "Col Sets 98-Pic, $130 Mil Slate," *DV*, 21 April 1959, 1, 4.

64. The eighteen-month production slate announced by Columbia in 1959 included ninety-eight films budgeted at a total of $130 million, including *Song Without End* (formerly *A Magic Flame*), *Suddenly, Last Summer*, *Anatomy of a Murder*, and *A Raisin in the Sun*: "Col Sets 98-Pic, $130 Mil Slate," *DV*, 21 April 1959, 1, 4.

65. Philip K. Scheuer, "Fuller in Running With 'Mob' Movie," *Los Angeles Times*, 2 July 1959, III:7; "Film Production Chart," *DV*, 13 March 1959, 12.

66. Fuller objected to the use of race in exploitation-style taglines like, "She had to choose between the handsome American and the strangely fascinating

Japanese": Fuller, *A Third Face*, 380–381; see print ad from *Los Angeles Times*, 4 November 1959, 26.

67. "Picture Grosses" column, *V*, 30 September through 4 November 1959.

68. Reviews of *The Crimson Kimono* in *Motion Picture Herald*, 12 September 1959, 403; *Kinematograph Weekly*, 7 April 1960, 25; see also Reviews of *The Crimson Kimono* in *V*, 9 September 1959; *Monthly Film Bulletin*, May 1960, 63.

69. "Sam Fuller Starts Casting Col 'Underworld,'" *DV*, 14 June 1960, 7; Philip K. Scheuer, "Fuller in Running With 'Mob' Movie," III:7; "'Underworld' to Studio," *DV*, 3 August 1960, 2; "Film Production Chart," *DV*, 12 August 1960, 6.

70. "'Frankly, My Next Pic Is All Action, Sex 'n' Violence,'" *V*, 28 October 1959, 4.

71. Letter from Geoffrey Shurlock to Samuel Briskin, Columbia Pictures Corporation, 10 November 1959, *Underworld, U.S.A.* PCA File, Production Code Administration Collection, MHL.

72. Letter from Geoffrey Shurlock to Samuel Briskin, Columbia Pictures Corporation, 25 January 1960, *Underworld, U.S.A.* PCA File, Production Code Administration Collection, MHL.

73. Letter from Geoffrey Shurlock to Samuel Briskin, Columbia Pictures Corporation, 23 May 1960, *Underworld, U.S.A.* PCA File, Production Code Administration Collection, MHL.

74. Ibid. In interviews, Fuller more than once recounted actually filming the scene of the stand-up strike:

"It was in the script, but they didn't really think I'd shoot it. I open up with a girl wearing a little bikini, but her legs are crossed and we assume she's naked. I'm on the big stage, stage seven, and we're shooting from up high. And you see the girl is in Indiana or someplace, on the floor. You see other girls, they're crossing their legs—you see a map of the United States of America. And, as all of this is happening, this girl says, "It's time we had a revolution. We don't want to support pimps. We don't want to support relatives of gangsters who are moving in. We're doing all the hard work. We want all the profits. So I am forming now a union of prostitutes of the United States . . ." It was very funny. In a way, they regretted taking it out, but they had to, because it was too rough. And I didn't argue about it." Eric Monder, "A Fuller View: An Interview with Sam Fuller," *Filmfax* 49 (March/April 1995): 75–76.

As the lines pertaining to the prostitutes' union and stand-up strike are not flagged by the PCA in either of the two subsequent June revisions of the script, it seems likely that the dialogue was cut from the script before the film went into production in July. While Fuller may still have shot the scene as he describes, it was most likely Columbia, and not the PCA, that asked the scene to be cut from the film, as the list of PCA cuts requested during the screening of the completed film does not include any references to the strike or the prostitute's union.

75. Letter from Geoffrey Shurlock to Samuel Briskin, Columbia Pictures Corporation, 8 June 1960, *Underworld, U.S.A.* PCA File, Production Code Administration Collection, MHL.

76. Letter from Geoffrey Shurlock to Samuel Briskin, Columbia Pictures Corporation, 23 May 1960, *Underworld, U.S.A.* PCA File, Production Code Administration Collection, MHL.

77. Memo for the PCA files, 17 November 1960, *Underworld, U.S.A.* PCA File, Production Code Administration Collection, MHL.

78. Letters from Geoffrey Shurlock to Samuel Briskin, Columbia Pictures Corporation, 25 January 1960 and 23 May 1960, *Underworld, U.S.A.* PCA File, Production Code Administration Collection, MHL.

79. Letter from Geoffrey Shurlock to Samuel Briskin, Columbia Pictures Corporation, 8 June 1960, *Underworld, U.S.A.* PCA File, Production Code Administration Collection, MHL.

80. Letter from Geoffrey Shurlock to Samuel Briskin, Columbia Pictures Corporation, 21 June 1960, *Underworld, U.S.A.* PCA File, Production Code Administration Collection, MHL.

81. Memo for the PCA files, 17 November 1960, *Underworld, U.S.A.* PCA File, Production Code Administration Collection, MHL.

82. "'Frankly, My Next Pic Is All Action, Sex 'n' Violence,'" 4.

83. "Departure in Trailers—Writer Addresses Audience," *Hollywood Reporter,* 7 September 1960.

84. Review of *Underworld, U.S.A.* in *Monthly Film Bulletin,* October 1962, 138; see also Reviews of *Underworld, U.S.A.* in *V,* 22 February 1961; *New York Times,* 13 May 1961, 10; *Motion Picture Herald,* 4 March 1961, 37; *Movie,* December 1962, 3–6.

85. Review of *Underworld, U.S.A.* in *V,* 22 February 1961.

86. Review of *Underworld, U.S.A.* in *New York Times,* 13 May 1961, 10; "Picture Grosses" column, *V,* 10 May through 6 September 1961.

*Chapter Four: The Freelance Years, 1961–1964 (pages 141–170)*

1. Testimony of Ira D. Riskin, court-appointed receiver for Samuel Fuller, in *Marta Fuller vs. Samuel Fuller,* Superior Court of the State of California, County of Los Angeles, as based on materials submitted by Fromkess & Firks Productions, Inc.

2. "Fromkess Making 5 Pix for AA Release," *DV,* 12 November 1962.

3. Samuel Fuller, *A Third Face: My Tale of Writing, Fighting, and Filmmaking* (New York: Knopf, 2002), 391.

4. "Sperling's 'Marauders,'" *DV,* 20 May 1959, 13.

5. See Interoffice memo from Michael Ludmer to Milton Sperling, 2 July 1959, Interoffice memo from Milton Sperling to Jack Warner, 25 November 1960, and Interoffice memo from Milton Sperling to Walter MacEwan, 10 February 1961, all in Script File, *Merrill's Marauders* Collection, WB.

6. Production budget, Budget File, *Merrill's Marauders* Collection, WB; Letter from Milton Sperling to Jack Warner, 14 March 1961, Production Misc. File, *Merrill's Marauders* Collection, WB.

7. Letter from Milton Sperling to Jack Warner, 14 March 1961, and Letter from Jack Warner to Milton Sperling, 20 March 1961, both in Production Misc.

File, *Merrill's Marauders* Collection, WB; see also Daily Progress Reports File, *Merrill's Marauders* Collection, WB; Letter from Milton Sperling to Charles Greenlaw, 20 March 1961, and Telegram from Milton Sperling to Yoss, 7 April 1961, both in Production Misc. File, *Merrill's Marauders* Collection, WB.

8. Fuller, *A Third Face*, 164.

9. See Reviews of *Merrill's Marauders* in *V,* 9 May 1962; *New York Times,* 14 June 1962, 23; *Film Daily,* 15 May 1962, 8; *Motion Picture Herald,* 23 May 1962, 563; *Boxoffice,* 21 May 1962, 2631; *Commonweal,* 22 June 1962, 330; *Time,* 8 June 1962, 66; *Movie* 2 (September 1962): 32; *Monthly Film Bulletin* 29, no. 343 (August 1962): 107; *Los Angeles Times Calendar,* 27 May 1962, 7.

10. *Boxoffice,* 21 May 1962, 2631; "Picture Grosses" column, *V,* 20 June through 8 August, 1962; "Picture Grosses" column, *V,* 18 September and 25 September 1963.

11. "Big Rental Pictures of 1962," *V,* 9 January 1963, 13.

12. "Fuller in Running With 'Mob' Movie," *Los Angeles Times,* 2 July 1959, III:7; Columbia Studios Biography of Samuel Fuller, 2 September 1959, *The Crimson Kimono* Clipping File, Core Collection, MHL.

13. "Film Production Chart," *DV,* 1 March 1963, 10; Testimony of Ira D. Riskin, court appointed receiver for Samuel Fuller, in *Marta Fuller vs. Samuel Fuller,* Superior Court of the State of California, County of Los Angeles, as based on materials submitted by Fromkess & Firks Productions, Inc.

14. For publicity, see "Cool Tall Connie Towers: Singer Stars as Stripper," *Milwaukee Journal,* 13 October 1963, 23; Bosley Crowther, "Coincidence," *New York Times,* 21 July 1963, II:5; Philip K. Scheuer, "Nerves All Jangled in 'Shock Corridor,'" *Los Angeles Times,* 10 October 1963, VI:9; Louella O. Parsons, "'Nice Girl' Signs for Strip-Tease Role," *Los Angeles Herald-Examiner,* 14 February 1963, A21. For print ads and information on radio and TV spots, see ad mats in *Shock Corridor* Press Book, Press Book Collection, MHL. For television spots, see Samuel Fuller Film Collection, Academy of Motion Picture Arts and Sciences, Beverly Hills, California.

15. "Picture Grosses" column, *V,* 18 September through 6 November 1963; "National Boxoffice Survey," *V,* 2 October 1963, 5.

16. Review of *Shock Corridor, Film Quarterly* (Winter 1963–1964): 62; see also Reviews of *Shock Corridor* in *Motion Picture Herald,* 24 July 1963, 857; *Boxoffice,* 15 July 1963, 2747; *New York Times,* 12 September 1963, 32; *Film Daily,* 3 July 1963, 6; *Saturday Review,* 10 August 1963, 34; *Commonweal,* 4 October 1963, 48.

17. See Reviews of *Shock Corridor* in *Boxoffice,* 15 July 1963, 2747; *V,* 10 July 1963.

18. Figure current as of June 19, 1968. Testimony of Ira D. Riskin, court appointed receiver for Samuel Fuller, in *Marta Fuller vs. Samuel Fuller,* Superior Court of the State of California, County of Los Angeles, as based on materials submitted by Fromkess & Firks Productions, Inc.

19. "'Naked Kiss' Premiere in Whitefish, Montana," *Film Daily,* 13 January 1964, 2; "Picture Grosses" column, *V,* 13 and 20 May 1964.

20. Reviews of *The Naked Kiss* in *V,* 20 January 1965; *New York Times,* 29 October 1964, 38. See also *Boxoffice,* 15 June 1964, 2835.

21. For a complete script of *The Rifle,* see *The Rifle* File, Unrealized Scripts Collection, MHL.

22. William Ornstein, "AA 'Wide Open' for Indie Producer Deals," *Film Daily,* 6 March 1964, 1, 6; "Allied Artists Earnings And Revenue Declined In First Fiscal Period," *Wall Street Journal,* 1 December 1965, 32.

## Chapter Five: The Final Battles, 1965–1997 (pages 171–202)

1. Andrew Sarris, *The American Cinema: Directors and Directions, 1929–1968* (Chicago: University of Chicago Press, 1968), 94.

2. See Lee Server, *Sam Fuller: Film Is a Battleground* (Jefferson, N.C.: McFarland & Company, 1994), 144; Richard Thompson, "3X Sam: The Flavor of Ketchup," *Film Comment* 13, no. 1 (January/February 1977): 30.

3. Ibid.; "International Sound Track," *V,* 16 February 1966, 27.

4. For a complete script of *The Eccentrics,* see *The Eccentrics* File, Tim Hunter Gift Collection, MHL.

5. Server, *Sam Fuller,* 145; Peter Bogdanovich, "Small Talk: Hollywood," *Movie* 16 (Winter 1968): 36.

6. For the complete thirty-three page treatment, see *Sound of Murder* File, Unrealized Scripts Collection, MHL.

7. Stuart Byron, "Steloff's Mexican Coproductions: Based on 'Faith' in Its Film Bank; Buffs' Idol, Sam Fuller, Returns," *V,* 21 June 1967, 5.

8. Ibid.; see also "Steloff in 13-Picture Deal with Calderón," *Hollywood Reporter,* 26 January 1968.

9. For production budget, see Earl C. Gottschalk, Jr., "In the Shark's Wake, Watch for Piranhas, Gators, More Sharks," *Wall Street Journal,* 10 September 1975, 1, 36. For description of production, see "Stuntman Tangles With Tiger Shark—Loses," *DV,* 25 July 1967; "Shark Kills a Man," *Life* 64, no. 23 (7 June 1968): 86–87; Samuel Fuller, *A Third Face: My Tale of Writing, Fighting, and Filmmaking* (New York: Knopf, 2002), 442–445.

10. Quoted in Mark Shivas, "Samuel Fuller: Two Interviews, California, 1969," *Movie* 17 (1970): 30.

11. Byron, "Steloff's Mexican Coproductions," 5, 71.

12. "Heritage Pic Dates Set," *The Hollywood Reporter,* 17 October 1969.

13. See Review of *Shark!, New York Times,* 16 June 1970, 54; Academy card in *Shark!* Clipping File, Core Collection, MHL.

14. Gottschalk, Jr., "In the Shark's Wake," 36.

15. Fuller, *A Third Face,* 449; "Robert [sic] Fuller to Write, Direct Film in West Germany," *The Hollywood Reporter,* 30 December 1971.

16. Samuel Fuller, "'Dead Pigeon' Livens Up Munich With Many 'Firsts' in Filming," *DV,* 39th Anniversary Edition, October 1972, 15.

17. See "Backstage with Syd Cassyd," *Boxoffice,* 19 November 1973; also Reviews of *Dead Pigeon on Beethoven Street* in *Los Angeles Times,* 8 November, 1974, IV:26; *Boxoffice,* 7 January 1974; *Monthly Film Bulletin* 51, no. 601 (February 1984): 56–57.

18. Fuller, *A Third Face,* 455.

19. For select quotes from English reviews, see Fuller, *A Third Face,* 455; American release ad, *DV* 40th Anniversary Issue, 1973, in the *Dead Pigeon on Beethoven Street* Clipping File, Core Collection, MHL.

20. See Review of *Dead Pigeon on Beethoven Street, V,* 29 November 1972.

21. Review of *Dead Pigeon on Beethoven Street, Take One* 4, no. 1 (September/October 1972): 32.

22. "Fuller Will Give Piece of War Pic to First Division," *Hollywood Reporter,* 18 January 1955.

23. Interoffice memo from R. J. Obringer to Hal Holman, 22 October 1957, Miscellaneous Fuller Files, *The Big Red One* Collection, WB.

24. Memo from Walter MacEwen to Charlie Greenlaw, 4 March 1958; Memo from Walter MacEwen to Steve Trilling, 6 March 1958; Memo from Walter MacEwen to R. J. Obringer, 13 March 1958; Memo from Charles F. Greenlaw to Dick Pease, 21 March 1958, all in Script File, *The Big Red One* Collection, WB.

25. Production and Military Note, *The Big Red One* Estimating Script, 20 March 1958, Script File, *The Big Red One* Collection, WB.

26. Memo from Charles F. Greenlaw to Dick Pease, 21 March 1958, Miscellaneous Fuller File, *The Big Red One* Collection, WB; notes written on *The Big Red One* Estimating Script, 20 March 1958, Script File, *The Big Red One* Collection, WB; unsigned, undated handwritten notes with page-by-page assessment of necessary locations, equipment, and special effects, Script File, *The Big Red One* Collection, WB.

27. See *The Big Red One* Estimating Script, 20 March 1958, Script File, *The Big Red One* Collection, WB.

28. Lawrence Cohn, "Long Road to 'The Big Red One,'" *DV,* 3 July 1980, 2.

29. Ibid.; Fuller, *A Third Face,* 476.

30. Cohn, "Long Road," 2; "Production Logistics Stalling Start of 'The Big Red One,'" *DV,* 14 July 1977, 3.

31. Ibid.; Edna Fainaru, "Israel Shakes Off Biblical Image With 'Big Red One's' Locationing," *V,* 2 August 1978, 31; "'Big Red One' Due Via Lorimar; Once Wayne, 20 Yrs. Ago," *V,* 11 October 1978, 5.

32. For production details, see Fuller, *A Third Face,* 477–481; Joan Borsten, "A D-Day Landing by 'Big Red One' Outside Tel Aviv," *Los Angeles Times Calendar,* 13 August 1978, 26, 29; *The Real Glory: Reconstructing The Big Red One* (Lorac Productions, Warner Bros. Entertainment, Inc., 2005); Author's interview with Kelly Ward, October 2005.

33. Roderick Mann, "Sam Plays It Again With 'Big Red One,'" *Los Angeles Times Calendar,* 1 June 1980, 28.

34. "Retro Screenings of Sam Fuller Pix Mark Debut of 'Big Red One,'" *DV,* 26 June 1980, 7; "Lorimar's Morpurgo On European Promo Swing," *V,* 17 September 1980, 50.

35. Richard Schickel, "Belated Victory," *Time,* 21 July 1980, 73. See also Reviews of *The Big Red One* in *New York Times,* 18 July 1980, C6; *Newsweek,* 28 July 1980, 68; *Sight and Sound* 49, no. 4 (Autumn 1980): 256–257; *Film Comment* 28, no. 4 (July 1992): 12.

36. Review of *The Big Red One, V,* 14 May 1980.

37. "50 Top-Grossing Films," *V,* 30 July 1980, 9; "Big Rental Films of 1980," *V,* 14 January 1981, 50.

38. "Sam Fuller Set for 'White Dog;' First H'wood Pic in 16 Years," *V,* 1 April 1981, 30; Todd McCarthy, "Samuel Fuller Brings in Par's Thriller 'White Dog' On Sked; Release In Early '82," *DV,* 19 June 1981, 2.

39. Author's interview with Jon Davison, August 2005.

40. "Sam Fuller Set for 'White Dog,'" 30.

41. *White Dog* Production Budget, *White Dog* Cost Reports File, Jon Davison Collection, MHL; McCarthy, "Samuel Fuller Brings in Par's Thriller," 2.

42. Memo from David L. Crippens to Richard Zimbert, 11 May 1981, *White Dog* Notes From Executives on Re-Editing File, Jon Davison Collection, MHL; Memo from Willis Edwards, undated, *White Dog* Consultants File, Jon Davison Collection, MHL.

43. Memo from Don Simpson to Jeff Katzenberg, 26 May 1981, *White Dog* Consultants File, Jon Davison Collection, MHL; Memo from Don Simpson to Jeff Katzenberg, 1 June 1981, *White Dog* Consultants File, Jon Davison Collection, MHL; Memo from Jeff Katzenberg to Jon Davison, 12 June 1981, *White Dog* Consultants File, Jon Davison Collection, MHL.

44. Memo from Ricardo Mestres to Jeff Katzenberg, 12 June 1981, *White Dog* Notes From Executives on Re-Editing File, Jon Davison Collection, MHL.

45. See Fuller's handwritten notes on memos from Jeffrey Katzenberg to Jon Davison, 16 June 1981 and 12 June 1981, *White Dog* Consultants File, Jon Davison Collection, MHL.

46. Memo from Paramount Pictures to Edgar Scherick, 25 February 1981, *White Dog* Script Notes on Kazan Draft File, Jon Davison Collection, MHL.

47. Memo from Paramount Pictures to Edgar Scherick, 10 November 1980, *White Dog* Script Notes on Kazan Draft File, Jon Davison Collection, MHL; Larry Wilson Notes on *White Dog* Script dated 27 October 1980, *White Dog* Script Notes on Kazan Draft File, Jon Davison Collection, MHL.

48. Nick Kazan, Curtis Hanson, and Tom Baum, *White Dog* Script, *White Dog* Kazan Draft File, Jon Davison Collection, MHL.

49. Memo from Paramount Pictures, 20 October 1981; Memo from Jon Davison to Jeffrey Katzenberg, 26 October 1981; Memo from Paramount Pictures to Jon Davison and Samuel Fuller, 10 November 1981, all in *White Dog* Notes From Executives on Re-Editing File, Jon Davison Collection, MHL.

50. Todd McCarthy, "Par Puts 'White Dog' On Shelf, Now for Homevideo, Cable Mkts.," *V,* 9 February 1983, 3, 44.

51. Review of *White Dog, V,* 23 June 1982.

52. McCarthy, "Samuel Fuller Brings in Par's Thriller," 44.

53. Lisa Katzman, "'White Dog' Is Set Loose at Last," *New York Times,* 7 July 1991, II:17.

54. Jean Callahan, "Hot *Dog,*" *American Film* 8, no. 7 (May 1983): 10.

55. Ibid.

56. Ibid.; Katzman, "'White Dog' Is Set Loose at Last," 17; Samuel Fuller, "The Dog That Didn't Bark," *The Guardian,* 26 April 1984.

57. Fuller, *A Third Face,* 493.

58. Fuller, *A Third Face,* 499–500.

59. Todd McCarthy, "Fuller Eyes 'Tough' Yank Mkt," *V*, 25 May 1983, 4, 37; Dave Kehr, "Fuller's Brush With Critics," *American Film* 9, no. 8 (June 1984): 13.

60. See Kehr, "Fuller's Brush With Critics," 13; Fuller, *A Third Face*, 500–501.

61. Review of *Thieves After Dark*, *V*, 7 March 1984.

62. "Howard A. Rodman, "Tobacco Road," *Village Voice* 33, no. 40 (4 October 1988): 89–90; Fuller, *A Third Face*, 526–527.

63. Fuller, *A Third Face*, 528.

64. Georgia Brown, "Quai It Again, Sam," *Village Voice* 36, no. 33 (13 August 1991): 60.

65. Review of *Street of No Return*, *V*, 31 May 1989.

66. Brown, "Quai It Again, Sam," 60.

67. Interview with Bryan McKenzie in *The Real Glory: Reconstructing The Big Red One* (2004); Panel discussion following the New York Film Festival screening of *The Big Red One: The Reconstruction*, 2 October 2004.

## Conclusion (pages 203–206)

1. Kenneth Turin, "Portrait of the Auteur," *New West*, 11 August 1980.

# Filmography

## Films as Director

*I Shot Jesse James.* 1949. Production: Lippert Productions, Inc. Distribution: Screen Guild Productions, Inc. Producer: Carl K. Hittleman. Screenplay: Samuel Fuller. Cinematography: Ernest Miller. Editing: Paul Landres. Music: Albert Glasser. Cast: John Ireland, Preston Foster, Barbara Britton, Reed Hadley.

*The Baron of Arizona.* 1950. Production: Deputy Corporation. Distribution: Lippert Pictures, Inc. Producer: Carl K. Hittleman. Screenplay: Samuel Fuller. Cinematography: James Wong Howe. Editing: Arthur Hilton. Music: Paul Dunlap. Cast: Vincent Price, Ellen Drew, Reed Hadley.

*The Steel Helmet.* 1951. Production: Deputy Corporation. Distribution: Lippert Pictures, Inc. Producer: Samuel Fuller. Screenplay: Samuel Fuller. Cinematography: Ernest W. Miller. Editing: Philip Cahn. Music: Paul Dunlap. Cast: Gene Evans, Steve Brodie, James Edwards, Robert Hutton, Richard Loo, William Chun.

*Fixed Bayonets.* 1951. Production and Distribution: Twentieth Century–Fox Film Corporation. Producer: Jules Buck. Screenplay: Samuel Fuller. Cinematography: Lucien Ballard. Editing: Nick DeMaggio. Music: Roy Webb. Cast: Richard Basehart, Gene Evans, Michael O'Shea.

*Park Row.* 1952. Production: Samuel Fuller Productions. Distribution: United Artists. Screenplay: Samuel Fuller. Cinematography: Jack Russell. Editing: Philip Cahn. Music: Paul Dunlap. Cast: Gene Evans, Mary Welch, Herbert Heyes.

*Pickup on South Street.* 1953. Production and Distribution: Twentieth Century–Fox Film Corporation. Producer: Jules Schermer. Screenplay: Samuel Fuller. Story: Dwight Taylor. Cinematography: Joe MacDonald. Editing: Nick DeMaggio. Music: Leigh Harline. Cast: Richard Widmark, Jean Peters, Thelma Ritter, Murvyn Vye.

*Hell and High Water.* 1954. Production and Distribution: Twentieth Century–Fox Film Corporation. Producer: Raymond A. Klune. Screenplay: Jesse L.

Lasky, Jr., and Samuel Fuller. Story: David Hempstead. Cinematography: Joe MacDonald. Editing: James B. Clark. Music: Alfred Newman. Cast: Richard Widmark, Bella Darvi, Victor Francen, Cameron Mitchell.

*House of Bamboo.* 1955. Production and Distribution: Twentieth Century–Fox Film Corporation. Producer: Buddy Adler. Screenplay: Harry Kleiner. Additional Dialogue: Samuel Fuller. Cinematography: Joe MacDonald. Editing: James B. Clark. Music: Leigh Harline. Cast: Robert Ryan, Robert Stack, Shirley Yamaguchi, Cameron Mitchell, Sessue Hayakawa.

*Run of the Arrow.* 1957. Production: Globe Enterprises/RKO Radio Pictures. Distribution: Universal-International. Producer: Samuel Fuller. Screenplay: Samuel Fuller. Cinematography: Joseph Biroc. Editing: Gene Fowler, Jr. Music: Victor Young. Cast: Rod Steiger, Sarita Montiel, Brian Keith, Ralph Meeker, Jay C. Flippen, Charles Bronson.

*China Gate.* 1957. Production: Globe Enterprises. Distribution: Twentieth Century–Fox Film Corporation. Producer: Samuel Fuller. Screenplay: Samuel Fuller. Cinematography: Joseph Biroc. Editing: Gene Fowler, Jr. Music: Victor Young, Max Steiner. Cast: Gene Barry, Angie Dickinson, Nat "King" Cole, Paul Dubov, Lee Van Cleef.

*Forty Guns.* 1957. Production: Globe Enterprises. Distribution: Twentieth Century–Fox Film Corporation. Producer: Samuel Fuller. Screenplay: Samuel Fuller. Cinematography: Joseph Biroc. Editing: Gene Fowler, Jr. Music: Harry Sukman. Cast: Barbara Stanwyck, Barry Sullivan, Dean Jagger, John Ericson, Gene Barry.

*Verboten!* 1959. Production: Globe Enterprises/RKO Radio Pictures. Distribution: J. Arthur Rank/Columbia Pictures. Producer: Samuel Fuller. Screenplay: Samuel Fuller. Cinematography: Joseph Biroc. Editing: Philip Cahn. Music: Harry Sukman. Cast: James Best, Susan Cummings, Tom Pittman, Paul Dubov.

*The Crimson Kimono.* 1959. Production: Globe Enterprises. Distribution: Columbia Pictures. Producer: Samuel Fuller. Screenplay: Samuel Fuller. Cinematography: Sam Leavitt. Editing: Jerome Thoms. Music: Harry Sukman. Cast: Victoria Shaw, Glenn Corbett, James Shigeta, Anna Lee.

*Underworld, U.S.A.* 1961. Production: Globe Enterprises. Distribution: Columbia Pictures. Producer: Samuel Fuller. Screenplay: Samuel Fuller. Cinematography: Hal Mohr. Editing: Jerome Thoms. Music: Harry Sukman. Cast: Cliff Robertson, Beatrice Kay, Larry Gates, Dolores Dorn, Richard Rust.

*Merrill's Marauders.* 1962. Production: United States Productions. Distribution: Warner Bros. Pictures. Producer: Milton Sperling. Screenplay: Samuel Fuller and Milton Sperling. Story: Charlton Ogburn, Jr. Cinematography: William

Clothier. Editing: Folmar Blangsted. Music: Howard Jackson. Cast: Jeff Chandler, Ty Hardin, Peter Brown, Andrew Duggan.

*Shock Corridor*. 1963. Production: Leon Fromkess–Sam Firks Productions. Distribution: Allied Artists Picture Corporation. Producer: Samuel Fuller. Screenplay: Samuel Fuller. Cinematography: Stanley Cortez. Editing: Jerome Thoms. Music: Paul Dunlap. Cast: Peter Breck, Constance Towers, Gene Evans, James Best, Hari Rhodes.

*The Naked Kiss*. 1964. Production: Leon Fromkess–Sam Firks Productions. Distribution: Allied Artists Picture Corporation. Producer: Samuel Fuller. Screenplay: Samuel Fuller. Cinematography: Stanley Cortez. Editing: Jerome Thoms. Music: Paul Dunlap. Cast: Constance Towers, Anthony Eisley, Michael Dante, Virginia Grey, Patsy Kelly.

*Shark!* 1969. Production: Heritage Enterprises/Cinematográfica Calderón. Distribution: Excelsior Distributing Company. Producers: José Luis Calderón, Skip Steloff, Marc Cooper. Screenplay: Samuel Fuller, John Kingsbridge. Story: Victor Canning. Cinematography: Raúl Martínez Solares. Editing: Carlos Savage. Music: Rafael Moroyoqui. Cast: Burt Reynolds, Barry Sullivan, Arthur Kennedy, Silvia Pinal.

*Dead Pigeon on Beethoven Street*. 1972. Production: Bavaria Atelier Studios. Distribution: Emerson Film Enterprises. Screenplay: Samuel Fuller. Cinematography: Jerzy Lipman. Editing: Liesgret Schmitt-Klink. Music: Can. Cast: Glenn Corbett, Christa Lang, Stephanie Audran, Anton Diffring.

*The Big Red One*. 1980. Production: Lorimar Productions. Distribution: United Artists. Producer: Gene Corman. Screenplay: Samuel Fuller. Cinematography: Adam Greenberg. Editing: David Bretherton, Morton Tubor. Music: Dana Kaproff. Cast: Lee Marvin, Mark Hamill, Robert Carradine, Bobby Di Cicco, Kelly Ward.

*White Dog*. 1982. Production and Distribution: Paramount Pictures Corporation. Producer: Jon Davison. Screenplay: Samuel Fuller, Curtis Hanson. Story: Romain Gary. Cinematography: Bruce Surtees. Editing: Bernard Gribble. Music: Ennio Morricone. Cast: Kristy McNichol, Paul Winfield, Burl Ives, Jameson Parker.

*Les Voleurs de la Nuit/Thieves After Dark*. 1984. Production and Distribution: Parafrance Films. Producer: Michel Gue. Screenplay: Samuel Fuller, Olivier Beer. Story: Olivier Beer. Cinematography: Philippe Rousselot. Editing: Catherine Kelber. Music: Ennio Morricone. Cast: Véronique Jannot, Bobby Di Cicco, Victor Lanoux.

*Street of No Return*. 1989. Production: Thunder Films International/FR 3 Films Production/Animatógrafo. Distribution: Jacques Bral. Producer: Jacques Bral.

Screenplay: Samuel Fuller, Jacques Bral. Story: David Goodis. Cinematography: Pierre-William Glenn. Music: Karl-Heinz Schafer. Cast: Keith Carradine, Valentina Vargas, Bill Duke, Andrea Ferreol.

## Screen Stories and Screenplays

*Hats Off.* 1936. Production: Boris Petroff Productions. Distribution: Grand National. Producer: Boris Petroff. Director: Boris Petroff. Screenplay: Samuel Fuller, Edmund Joseph.

*It Happened in Hollywood.* 1937. Production and Distribution: Columbia Pictures. Executive Producer: William Perlberg. Director: Harry Lachman. Screenplay: Samuel Fuller, Ethel Hill, Harvey Ferguson. Story: Myles Connolly.

*Gangs of New York.* 1938. Production and Distribution: Republic Pictures. Producer: Armand Schaefer. Director: James Cruze. Screenplay: Wellyn Totman, Samuel Fuller, Jack Townley, Charles Francis Royal. Story: Samuel Fuller, based on novel by Herbert Asbury.

*Adventure in Sahara.* 1938. Production and Distribution: Columbia Pictures. Producer: Louis B. Appleton, Jr. Director: D. Ross Lederman. Screenplay: Maxwell Shane. Story: Samuel Fuller.

*Federal Man-Hunt.* 1939. Production and Distribution: Republic Pictures. Associate Producer: Armand Schaefer. Director: Nick Grinde. Screenplay: Maxwell Shane. Story: Samuel Fuller, William Lively.

*Bowery Boy.* 1940. Production and Distribution: Republic Pictures. Associate Producer: Armand Schaefer. Director: William Morgan. Screenplay: Robert Chapin, Harry Kronman, Eugene Solow. Story: Samuel Fuller, Sidney Sutherland.

*Confirm or Deny.* 1941. Production and Distribution: Twentieth Century–Fox Film Corporation. Producer: Len Hammond. Directors: Archie Mayo, Fritz Lang. Screenplay: Jo Swerling. Story: Samuel Fuller, Henry Wales.

*Power of the Press.* 1943. Production and Distribution: Columbia Pictures. Producer: Leon Barsha. Director: Lew Landers. Screenplay: Robert Hardy Andrews. Story: Samuel Fuller.

*Gangs of the Waterfront.* 1945. Production and Distribution: Republic Pictures. Associate Producer: George Blair. Director: George Blair. Screenplay: Albert Beich. Story: Samuel Fuller.

*Shockproof.* 1949. Production and Distribution: Columbia Pictures. Producers: Helen Deutsch, S. Sylvan Simon. Director: Douglas Sirk. Screenplay: Helen Deutsch, Samuel Fuller.

*The Tanks Are Coming.* 1951. Production and Distribution: Warner Bros. Pictures. Producer: Bryan Foy. Directors: D. Ross Lederman, Lewis Seiler. Screenplay: Robert Hardy Andrews. Story: Samuel Fuller.

*Scandal Sheet.* 1952. Production: Edward Small Productions. Distribution: Columbia Pictures. Producer: Edward Small. Director: Phil Karlson. Screenplay: Ted Sherdeman, Eugene Ling, James Poe. Story: Samuel Fuller.

*The Command.* 1954. Production and Distribution: Warner Bros. Pictures. Producer: David Weisbart. Director: David Butler. Screenplay: Russell S. Hughes, Samuel Fuller. Story: James Warner Bellah.

*The Cape Town Affair.* 1967. Production: Killarney Film Studios/Twentieth Century–Fox Film Corporation. Distribution: Reel Media International/Twentieth Century–Fox Film Corporation. Producer: Robert D. Webb. Director: Robert D. Webb. Screenplay: Samuel Fuller, Harold Medford. Story: Dwight Taylor.

*The Deadly Trackers.* 1973. Production: Cine Films, Inc. Distribution: Warner Bros. Pictures. Producer: Fouad Said. Director: Barry Shear. Screenplay: Lukas Heller. Story: Samuel Fuller.

*The Klansman.* 1974. Production: Atlanta Productions/Paramount Pictures. Distribution: Paramount Pictures. Producer: William Alexander. Director: Terence Young. Screenplay: Millard Kaufman, Samuel Fuller. Story: William Bradford Huie.

*Let's Get Harry.* 1986. Production: Delphi V Productions/Tri-Star Pictures. Distribution: Tri-Star Pictures. Producers: Daniel H. Blatt, Robert Singer. Director: Alan Smithee (Stuart Rosenberg). Screenplay: Charles Robert Carner. Story: Mark Feldberg, Samuel Fuller.

## Television

SERIES EPISODES

*The Virginian.* "It Tolls For Thee." 1962. NBC TV. Executive Producer: Charles Marquis Warren. Director: Samuel Fuller. Script: Samuel Fuller.

*The Dick Powell Show.* "330 Independence S.W." 1962. NBC TV. Executive Producer: Dick Powell. Director: Samuel Fuller. Script: Allan Sloane.

*Iron Horse.* "The Man From New Chicago." 1966. ABC TV. Executive Producer: Charles Marquis Warren. Director: Samuel Fuller. Script: Mort R. Lewis.

*Iron Horse.* "High Devil." 1966. ABC TV. Executive Producer: Charles Marquis Warren. Director: Samuel Fuller. Script: Samuel Fuller.

*Iron Horse.* "Hellcat." 1966. ABC TV. Executive Producer: Charles Marquis Warren. Director: Samuel Fuller. Script: Samuel Fuller, Oliver Crawford.

*Iron Horse.* "Volcano Wagon." 1967. ABC TV. Executive Producer: Charles Marquis Warren. Director: Samuel Fuller. Script: Ken Trevey.

*Iron Horse.* "Banner with a Strange Device." 1967. ABC TV. Executive Producer: Charles Marquis Warren. Director: Samuel Fuller. Script: John O'Dea, Arthur Rowe.

*Iron Horse.* "The Red Tornado." 1967. ABC TV. Executive Producer: Charles Marquis Warren. Director: Samuel Fuller. Script: Warren Douglas.

TELEVISION MOVIES

*Le Jour du châtiment/The Day of Reckoning.* 1990. Harlech Television. Producer: Nicole Flipo. Director: Samuel Fuller. Script: Samuel Fuller, Christa Lang. Based on a story by Patricia Highsmith.

*The Madonna and the Dragon.* 1990. Canal +/Flach Film/TF1. Producer: Jean-François Lepetit. Director: Samuel Fuller. Script: Samuel Fuller, Christa Lang. Story: Reza Degathi, Selim Nassib.

## Selected Documentaries on Fuller

*Samuel Fuller and The Big Red One.* 1979. Producers: Tom Burghard, Thys Ockersen. Director: Thys Ockersen.

*Fuller, Frame By Frame.* 1983. Producers: Jacques Audrain, Jean Minodo, André S. Lebarthé, Guy Girard. Director: André S. Lebarthé.

*Falkenau, The Impossible.* 1988. Production: Michklan World Productions. Producer and Director: Emil Weiss.

*Tigrero: A Film That Was Never Made.* 1994. Production: Marianna Films. Producer and Director: Mika Kaurismäki.

*The Typewriter, the Rifle & the Movie Camera.* 1996. Production and Distribution: British Film Institute, Independent Film Channel. Producers: Paula Jalfon, Colin McCabe. Director: Adam Simon.

*The Men Who Made the Movies: Samuel Fuller.* 2003. Production: Turner Classic Movies. Producer and Director: Richard Schickel.

*The Real Glory: Reconstructing The Big Red One.* 2004. Production: Lorac Productions/Warner Bros. Entertainment, Inc. Executive Producer: Richard Schickel. Producer and Editor: Brian Hamblin. Co-Producer: Doug Freeman.

# Selected Bibliography

## Periodicals

*Boxoffice*, 1951–1980.
*Commonweal*, 1951–1955, 1962–1963.
*Daily Film Renter*, 1955–1957.
*Daily Variety*, 1950–1997.
*Film Daily*, 1950–1964.
*Hollywood Citizen News*, 1951–1957.
*Hollywood Reporter*, 1949–1991.
*Kinematograph Weekly*, 1949–1957.
*Los Angeles Daily News*, 1949–1954.
*Los Angeles Examiner*, 1951–1962.
*Los Angeles Herald Examiner*, 1980–1981.
*Los Angeles Times*, 1950–1997.
*Los Angeles Weekly*, 1990–1997.
*Monthly Film Bulletin*, 1949–1984.
*Motion Picture Herald*, 1949–1963.
*Movie*, 1962–1970.
*Newsweek*, 1951–1955, 1980, 1984.
*New Yorker*, 1951–1954, 1991.
*New York Times*, 1949–1997.
*Saturday Review*, 1953–1963.
*Scenario: The Magazine of Screenwriting Art*, 1998.
*Theatre Arts*, 1952–1953.
*Time*, 1952–1962, 1980, 1994, 1997.
*Variety*, 1949–1997.
*Village Voice*, 1976–1997.

## Books and Articles

Agabiti, Thomas. "Samuel Fuller's *Run of the Arrow* and the Mythos of Romance: An Archetypical Analysis." *Film Reader* 2 (January 1977): 96–110.
Bacher, Lutz. *Max Ophuls in the Hollywood Studios*. New Brunswick, N.J.: Rutgers University Press, 1996.

Balio, Tino, ed. *The American Film Industry*. Revised ed. Madison: University of Wisconsin Press, 1985.

———. *The Grand Design: Hollywood as a Modern Business Enterprise*. Berkeley: University of California Press, 1993.

———. *United Artists: The Company That Changed the Film Industry*. Madison: University of Wisconsin Press, 1985.

Basinger, Jeanine. *The World War II Combat Film: Anatomy of a Genre*. New York: Columbia University Press, 1986.

Belton, John. "Are You Waving the Flag at Me? Samuel Fuller and Politics." *Velvet Light Trap* 4 (Spring 1972): 10–13.

Björkman, Stig, and Mark Shivas. "Samuel Fuller: Two Interviews." *Movie* 17 (Winter 1969/1970): 25–29.

Bogdanovich, Peter. "B-Movies." In *Picture Shows*. London: George Allen & Unwin, 1975.

Bordwell, David, Janet Staiger, and Kristin Thompson. *The Classical Hollywood Cinema: Film Style and Mode of Production to 1960*. New York: Columbia University Press, 1985.

Browne, Nick, ed. *Refiguring American Film Genres: Theory and History*. Berkeley: University of California Press, 1998.

Canham, Kingsley, "Samuel Fuller's Action Films." *Screen* 10, no. 6 (November/December 1969): 80–101.

———. "The World of Samuel Fuller." *Film* 55 (Summer 1969): 4–10.

Caughie, John, ed. *Theories of Authorship: A Reader*. London: Routledge, 1981.

Clark, Randall. *At a Theater or Drive-In Near You: The History, Culture, and Politics of the Exploitation Film*. New York: Garland Publishing, 1995.

Corman, Roger, with Jim Jerome. *How I Made a Hundred Movies in Hollywood and Never Lost a Dime*. New York: Da Capo Press, 1990.

Coursodon, Jean-Pierre, and Pierre Sauvage. *American Directors: Volume II*. New York: McGraw-Hill, 1983.

Crawley, Tony. "In War, as in Movies, There Are No Heroes. Only Survivors." *Films Illustrated* 9, no. 107 (August 1980): 434.

Doherty, Thomas. *Teenagers and Teenpics: The Juvenilization of American Movies in the 1950s*. Boston: Unwin Hyman, 1988.

Farber, Manny. "The Films of Sam Fuller and Don Siegel." *December* 12, no. 1/2 (1970): 170–172.

Fuller, Samuel. "The Dog That Didn't Bark." *The Guardian*, 26 April 1984.

———. "Film Fiction: More Factual than Facts." *Projections* 1 (1992): 131–132.

———. "News That's Fit to Film." *American Film* 1, no. 1 (October 1975): 20–24.

———. *A Third Face: My Tale of Writing, Fighting, and Filmmaking*. New York: Knopf, 2002.

———. "War That's Fit to Shoot." *American Film* 2, no. 2 (November 1976): 58–62.

———. "What Is a Film?" *Cinema* 2, no. 2 (July 1964): 22–24.

Gardner, Gerald. *The Censorship Papers: Movie Censorship Letters From the Hays Office, 1934 to 1968*. New York: Dodd, Mead & Company, 1987.

Garnham, Nicholas. *Samuel Fuller.* New York: Viking, 1971.

Gehring, Wes D., ed. *Handbook of American Film Genres.* New York: Greenwood Press, 1988.

Gerstner, David A., and Janet Staiger, eds. *Authorship and Film.* New York: Routledge, 2003.

Goodman, Ezra. "Low Budget Movies with POW!" *New York Times Magazine,* 28 February 1965, 42–50.

Gordon, Marsha. "'What Makes a Girl Who Looks Like That Get Mixed Up in Science?': Gender in Sam Fuller's Films of the 1950s." *Quarterly Review of Film and Video* 17, no. 1 (2000): 1–17.

Grant, Barry Keith, ed. *Film Genre Reader II.* Austin: University of Texas Press, 1995.

Hardy, Phil. *Samuel Fuller.* New York: Praeger, 1970.

Hoberman, J. "American Abstract Sensationalism." *Artforum* (January 1981): 42–49.

———. "Sam Fuller: Gate Crasher at the Auteur Limits." *Village Voice,* 2 July 1980, 39.

Horton, Robert. "Sam's Place." *Film Comment* 32, no. 3 (May/June 1996): 4–9.

"Interview with Sam Fuller, An." *Framework* 19 (1982): 26–28.

Jacobs, Lea. "The B Film and the Problem of Cultural Distinction." *Screen* 33, no. 1 (Spring 1992): 1–13.

Jowett, Garth. *Film: The Democratic Art.* Boston: Little, Brown and Company, 1976.

Klinger, Barbara. *Melodrama and Meaning.* Bloomington: Indiana University Press, 1994.

Lev, Peter. *Transforming the Screen: 1950–1959.* Berkeley: University of California Press, 2003.

Macdonald, Dwight. "A Caste, a Culture, a Market." *New Yorker* 34, no. 40 (22 November 1958): 57–95.

McCarthy, Todd, and Charles Flynn, eds. *Kings of the Bs: Working Within the Hollywood System.* New York: E. P. Dutton & Co., 1975.

McConnell, Frank. "Pickup on South Street and the Metamorphosis of the Thriller." *Film Heritage* 8, no. 3 (Spring 1973): 9–18.

McGee, Mark Thomas. *Fast and Furious: The Story of American International Pictures.* Jefferson, N.C.: McFarland & Company, 1984.

Merritt, Russell, and Peter Lehman. "An Interview with Samuel Fuller." *Wide Angle* 4, no. 1 (1980): 66–75.

Miller, Frank. *Censored Hollywood: Sex, Sin, and Violence on Screen.* Atlanta, Ga.: Turner Publishing, 1994.

Monder, Eric. "A Fuller View: An Interview with Sam Fuller." *Filmfax* 49 (March/April 1995): 73–76.

Moullet, Luc. "Sam Fuller—Sur les brisées de Marlowe." *Cahiers du Cinéma* 93 (March 1959): 11–19.

Neale, Steve. *Genre and Hollywood.* London: Routledge, 2000.

———. "Melo Talk: On the Meaning and Use of the Term 'Melodrama' in the American Trade Press." *The Velvet Light Trap* 32 (Fall 1993): 66–89.

Okuda, Ted. *Grand National, Producers Releasing Corporation, and Screen Guild/Lippert: Complete Filmographies and Studio Histories.* Jefferson, N.C.: McFarland & Company, 1989.

Orgeron, Marsha. "Liberating Images? Samuel Fuller's Film of Falkenau Concentration Camp." *Film Quarterly* 60, no. 2 (Winter 2006/2007): 38–47.

Rhodes, Colin. *Primitivism and Modern Art.* London: Thames and Hudson, 1994.

Rosenbaum, Jonathan. "His Master's Vice: Fuller's *White Dog.*" In *Placing Movies.* Berkeley: University of California Press, 1995.

———. "Paris Journal." *Film Comment* 8, no. 2 (Summer 1972): 2–4.

Routt, William D. "The Wild Old Men of the Movies." *American Film* 1, no. 10 (September 1976): 54–59.

Ryan, Tom. "Sam Fuller: Survivor." *Cinema Papers* 30 (December 1980/January 1981): 423–426, 498–500.

Salt, Barry. *Film Style and Technology: History and Analysis.* 2nd ed. London: Starword, 1992.

"Samuel Fuller." *Film Dope* 18 (September 1979): 16–18.

"Samuel Fuller: Two Interviews." *Movie* 17 (Winter 1969/1970): 25–31.

Sanjek, David. "'Torment Street Between Malicious and Crude': Sophisticated Primitivism in the Films of Samuel Fuller." *Literature/Film Quarterly* 22, no. 3 (1994): 187–194.

Sarris, Andrew. *The American Cinema: Directors and Directions, 1929–1968.* Chicago: University of Chicago Press, 1968.

———. "Fuller Up." *Village Voice,* 17 January 1984, 49.

Schaefer, Eric. *Bold! Daring! Shocking! True!: A History of Exploitation Films, 1919–1959.* Durham, N.C.: Duke University Press, 1999.

Schatz, Thomas. *Hollywood Genres: Formulas, Filmmaking, and the Studio System.* New York: McGraw-Hill, 1981.

———. *Boom and Bust: American Cinema in the 1940s.* Berkeley: University of California Press, 1997.

Schickel, Richard. "Sam Fuller: Movie Bozo." In Philip Lopate, ed. *American Movie Critics: An Anthology From the Silents Until Now.* New York: Library of America, 2006.

Selznick, Daniel. "An Old Pro on the Go Again." *New York Times Magazine,* 4 May 1980, 48–49, 58–70, 74–78.

Server, Lee. *Sam Fuller: Film Is a Battleground.* Jefferson, N.C.: McFarland & Company, 1994.

Sherman, Eric, and Martin Rubin. *The Director's Event: Interviews with Five American Filmmakers.* New York: Atheneum, 1970.

Silver, Alain, and James Ursini. *What Ever Happened to Robert Aldrich? His Life and His Films.* New York: Limelight Editions, 1995.

Simon, Adam. "Sam Fuller: Perfect Pitch." *Sight and Sound* 8, no. 3 (March 1998): 18–22.

Singer, Ben. *Melodrama and Modernity: Early Sensational Cinema and Its Contexts.* New York: Columbia University Press, 2001.

Solomon, Aubrey. *Twentieth Century–Fox: A Corporate and Financial History.* Metuchen, N.J.: Scarecrow Press, 1988.

Thompson, Richard. "3X Sam: The Flavor of Ketchup." *Film Comment* 13, no. 1 (January/February 1997): 25–31.

Turan, Kenneth. "Portrait of an Auteur." *New West,* 11 August 1980.

Wexman, Virginia Wright, ed. *Film and Authorship.* New Brunswick, N.J.: Rutgers University Press, 2003.

Will, David, and Peter Wollen, eds. *Samuel Fuller.* Edinburgh: Edinburgh Film Festival, 1969.


## Unpublished Materials and Manuscript Collections

Bernstein, Matthew. "Defiant Cooperation: Walter Wanger and Independent Production in Hollywood, 1934–1949." Ph.D. dissertation, University of Wisconsin–Madison, 1987.

*The Big Red One* Collection, Warner Bros. Archives, University of Southern California, Los Angeles, California.

Core Collection, Margaret Herrick Library, Academy of Motion Picture Arts and Sciences, Beverly Hills, California.

Columbia Pictures Collection, Arts Library Special Collections, Young Research Library, University of California–Los Angeles, Los Angeles, California.

Jon Davison Collection, Margaret Herrick Library, Academy of Motion Picture Arts and Sciences, Beverly Hills, California.

Giglio, Ernest D. "The Decade of the Miracle, 1952–1962: A Study in the Censorship of the American Motion Picture." Ph.D. dissertation, Syracuse University, 1965.

Hedda Hopper Collection, Margaret Herrick Library, Academy of Motion Picture Arts and Sciences, Beverly Hills, California.

James Wong Howe Collection, Margaret Herrick Library, Academy of Motion Picture Arts and Sciences, Beverly Hills, California.

*Marta Fuller vs. Samuel Fuller.* Superior Court of the State of California, County of Los Angeles.

Marty Weiser Collection, Margaret Herrick Library, Academy of Motion Picture Arts and Sciences, Beverly Hills, California.

*Merrill's Marauders* Collection, Warner Bros. Archives, University of Southern California, Los Angeles, California.

Press Book Collection, Margaret Herrick Library, Academy of Motion Picture Arts and Sciences, Beverly Hills, California.

Production Code Administration Collection, Margaret Herrick Library, Academy of Motion Picture Arts and Sciences, Beverly Hills, California.

RKO Pictures Collection, Arts Library Special Collections, Young Research Library, University of California–Los Angeles, Los Angeles, California.

Twentieth Century–Fox Collection, Arts Library Special Collections, Young Research Library, University of California–Los Angeles, Los Angeles, California.

Unrealized Scripts Collection, Margaret Herrick Library, Academy of Motion Picture Arts and Sciences, Beverly Hills, California.

# Index

Page numbers in *italics* indicate illustrations.

# About the Author

Lisa Dombrowski is associate professor of film studies at Wesleyan University, where she teaches courses on cinema history, film form and analysis, and the American film industry.